WHEN THE CENTER IS ON FIRE

# WHEN THE CENTER IS ON FIRE

## Passionate Social Theory for Our Times

*By*

DIANE HARRIFORD AND BECKY THOMPSON

UNIVERSITY OF TEXAS PRESS

AUSTIN

"To Du Bois" by Becky Thompson, from *Harvard Review* (Spring 2008).
Reprinted by permission.

"History in the Water," by Becky Thompson, from *My Soul Is Anchored: Poems from the Mourning Katrina National Writing Project* (2006), copyright 2005 by Becky Thompson. Reprinted by permission of the Furious Flower Poetry Center, Joanne Gabbin, director.

"Beirut 2006" and "Questions," by Becky Thompson, from *We Begin Here: Poems on Palestine and Lebanon* (2007), edited by Kamal Boullata and Kathy Engel, copyright 2006 by Becky Thompson. Reprinted by permission of Interlink Books, an imprint of Interlink Publishing, Northampton, MA.

"Post-Attica Visit," by Becky Thompson, from *Warpland: A Journal of Black Literature and Ideas* 12, no. 1 (2005), copyright 2005 by Becky Thompson. Reprinted by permission of the Gwendolyn Brooks Center for Black Literature and Creative Writing.

"Tanka," by Becky Thompson, from *Illuminations: An International Magazine of Contemporary Writing* (August 2006), copyright 2006 by Becky Thompson. Reprinted by permission of Rathasker Press. Appears here as "Canopy."

Requests for permission to reproduce material from this work should be sent to:
Permissions
University of Texas Press
P.O. Box 7819
Austin, TX 78713-7819
www.utexas.edu/utpress/about/bpermission.html

♾ The paper used in this book meets the minimum requirements of
ANSI/NISO Z39.48-1992 (R1997) (Permanence of Paper).

Library of Congress Cataloging-in-Publication Data
Harriford, Diane Sue.
When the center is on fire : passionate social theory for our times /
Diane Harriford and Becky Thompson. — 1st ed.
    p.    cm.
Includes bibliographical references and index.
ISBN 978-0-292-71775-6 (cl. : alk. paper) —
ISBN 978-0-292-71776-3 (pbk. : alk. paper)
1. Sociology.   2. Social sciences — Philosophy.   I. Thompson, Becky W.   II. Title.
HM585.H37   2008
301.0973 — dc22
2008003458

*For*
*Sally Abood*
*and*
*Thelma Harriford*
*(1911–1990)*

# CONTENTS

# ACKNOWLEDGMENTS

From its genesis on a late summer evening in San Francisco in 2004 to its completion a few months after we returned from Tunisia in 2006, this book has traveled the distance in our psyches. Coming together, we wrote a book neither of us could have written alone. Diane had been thinking about writing a book about sexuality for years. Becky had been writing poetry and earlier books in qualitative sociology and social justice movements. These concerns are embedded in this book, but in transmigrated form. What had kept Diane from writing before was a feeling that she could not write in her own voice, that writing would deaden ideas she wanted to keep alive. Becky was eager to find ways to translate our many animated conversations over the years onto the written page while trying to make social theory poetic. The writing process has been so quirky that we have been able to "do sociology" in a way that feels like us.

Along the way, many people have read chapters and drafts, each helping us immeasurably. Novelist and friend Andrea Herrera—after learning that a press that had solicited our book had subsequently named it "too imaginative and creative"—knew immediately that the editor in chief of the University of Texas Press would only see those adjectives as positive. Theresa May read the manuscript in two days and within a week had fully embraced the project. It has been a great pleasure to work with her. Monisha Das Gupta devoted her critical and savvy political eye to the text, while appreciating our collaborative process. The intellectual sophistication Monisha brought improved our thinking immeasurably. The Sister Scholars in New York City affirmed that this project had merit and insisted that we go forward; over the years this group has been a place to develop new language and do creative thinking about the world. Ismail Rashid has been Diane's colleague and comrade for many years, and, from the beaches of Tunisia to the weekly dinners they shared to revive their sanity, he has always reminded Diane that this book was a political project. Maury Stein,

Becky's mentor of thirty-plus years, graced us with his gutsy and encouraging suggestions. Pinar Batur, George Katsiaficas, Joshua Schreier, David Wellman, Mootacem Bellah Mhiri, and Shannon Farrington also gave us brave and crucial comments on earlier versions of this book.

Kay and Kim Elliot, sisters in the realm of word magic, copyedited and handled the challenges of virtual citations with great humor and patience. The Press brought us to Rosemary Wetherold, whose copyediting showed a stunning level of professionalism and intellectual engagement. Thanks as well to Leslie Tingle for her respectful coordination of all the stages of the book's production. The librarians at both Vassar College and Simmons College were ingenious and generous in their constant help on this project, especially Rex Krajewski, Carol Demos, Mark Christel, Gretchen Lieb, and Carol Lynn Marshall. We both also appreciate the funding we received from the Simmons College Fund for Research and the Jane Rosenthal Heimerdinger Fund at Vassar College. Thanks as well to many colleagues in both locations, especially Patricia Turner, Sheila Stukes, Judy Cadwallader, Rachel Kitzinger, Don Basch, Lisa Smith-McQueenie, Gary Bailey, Loretta Williams, Peter Stillman, Adelaide Villmoare, and Edward Pittman. We have greatly appreciated working with such smart and politically committed students in recent years, especially Eleanor Chin, Maria Velazquez, Raquel Evita Saraswati, Amy St. Martin, Nell Maggio, Gray Sutherland-Rice, Katie Klumpp, Tina Boisseau, Christopher Beach, Carol Harper, Hayden Nelson-Major, Victor Ray, Jason Wu, Steven Lavoie, Gina Gambone, Melixza Gonzalez, the Sister Power crew, and SLAP.

The following artists, activists, and intellectuals have shaped this book in ways both overt and subtle: Bassam Tibi, Mel King, Samuel Lind, Sherman Alexie, Howard Winant, Charlotte Pierce-Baker, Beverly Tatum, Akasha Gloria Hull, Margaret Andersen, Joy Harjo, Horace Seldon, Mary Romero, the Black Radical Congress, Charlene Mitchell, Louise Merriweather, Robin Kelley, Carol Boyce Davies, Beverly Wright, Nina Simone, Curtis Mayfield, Pablo Milanés, and the Dixie Chicks. Becky wants to thank Ethelbert Miller, Randall Horton, Dwayne Betts, Claudette Webster, Vijay Seshadri, Marie Howe, Martín Espada, Rafael Campo, and especially Sonia Sanchez for their gifts as teachers of poetry. Thanks also to *Harvard Review, Illuminations, Warpland,* Kamal Boullata, Kathy Engel, Joanne Gabbin, and the Furious Flower Poetry Center's project *My Soul Is Anchored: Poems from the Mourning Katrina National Writing Project,* for earlier publication of several of Becky's poems. Thank you, as well, to the Provincetown Fine Arts Work Center, a place of annual regeneration.

Through this project, we have tried to spend as much time as possible in the realm of love. Thanks to all for holding us there: Sangeeta Tyagi, Aimee Carrillo Rowe, Bonnie Kerness, Brandy Cruthird, David Gilbert, Sohaila Abdulali, Rachel Hall, Regie Gibson, Nachum Cohen, Sheena Malhotra, Esther Leidolf, Taina and Simone, Beverly Decker, Charlotte Ledoux, Marcela Lopez, Ruth Spencer, Barbara Page, and Tyrone Simpson. For love in the name of timbales and indigo blue, Becky thanks Cornell Coley. Thanks also to Becky's idiosyncratic and loving family: Sally Abood; Ginny and the Onysko family; Becky's ninety-five-year-old intellectual grandmother, Beth Fillmore; Maury, Phyllis, and Ninian Stein; Stuart and Rosie Thompson and Becky's beautiful new goddaughter, Alexandra; Emily on-your-way-to-college Kosoff; and Becky's way grown-up son, La Mar Delandro. To Susan Kosoff, Becky says: "This will be seven we have done together, you and me. Thank you and Emily for giving me 'no matter what' love, all these years."

Our last thank-yous, for now, go out to each other. To Becky, Diane says: "You must have worked some magic on me because everyone has been waiting for me to write, including me. Now, here it is. It is a good thing you are a strong person." To Diane, Becky says: "You are marvelous, still and more so. You give new meaning to the word 'irrational.' Thank you." To the readers, may this book infuriate and resonate, incite and captivate, help turn us toward a finer vision.

WHEN THE CENTER IS ON FIRE

# INTRODUCTION

## *An Offering . . . Can We Talk?*

A few months after 9/11, one of our friends began to speak about his memories of living in New York City during the attacks on the World Trade Center. As he continued to talk about the tragedy, we began to see how profoundly he wanted to understand the assault and how few words he had to do so. He talked about the event as if it were a natural disaster or some cataclysmic event brought on by God that happened completely out of context. At the time, we noted that both the tragedy itself and the man's reaction to it were revealing; he was mirroring a reaction we were seeing all around us. Typically, the American way of dealing with socially induced trauma has been to quickly move forward with hopes that time will wash it away. Immediately following 9/11, there was a momentary opening of political commentary across the country—meetings in faith communities, schools, and local organizations attempting to make sense of the atrocity. Within weeks, however, we began to witness a kind of closing down, a pulling up of the drawbridge, a reduction of public conversation. Given the enormity of the event, it has been striking how very little coming together there has been of leading intellectuals, social activists, and religious leaders to talk collectively about the meaning of 9/11.

As sociologists, we found ourselves wanting to understand why the most visible national response to 9/11 was to send troops to Afghanistan and then to Iraq to fight wars many people didn't support or understand, leaving fundamental questions about the causes and consequences of the attacks unanswered. We wanted to know why a group of suicide bombers were willing to give up their lives, leaving their friends and loved ones, including their children, behind. We needed to know the costs and consequences of the terror of 9/11 on the families of those who died. We needed to know what spiritual, artistic, and intellectual contributions could serve as a salve and antidote to such pain.

The atrocity also required us to look anew at the consequences of exporting and enforcing a particular economic, political, and religious system throughout many regions of the world. The terrorism was, in part, a conflict between militant Islam and US imperialism. It was also a challenge to continued white domination, since the United States, currently the sole superpower in the world, is also the most powerful white-controlled country. The attacks on 9/11 signaled a wobbling of white supremacy, a sign that an increasing number of mostly young, well-educated people of Arab descent were willing to take their own lives, to martyr themselves, if necessary, before they were willing to accept domination by the United States. As public sociologists—those who seek to make links between the academy and social justice issues—we found ourselves particularly interested in how social theory might help us grapple with the factors leading to the terrorism and the silences following it.

We come to this volume deeply troubled about contemporary US society and its relationship to the world community. We have seen people so frightened that they have allowed fundamentals of US democracy—the Bill of Rights and the First and Fourteenth Amendments—to be compromised, if not demolished, under the Patriot Act. People seem willing to have their bags searched before getting on a subway in New York City without questioning how the violation of privacy in that context undermines civil liberties. Are we safe when we can't be sure that a record of the books we check out of a public library won't be scrutinized and when our e-mail can be searched with no warning or reason? Are we safe when people in our communities can be picked up and detained without any semblance of due process? One promise of social theory is to look beneath surface understandings of "safety" and other words that are used as codes to obscure power inequalities.

This book is our attempt to offer a sophisticated yet accessible analysis of several of the most troubling and transformative social upheavals in recent US history, using social theory to help us. We want to offset superficial interpretations of these events that have fueled fear, rage, and confusion. The unrelenting pace of these upheavals has left little room to understand their importance and the links between them. With the explosion of the information age, people are constantly bombarded with images of war, inequalities, violence, and disease, so much so that it is easy, and in some ways understandable, to tune out and become numb to the media barrage. And yet, the most egregious, complicated, and important social upheavals stay with us, haunting our collective unconscious. These upheavals insist upon discussion—to be understood and engaged with in a deep way.

The upheavals and traumas that we examine—the 2005 Hurricane

Katrina disaster, the 2001 terrorist attacks, the 2003 Abu Ghraib prison abuses, and the 1999 Columbine murders/suicides—have in common a destabilizing effect on people's sense of belonging to a society they can understand and rely upon. Each of these upheavals has forced people to see inequalities most people do not want to see—to confront collective denial about racism, imperialism, patriarchy, and other oppressions. White middle-class teenagers indiscriminately shooting their classmates and themselves; thousands of people in New Orleans on rooftops for days after Katrina, waiting for rescues that never came; elderly and sick people left on baggage carousels in the aftermath of the hurricane; a young female soldier deliberately humiliating Iraqi detainees while willingly being photographed doing so—all are examples of a deeply troubled society. In the face of the collective disorientation that has ensued as a consequence of these and other events, we need to see conceptual connections between these seemingly individual catastrophes and find strategies for repairing the torn social fabric.

The book's method reflects our belief in linking current catastrophes to history. Reaching back to social theory in the nineteenth and twentieth centuries recovers the past in a way that makes it usable to us now. Sociologist W. E. B. Du Bois's brilliant writing on the souls of black people underscores why the Katrina disaster not only exposed two, unequal Americas but also dredged up deep historical memories about the Middle Passage, slavery, and lynching. Calling upon economist and sociologist Karl Marx's concept of alienation provides an essential, irreplaceable explanation of why the Abu Ghraib prison photographs were taken and what these photos reveal about labor in a postindustrial, militarized society.

The German sociologist Max Weber shows us that when people cannot find rational explanations for unanticipated events, they fall back on irrational thought—hence our friend and many others who see 9/11 as an act of God. Weber's work opens a way to see why intellectually grounded and politically engaged knowledge of world politics is essential to dealing with terrorism. Drawing upon the questions that troubled French sociologist Émile Durkheim about factors that undermined a sense of collectivity and belonging in the nineteenth century enables us to see the Columbine murders/suicides as a cry for help in an increasingly atomized society. We believe that classical social theory can help us recover a humane, life-giving, and connective social ethic that can fruitfully counteract the dehumanization and emptiness that each of these recent events has uncovered.

Each chapter calls attention to the continued relevance of classical theorists and also augments their work with analyses provided by contemporary social thinkers. Du Bois's limited gender analysis and his biracial (black/white) focus led us to call upon the work of contemporary historian Darlene Clark Hine and cultural theorist Gloria Anzaldúa for an expanded understanding of consciousness that is both multiracial and transnational. The limits of Marx's work in terms of the psychological impact of alienation led us to contemporary trauma theory—a connection that allows us to understand the Abu Ghraib torture from economic and psychological perspectives simultaneously. The limits of Weber's work, in terms of not anticipating a reemergence of religious fundamentalism, led us to consider calls for the sacred across the globe. Durkheim's limited attention to the means of countering violence and suicide in a postindustrial society led us to the work of Audre Lorde and others who believe that embracing racial, sexual, and religious diversity is key to being human.

Our book makes a plea to find a narrative that sees human beings as inevitably linked to a larger social community. In this way, it challenges a certain trend in postmodernist theory in the 1980s and 1990s that assumes that power is everywhere and nowhere at the same time. As an intellectual movement begun in France and then incorporated into much scholarship in the academy in the US, "postmodernism" has been used to describe such a wide range of theoretical innovations that any brief critique would, by definition, be reductionist.[1] Our worry, however, has been the tendency within some postmodernist theory to reject the possibility of core social, political, and cultural truths. When theorists assume that class, power, and race are essentially empty of meaning—that they have no historical significance beyond what individuals give them—it becomes increasingly difficult to identify who benefits from and who is injured by inequalities. When power can't ultimately be held accountable or resisted, then all points of view are equally valuable.

An example of this relativism occurred in one of Diane's college courses, Black Intellectual Thought, when one of the students complained about an assumption in the class that slavery is wrong. He argued that the professor could not start with that assumption since the class needed to take the point of view of both the slave master and the slave. His comment made Diane realize that the notion of social justice had slipped from view, lost to endless relativism. His argument was devoid of a moral center and ran the risk of devolving into a destructive individualism.

This relativism, of course, is not the promise of public sociology. With its roots in the work of Karl Marx, W. E. B. Du Bois, the Chicago School of Sociology, and other scholars committed to social activism, public sociology has always had a social justice mission to name and subvert specific oppressions.[2] Although postmodernism continued to curry favor within academic settings in the 1990s, public sociologists and other social theorists remained determined to make links between studied reflection and social change. As drastic shifts in political power in the 1980s and 1990s undermined democracy in frightening ways, public sociologists continued to identify and stand against the state's increasing misuse of power.

In response to a period that is replete with analyses that consider only the individual, the local, and the present, our book makes a plea to embrace a narrative that sees human beings as historically and politically linked. Over the last decade, the obvious distress of many communities as a result of escalating poverty and discrimination and the eventual dissatisfaction with postmodernism as an intellectual framework have ushered in a renewed interest in an activist-based, public sociology. Many people are finding ways to understand and relieve the stresses they feel in their own lives and communities. To us it is clear that while we can't risk buying into a relativism that ultimately sees people as disconnected and fragmented, a rigid grand narrative, such as that offered by fundamentalist religion, risks another extreme by cementing people into narrow roles and behaviors. By highlighting the work of leading social thinkers, we seek to offer inclusive, hopeful, and spiritually inspired narratives of belonging. We seek a vision beyond the relativity of postmodernism and the rigidity of fundamentalist religion that recognizes social justice as key to what makes us human.

### FIRST LOVES

While unresolved recent catastrophes were our initial reason for writing this book, ultimately it was our seemingly benign decision to attend a panel on the work of W. E. B. Du Bois that finally pushed us to apply our longstanding interest in social theory to examine these upheavals. In the summer of 2004, we attended the American Sociological Association meetings in San Francisco together, wanting to enjoy a few days in that glorious city and wiggle our toes before the rush and pressure of another school year. While there, we attended a well-publicized and long-awaited plenary on the legacy of Du Bois, a political activist, an essayist, a poet, a founder of the NAACP and the Pan African Movement, and a scholar considered one of the founding figures in sociology. We came to the plenary early, to make sure we got good seats, both lamenting about how what promised to be the most important session of the conference was taking place in a space entirely too small for the most integrated crowd of this year's conference.

We listened as one speaker after another repeated what had already been said and written about Du Bois, his life, and his scholarship. We rolled our eyes and passed notes about longing to eat dinner. We commented about how sociology seemed to be going nowhere fast, honoring a man whose work we so admired while bringing almost nothing new to the conversation. The crowd was polite but restless, perhaps as eager as we were for a more thoughtful and original presentation.

Then, plenary panelist Patricia Hill Collins, a leading black intellectual and a sociologist, began her talk, speaking with an intensity that made the crowd, for the first time, sit up in their seats.[3] She refocused the discussion from suggesting that Du Bois had heirs in other well-known black intellectuals (Cornel West, Henry Louis Gates, Manning Marable, Charles Ogletree) to underscoring the uniqueness of Du Bois's position. Unlike his contemporaries, Du Bois spent most of his career outside of the academy. He was a lone voice, did not have the patrons others have had, and stayed close to the black community. Collins asked sociologists to look at who currently truly embodies his legacy. Who are those who are still marginalized, have an unbending integrity, and consider the lives of black people important? Collins also cautioned against romanticizing Du Bois, reminding the audience that, when it came to gender, Du Bois had much to learn. He was unwilling to see anti-lynching activist Ida B. Wells and educator Anna Julia Cooper as his peers and was unable to consider gender as a category on a par with race and class.

We left the plenary pleased that Collins had, rightfully, gotten a standing ovation, while still frustrated that, again, she had been the only woman on the panel. We left asking ourselves why, with all of these contradictions, we were still sociologists, choosing to spend some of our last summer days at a sociology conference? Were we mad, sad, tired, or just crazy to still be teaching classical and contemporary sociology? Why, after we had held appointments in African American studies and women's studies at various universities across the country over a twenty-year span, did we now find ourselves with appointments in sociology departments, teaching sociology? Why that commitment, when Patricia Hill Collins was having to explain, yet another time, what the now classic text *All the Women Are White, All the Blacks Are Men, But Some of Us Are Brave* identified almost twenty-five years ago?[4]

We began walking in search of a healthy dinner that we would, no doubt, follow with an outrageously rich dessert. A block from Glide Memorial, a church with a long-standing mission to advance urban justice and gay and lesbian communities, we watched as a long line of people snaked around the building and then around the block, waiting for dinner. We both looked at each other, plaintively acknowledging that in all our years of living in or visiting San Francisco, we had never seen so many homeless people—young, pierced women; too-thin gay men; mothers with two children holding on tightly; men with children; young men in work clothes, with bottles, with beards or shaven heads. Everyone was there, in line, waiting. How could sociology possibly be an antidote to that poverty, to that injustice, to such despair, when we were so far from Du Bois's solutions, from his vision?

After Collins's talk, we had to acknowledge that, in our teaching, we still looked to social theory to address poverty and other social injustices. We were still invested in sociology, still trying to pass on some torch that, on some level, we thought worth passing. Even though much of our intellectual energy had focused on women's studies (for Diane) and African American studies (for Becky) over the last two decades, we had also continued to teach sociology, suggesting that there might be something to the old saying, "You never forget a first love." It was to sociologists that academics across many disciplines turned when they wanted to study social problems, cataclysmic historical changes, and what gave people meaning in the midst of economic, political, and social change.

We had to admit that some of the ideas that first thrilled us about sociology still did—and they still do. Karl Marx's *Communist Manifesto* was, arguably, the most influential political pamphlet in the nineteenth century, explicating the economic world for people leaving peasant labor in the fields to become wage workers in cities.[5] Marx rightfully predicted that late capitalism would depend upon unemployment, hence lines of homeless people in San Francisco and other cities all over the world whose joblessness guarantees low wages among those who can find work. German social theorist Max Weber's concept of the "iron cage" still provides a graphic metaphor for the perils of bureaucracy, the impersonal occupations that lock people into soulless and passionless work.[6] The idea of the iron cage anticipated the Holocaust and other bureaucratically justified acts against humanity—including the abuses at Abu Ghraib prison—by predicting the danger of positions robbed of a moral sensibility, positions in which people are asked to follow their superiors no matter the ethical consequences.

In the twentieth century, the list of sociologists whose work has forever changed how people understand themselves and their world is long and colorful. Sociologists have always been players in identifying the roots of social injustice and steps for social change, although they have not necessarily garnered the attention needed to have substantial public impact.

While the history of public sociologists is a proud one, the two twentieth-century texts that may be most representative of this tradition are Du Bois's *The Souls of Black Folk,* published in 1903, and C. W. Mills's 1959 book, *The Sociological Imagination.*[7] Public sociology circles back, again and again, to these two texts, which distinguish themselves because of their ability to speak to people in and outside of the academy. As a pair, *The Souls of Black Folk* and *The Sociological Imagination* give us examples of an impassioned, activist-based, interdisciplinary field of study where people's subject positions—their race, class, gender, sexuality, nationality, and politics—are not only relevant but also crucial to their arguments.

*The Souls of Black Folk,* Du Bois's most famous book, was published during the nadir of race relations in US history. Mills's most influential book, *The Sociological Imagination,* was able to ride the wave of the civil rights and women's movements in the United States in the 1960s. Academic sociology made room for Mills, a white man, in a way it never did for Du Bois. Du Bois left academia disillusioned about the academy as a location for substantial social change, aware that the white academy had yet to authorize studies that were vital for supporting racial justice. Mills, on the other hand, remained in the academy, as a tenured professor at Columbia University, spending his short but prolific life attempting to upend sociological doctrine bent on celebrating the status quo.

Du Bois knew that it was impossible to understand the struggles of African Americans in the United States without confronting the roots of imperialism and slavery. He traveled all over the world, making alliances with people in the Soviet Union, China, and many countries in Africa and South America. Mills also had an international perspective, writing about Cuba, Russia, and the United States, considering in particular their position in the world community. Among other contributions of the civil rights and black power movements was a message to sociology that it had to look outside the United States to understand what was going on internally. Not surprisingly, as anthropology in the 1980s and 1990s began to look inward, accepting some of the damage caused by exoticizing the "other" internationally, sociology had to face the damage caused by a routinely internal gaze that did not account for the slave trade and the history of colonialism.[8]

In many ways, Du Bois's work imagined the twentieth-century movements for social justice into existence. Some have wondered if Du Bois's death in Ghana on the eve of the 1963 march on Washington could be understood as anything less than an act of providence. His work leading up to the march spanned several decades. C. W. Mills also captured the beat of a people—in his case, the millions of people who, increasingly, were seeing their personal lives as deeply affected by social forces, often unfair ones at that. The term he coined, "the sociological imagination," describes a self-consciousness that enables people to see their deep connection to a larger community. In Mills's words, it is "a quality of mind that seems most dramatically to promise an understanding of the intimate realities of our selves in connection with larger social reality."[9]

The sociological imagination awakens people to the knowledge that their ostensibly private orbit is actually part of an entire world turning. This imagination offers a dynamic and socially engaged methodology that takes seriously the link between what is often deemed a private trouble and its connection to structural inequalities. The seemingly private trouble of Rosa Parks not wanting to sit at the back of the bus was actually a profoundly public issue of an entire people who were being publicly and privately disrespected. Rosa Parks was hardly one individual tired woman who just had to sit down. She was a trained activist, a preplanned provocateur who became a symbol of a people who refused to accept injustice. Our friend's seeming private misery surrounding 9/11 is also a deeply public concern. The events surrounding 9/11 cannot solely be attended to through individual solutions of therapy and grief work. It also requires leadership from all realms that refuses to scapegoat South Asians, Arabs, and Muslims and takes seriously the deep-seated conflict between Western values of consumerism and individualism on the one hand and fundamentalist Islamic understandings of life on the other.

While Du Bois and Mills imagined many of the problems we now face in the twenty-first century, they both owe a debt to the classical traditions that they simultaneously embraced and critiqued. It is hard to think of any theorist in the nineteenth or twentieth century who was more committed to social change than Karl Marx, a man who many activists believe was the most influential thinker on world politics in the twentieth century. His vision, which many would call utopian, contains an optimism that has given hope and strength to millions of people mired in poverty. Émile Durkheim's desire to locate a moral compass for societies that he believed needed a collective sense of belonging remains a powerful antidote to the cult of individualism that plagues much of the modern world. Max Weber was a scholar of dazzling erudition who, at the same time, understood the emotional components of human existence. Weber knew that people are both body and mind, emotion and intellect, and that the modern world would put these in conflict.

With that said, our interest is not in considering the entire life works of

Marx, Weber, Durkheim, or Du Bois. Rather we zero in on those specific classical sociological concepts that help us explain current catastrophes. While we ground the concepts we use in the historical contexts in which the theorists wrote, we also believe that these insights have transhistorical relevance. For example, while aspects of both Weber's and Durkheim's work have rightfully been criticized as maintaining the status quo in nineteenth-century European society (including deeply embedded social hierarchies), that criticism does not mean that all of their work needs to be discarded. Weber's focus on characteristics of Protestantism obscures white theft of native land and slavery in the United States (since Weber did not focus on either), but his identification of the Protestant ethic in relation to capitalist accumulation remains relevant to understanding 9/11. In fact, we believe that Weber's work makes possible a rich and innovative interpretation of 9/11 and its aftermath as illustrating a transnational hunger for the sacred in an increasingly secular world. While Durkheim did not concern himself with imperialism or patriarchy, he did offer keen insight into the rootlessness experienced by many people in postindustrial society, including the two young people who killed their classmates and then themselves on a 1999 spring day in Colorado.

This book, then, is an invitation to social theory that draws on the specific theoretical tools from sociology that continue to inspire us and concepts from other disciplines that we can't help but claim for sociology. The book comes from the tradition of public sociologists who have always applied an interdisciplinary gaze to their work and a questioning spirit to their theoretical scope. Our willingness, perhaps even compulsion, to both engage with and extend beyond sociology—and our hunger for a multiracial, interdisciplinary focus—is what we believe ultimately allows us to offer new theoretical formulations.

Our grounding in black studies, in the history of the African American experience in particular, nurtures new theoretical formulation on historical memory dredged up during and since Hurricane Katrina. In the section of the book on the 9/11 attacks, our interest in religion and spirituality allows us to move beyond US ethnocentrism to identify a search for the sacred as a transnational need. For our analysis on Abu Ghraib, drawing upon both trauma theory that is grounded in psychoanalytic study and Marx's scholarly work on alienation enables us to show how the psychology of witnessing torture has a materialist base. The link between trauma theory and Marxism makes the work relevant to people interested in psychology and mental health. Our grounding in feminist theory, which insists on placing concerns about the body on a par with attention to the mind, enables us to move conceptually from a discussion of the Columbine massacre in particular to an analysis of body consciousness as a necessary antidote in this information age. As a book that looks deeply at media and imagery, culture and consciousness, while maintaining a commitment to data as a source of theory production, we see this volume as a bridge between sociology and cultural studies. It is also our attempt to reanimate public sociology by attending to upheavals at the forefront of people's worries.

Our book also reflects a momentum that has been building over the last thirty years, fueled by an increasing number of intellectuals who see the limitations imposed by disciplines that maintain an exclusionary canon (focused primarily on the work of white US- or European-born men). With the multiracial selection of authors whose work this book draws upon—including critical race theorist and the *Nation* columnist Patricia Williams, sociologist Patricia Hill Collins, activist and poet Audre Lorde, cultural theorist Gloria Anzaldúa, historian Darlene Clark Hine, and others—we are cracking the canon wide open. This book demonstrates why we keep turning to sociology as a means of both explaining and ending social inequalities that are at the root of many recent social upheavals.

## CONNECTING THE DOTS:
### AN OVERVIEW OF OUR IDIOSYNCRATIC PLEA

This book is written from the perspective of two skeptical, race- and gender-attentive women who are unsatisfied with any telling of a discipline's history that serves as a cheerleader for that field of study. While work by US sociologists in the 1920s and 1930s allowed many working-class voices to be heard (with particular focus on immigrant communities in Chicago), by the 1940s and 1950s much of sociology had been hijacked by a focus on abstract empiricism—a scientific method that leaves little room for human agency. By the end of World War II, sociology had surrendered much of its critical edge. It is shocking, but not uncharacteristic, that it wasn't until 1940, years after the buildup of the Nazi regime, that the leading US sociology journal published its first article on the Nazi Party.[10] As the United States became a world power, exerting its economic and military might across the globe, sociology increasingly became a publicist for US domination. Mainstream sociologists joined in the anticommunist hysteria of the 1950s, causing the discipline to lose much of its commitment to subverting injustice. During this period, sociology also increasingly depended upon the government for funding, again watering down its independence.

To this day, many sociologists are still taught that they should deliver conference papers about poverty, human rights violations, the AIDS epidemic, and institutional racism with the same measured and distant tone one might use to report on fluctuations in marketing patterns in advertising or changes in the weather. In his contemporary social theory text, sociologist Steven Seidman writes of the pain and outrage he felt, as a gay man, when he arrived at a national sociology conference in 1989 held in San Francisco, only to learn that not one social theory panel at the entire conference included a talk on the AIDS crisis.[11] By 1989, the AIDS crisis was devastating gay and straight communities all over the country. AIDS organizers were already aware that the epidemic was, with lightning speed, becoming a pandemic. An emphasis on dispassionate, distanced scholarship comes from what sociologist Alvin Gouldner refers to as "the myth of a value-free sociology," a myth that he identifies as "a conquering one."[12]

This training to be an objective social scientist is an example of what Patricia Williams refers to as the practice of "spirit murder"—a "disregard for others whose lives qualitatively depend on our regard."[13] Asking people to testify against themselves and their communities in order to succeed in the law, in the academy, and in other occupations requires them to murder their own and others' spirits in order to advance professionally. The quest for objectivity and distance has also contributed to a long history in sociology of avoiding many compelling and influential social issues, just when society needs deeply considered and rigorous analyses.

We start from the premise that people's social locations—their race, class, gender, ethnicity, nationality, linguistic background—profoundly shape their work and outlooks on the world. This is as true for social theorists as for the rest of us. This is what Patricia Hill Collins refers to as "standpoint theory"—where one stands in society frames how she or he interprets the world; what poet and theorist Adrienne Rich refers to as the "politics of location"; and what Patricia Williams refers to as "subject position."[14] As teachers for the last twenty years, we have found that teaching about the lives of the theorists we study—their childhoods, their struggles to find a place in the world, their passions, their health, their intellectual journeys—is a way to bring those theorists alive. We are interested in showing how theorists' struggles, worries, activism, and heartbreaks have informed their scholarship. This is why, in each chapter of the book, we weave biographical information about the theorists into our analysis as a way to show the dialectical relationship between personal lives and the theory scholars create. To make the theory come alive on the page, we tried to keep their biographies central—an approach that moves us beyond the quest for "objectivity" and distance that has long plagued the social sciences.

This book, we warn you, is anything but dispassionate and distant. It is a selective perspective from the point of view of two feminists dedicated to racial justice who are not willing to give up on social theory, who will not concede it to corporate hands, and who will not let it be denuded of its activism. In our own way, we are taking possession of sociology, beginning from the stance that activism is the measuring stick needed to judge the worth and longevity of any sociologist and his or her work.

Part One, "Consciousness: Lessons from Hurricane Katrina," addresses a change in political consciousness in the United States during the last thirty years that has made it possible for many people to be surprised when Katrina's destruction uncovered poor black communities. Many of the residents of New Orleans could not leave and were abandoned to fend for themselves. To answer the question of why this erasure occurred, we examine the rise of the color-blind ideology in the last thirty years that has been orchestrated by a substantial solidification of white conservative forces. These forces have, among other priorities, helped to advance a rising number of black conservatives. Du Bois's theory of "double consciousness" illuminates the consequences when conservative black people are implicated in attempting to erase the realities of race and class inequities.[15] Du Bois's concept speaks to a dual psychic space as well as to the reality of only partial citizenship, a status that has required black people to choose between being American and being black in one way or another for centuries.

We then provide a profile of Secretary of State Condoleezza Rice, who represents black people who have become American to such a degree that they don't seem to be part of a despised group any longer. We ask if they are seen as individuals in ways that Du Bois could hope for but never imagined. And we grapple with the fallout when double consciousness seems to no longer apply to black conservatives. Our questions are answered as we look carefully at the reporting of the Katrina disaster and find that even though black conservatives have rejected double consciousness, it still resides among many African Americans who were profoundly disturbed when they witnessed Katrina or survived it themselves. Katrina linked people back to historical memory that ties them to each other and to past struggles. Drawing upon the work of historian Darlene Clark Hine and cultural theorist Gloria Anzaldúa, we conclude the section by acknowledging that we continue to need not merely double consciousness but a consciousness that has expanded to include many other identities. We are hopeful that out of the destruction of Katrina will come a reinvigoration of New Orleans's long struggle for cultural and political wholeness.

Part Two, "Spirit: The 9/11 Attacks," begins with an acknowledgment of the effect of 9/11 on New Yorkers and others around the world. We trace how the goodwill and compassion immediately following the attacks were replaced by business as usual when the politics of retaliation became the rational response to the irrationality of 9/11. These politics made it possible for the United States to invade Afghanistan and later to occupy Iraq, as well as to intensify fear of the Arab "other." We look to Max Weber and his work on modernity and rationality to see how the politics of compassion became the politics of retaliation. We are also able to see that both those responsible for 9/11 and those mourning the attacks may have a similar hunger for the mystical, which can provide a sense of joy, communion, and meaning that is often absent in contemporary society.

Part Three, "Labor: The Abu Ghraib Prison Abuses," begins with a question we have found ourselves asking, in despair—why are so many people in the United States perennially angry? Why the hostility, aggressiveness, and over-the-top xenophobia? When, like millions of other people throughout the world, we saw photographs of the US military humiliating detainees at the Abu Ghraib prison in Iraq, we were horrified by what, to us, looked like acts of great anger, anger writ large on a big screen that is reflected in many American acts around the globe.

To address this question, we reach to the work of Karl Marx, in particular his examination of the multiple consequences of alienated labor.[16] His insights help us understand what happens to people who spend their time doing work that has no creative or productive meaning. The photos can be considered a depraved attempt on the part of the military to create a product that would help the military overcome their alienation. Instead, as a result of digital camera technology, their photos were disseminated around the world, making the audience a witness to the abuse of the prisoners, giving the guards' alienated labor worldwide exposure. This exposure does not ignoble, as Marx hoped. By showing us the debased prisoners and the process of abuse, the photos implicated all of us who viewed them. We present parallels between Marx's analysis of people's separation from the process of production, on one hand, and psychoanalytic work on dissociation—sociological and psychological processes in response to social trauma—on the other.

While Marx remains helpful in predicting the problems of labor in a postindustrial, hypercapitalist society, the dead end for Marx is his inability to find solutions to these problems (short of the overthrow of capitalism). In search of solutions we turn to María Lugones, Dori Laub, Marilyn Buck, and Frantz Fanon, all of whom provide critical insights about alienation, twenty-first-century style. We conclude the section with profiles of grassroots social justice organizations that are committed to the process of what Frantz Fanon refers to as "decolonizing" people's minds.[17] These organizations are offering solutions Marx might well have endorsed but probably could not have imagined.

Part Four, "Body: The Columbine School Shooting," hinges on the question of whether, in this information age of seemingly endless possibilities, there is a moral compass that can be a guide for people's need for connection and community? Our focus on the 1999 Columbine High School murders/suicides in Colorado reflects our interest in moving the national discussion from attention on two disturbed young men to the reasons why white adolescent boys in our society would feel so disconnected from others that they would shoot their classmates and then themselves. To grapple with this question, we look to the scholarship of the French sociologist Émile Durkheim. In particular we ask whether his analysis of community, morality, and individualism as it relates to the nineteenth and twentieth centuries can be applied to twenty-first-century social problems.

Through his careful empirical and theoretical work Durkheim showed that while religion held people together in preindustrial societies, occupational groups, education, and government would bind individuals to each other in industrial society. Our question pivots on what will bind people to each other in the twenty-first century, when both religion and government are insufficient to the task? We ask in particular: How far can Durkheim's work take us in understanding why two teenagers—with race, class, and gender privilege, with seemingly the world and their lives in front of them—would premeditate one of the deadliest school murders in US history? Durkheim's work shows that community and connection—which are manifest in belonging to one's body and the body politic—are transhistorical necessities. His work suggests that a postindustrial, highly technological, and militarized society may make it impossible for people to live comfortably in either of these bodies. Durkheim underscores why the question of what provides people with a sense of social cohesion and connection remains paramount.

This reality has encouraged us to look to contemporary theorists for help in understanding ways of approaching current despairs. We look to Audre Lorde's work on the "erotic as power" as a way to connect us to others as well as to gain the wholeness that Durkheim recognized is necessary for people to experience joy in life.[18] We ask what antidotes are necessary to protect against the disembodiment and fragmentation that are part of Internet culture. We propose that body consciousness be recognized as a key resource of power to keep people grounded in their bodies and with each other in the face of cyberspace realities.

In the concluding chapter, we revisit key themes in the book through a dialogue between the two of us, based on a series of questions we ask each other. Throughout the book, we have asked for dialogue, so we thought it only proper to end with a conversation ourselves. After several substantive chapters focusing on classical theorists' lives and contributions, this last chapter takes the reader backstage, to our process, emotions, and personalities, and to the challenges in writing the book. We ask whether our initial admiration for classical theory remained by the end of the project—whether continuing to read and teach these theorists makes sense. We talk about inequalities that are still most troubling to us and whose activist work continues to inspire us.

### WRITING ON THE RUN

In the time we have spent writing this book, we have often grappled with how our social locations have shaped our arguments and intellectual collaboration. Sociologists rarely talk about the actual work of writing, whether individually or collaboratively. While poets and novelists attend to the lived practice of being writers, sociologists and other academics tend to treat this work as a privatized space, a silence that does little to open up the process for people to learn from. We have done much of the initial writing together, in the same room, slogging our ideas out in quick and slow snatches. When we haven't been able to be together (since we live in different states), we have written over the phone, the handset cradled in between Becky's neck and shoulder as she tried to type fast enough to keep up with Diane's lightning-speed ideas. The closest we can come to describing writing together is that it is like being in a cantankerous trance. While we are in this state, it feels like we are twisting our way through to more nuanced analyses by pushing against each other, our long-standing friendship the touchstone that lets us get cranky and argumentative. After this initial writing, we go back and refine our work, doing more background research and footnoting.

On the face of it, our identities—in terms of race, age, and, to some extent, sexuality and class—differentially influence the arguments we have made in the process of writing collaboratively. And yet, over the years, we have seen how deeply intertwined our histories and perspectives are, particularly as people growing up in the United States. For Diane, as a black person whose ancestors were dragged to this country more than three centuries ago and were responsible for creating most of the wealth of the country, it is hard to see oneself as anything but American, while still aware of an African past. Becky's Mormon background also gives her a uniquely American identity. This identity was born in upstate New York in the late 1820s among poor white people determined to find a way to distinguish themselves from black people and thereby to ensure success in US society. Trying to outdo the WASPs, in response to the threat of being seen as not quite white enough, members of the Mormon faith developed an intense Protestant ethic. Prohibiting alcohol, tobacco, and premarital sex was a way to prove their whiteness (their not-blackness)—a real challenge given that, structurally, they occupied a similar location to that of free black people. Both groups needed to sell their labor, did not own property, and did not have access to higher education. Mormons kept black people out of their church to distinguish themselves from blacks. After the Civil War, Mormons certainly did not want to be confused with the newly freed slaves—another trick, considering they had worked and lived beside each other for decades.

As a new religion, Mormonism was negatively tied to blackness, and in that way it is American to its core. This echoes Ralph Ellison, author of *Invisible Man,* who often said that white Americans are blacker than they know.[19] Psychic ties between Mormons and African Americans have been largely unexplored.[20] Meanwhile, in the last several years, we have seen Mormonism growing all over Africa and across US cities, including Harlem. It may be that Mormons had to leave black people to create an identity before they could embrace black people, with whom they have much in common. These shared values include Protestantism with a cultural twist; a primary identification with being American; an intense focus on family; a belief in circling the wagons while watching after your own, often with great protectiveness and judgment; and shared conservative beliefs about reproductive rights, monogamy, and heterosexuality.

In this context, we also both represent groups who, historically, have been running away from something, a running that, in a bizarre way, connects us. We both came from regions of the country that are running places. Historically, Mormons were running fast, from poverty, from strictures against polygamy, from anti-Mormon violence. In keeping with this tradition, Becky has certainly spent most of her life a far distance from a Mormon upbringing, a rebellion begun by her mother. The black people living in Sioux City, Iowa, where Diane was raised, all came running from somewhere else—from the South, many straight up from Arkansas and Alabama. With this running, they were desperately trying to situate themselves, first and foremost, as "Americans." Having grown up in this ideological context, the notion of an ethnic enclave was a foreign concept to Diane until she moved to New York City. There she saw Italian, Irish, and German communities—Little Italy, Hell's Kitchen, and Yorkville—where immigrants maintained a good deal of their cultural heritages from the old countries. By contrast, people living in the West and Midwest went there to make themselves Americans—in many ways devoid of their ethnic backgrounds.

The family Diane came from was full of runaway slaves, running from slavery and running toward patriarchy, a move to distinguish themselves from the myth of black matriarchal households. Diane was drawn to women's studies as a response to the extraordinarily patriarchal black community where she was raised. Becky was drawn to African American studies because she felt at home there intellectually and politically in a way she had not felt elsewhere. At seven years old, Becky saw a photograph of a slave ship with Africans tied down in rows, a reality that spoke to her unconsciously due to early childhood trauma.[21] Akasha Gloria Hull's extraordinary book, *Soul Talk: The New African American Women's Spirituality*, offers deep reflection on the ways that women heal from historical, sexual, and physical trauma—trauma that is both consciously named and unconsciously encoded in the flesh.[22] The depth of African American studies, as a discipline, is nourished by its ability to recognize connections between the past and the present, its willingness to privilege memory and honor the flesh.

Due to these overlapping histories, in many ways Diane and Becky have always been recognizable to each other. We don't want to say that our racial backgrounds make no difference in our lives and perspectives, but that difference is not what typically drives our dialogues. More relevant to us, in addition to our relation to Americanness, is our shared history of growing up in mixed-up families—which makes people ambitious in some key ways, prone to living in our heads, and watchful, a reality that drew both of us to sociology. Growing up fast also led us to think that change is our responsibility. There is a restlessness in that mission. Diane can remember, from when she was very young, talking about how she was going to go somewhere, learn something new, leave where she was in order to find a new place. As a child, when people would ask her where she was going, she couldn't answer. It was more about always pushing forward.

Like many people, we witnessed pain as children, a reality that, we believe, helped prepare us for the work, the almost obsessive need to spend weeks researching the abuses at Abu Ghraib prison, the psychic worlds of Dylan Klebold and Eric Harris in Colorado, and the other devastating issues we examine in this book. We, unfortunately or not, depending upon your perspective, have the stomach for facing that pain. Seeing pain early can give people a kind of empathy that can stay with us all of our lives. At the same time, that pain is seared into consciousness in a way that won't let people forget certain things, that compels us to call for a witness. This vision can, in some moments, take us to a place of grace. These are gifts we both received as children.

We also share a deep and abiding belief that an American identity carries a commitment to responsible dissent—to name and lessen the distance between US ideals and realities. Audre Lorde once said that the United States has been on the wrong side of every liberation struggle in recent history. US intervention in Chile, Cuba, and Grenada and the US government's support of Saddam Hussein and the Taliban prior to 9/11 are just a few examples that speak to Lorde's claim. Our belief is that it is our civic responsibility to see how what is done both domestically and internationally in the name of nation, the US nation, puts people at risk both inside and outside US borders—hence, the title of this book. "When the center is on fire" is a metaphor for a nation whose unbounded military and economic expansion has created the conditions for its own destruction. At the same time, on some level we must believe that there is still time to put the fire out. A global perspective is one that enables us to see that social movements both outside and inside the United States are working to put the fire out. In this way, while our heritage was born from US soil, our sense of ourselves is bigger than that as we attempt to hold ourselves accountable to a citizenship beyond national divides. Similarly, while the social upheavals we focus on in the book have particular significance for US readers, how people handle these upheavals will have transnational implications far into the future.

Through our collaborative process it has been impossible to imagine trying to grapple with the enormity and complications of the social problems we address in this book without having each other. We have cried, laughed, screamed, argued, pouted, and reasoned our way through this process together. "Ain't no mountain high enough" and "The last nerve is never really the last nerve" are how we feel about working together. May this process present itself in the following pages and invite the reader into the process as well.

# PART ONE

# CONSCIOUSNESS

*Lessons from Hurricane Katrina*

To Du Bois
after Randall Horton

**DuBois** (*due-boyz*) *v.* [*French Huguenot*]. *1*) *to write scholarly blues from a place that is deeper than black, as in, to* dubois *with fire where there once was only reason, Sam Hose's lynched knuckles hanging in an Atlanta butcher shop. 2) to Pan Africa a movement knowing that forty acres and a mule will never satisfy, as in I* dubois *my way to Ghana in my ninety-third year; see also Alice Walker's womanism: "Mama, I'm walking to Canada and I'm taking you and a bunch of other slaves with me." Reply: "It wouldn't be the first time." 3) to grieve the loss of one's only son:* his little soul leapt like a star / that travels in the night / and left a world / of darkness in its train. *4) to wear three piece suits in Atlanta's summer as in, I will* du bois *you with the finest of leather, the sweet smell of Tunisian cologne. syn West, Cornel. 4a) to smoke one cigarette after every meal, for 72 years; refining discipline that also woos the women, see also: Shirley Graham Du Bois.*

— BECKY THOMPSON

# ONE

# CONDOLEEZZA RICE,
# W. E. B. DU BOIS, AND
# DOUBLE CONSCIOUSNESS

In August 2005, Katrina, a category three hurricane, struck, virtually wiping out the city of New Orleans and wreaking havoc on the coasts of Louisiana, Alabama, and Mississippi. Thousands of poor people—mostly African American, but also Jamaican, Honduran, and Vietnamese; Houma, Chitimacha, and Choctaw; and white—were stranded in their houses, unable to escape the path of the storm. The federal and state agencies responsible for emergency assistance did virtually nothing to help evacuate the 100,000 people without cars.[1] Whole neighborhoods, patients in hospitals, elderly people, and young people were unable to escape, having to fend for themselves as the floodwaters rose. Governmental agencies provided almost no help for days and, in some locations, months following the storm.

While President Bush and Secretary of State Condoleezza Rice maintained that racism was not operating in the government's handling of the crisis, many people across the political spectrum knew racism when they saw it: "The color line separate[d] the drowned from the saved, and that line was laid a long time ago."[2] The media could not help but show the devastating differences in how middle-class white people and the poor—mostly black people—were faring after the storm. Many white people lost their homes but found safety with relatives or in hotel rooms that they drove to in cars containing their pets and other important valuables. In contrast, poor people were left to drown. If they managed to get out, they had no option but to be housed in unsafe, unsanitary, and overcrowded facilities with no plans in place for future shelter. From the Coast Guard to the Federal Emergency Management Agency (FEMA) and the National Guard, the list was long of agencies that failed to understand how race and class differentially affected the ways people were able to respond to the crisis.[3] In this instance, their negligence cost hundreds of lives.

While most of the critical attention following the catastrophe focused on the failures of the governmental agencies, the crisis also underscored, in perhaps the most dramatic way we could imagine, the damage done with the rise of black conservatives. Over the last twenty years, they have increasingly been portrayed as the voice for black people. The ascendancy of black conservatives—made possible through their empowerment by white leaders in the Republican Party—has silenced the progressive black leaders who have kept poor people on the radar screen. Katrina forced people across the world to acknowledge the widespread poverty in the United States, to see that many had been left behind while only a few black people realized the benefits of the civil rights movement. People were poor in New Orleans (and elsewhere) before Katrina hit. It took the storm to awaken people to the conditions poor people have long been enduring.

We see the rise of black conservative leadership as a sign of serious distress, because movements for racial justice in the United States have always been led by black people who see themselves as intricately connected with and responsible to black communities. Many were surprised to see the devastating scenes—graphic images of old people dying on airport baggage carousels after Katrina; children wandering around, separated from their relatives; and people waving emergency flags for days from their rooftops, hoping for a rescue—because we have been conditioned to think that racism and poverty had been eliminated, a conditioning that black conservatives helped to make possible. One reason that black people are 7.8 times as likely to be imprisoned as whites while the national discourse focuses on Michael Jackson and Tom Cruise is that we are missing black leadership that keeps the needs of the least empowered at the center of concern.[4] In many circles individual mobility seems to have become more important than social justice, more important than bearing witness to collective suffering. Black people have long been the conscience of the United States, the consciousness for racial progress, a reality that we fear is slipping.

Black conservatives are certainly not at the center of the turn away from racial justice in the United States. While they have played a part, their power and influence pale in comparison with white power. In the last quarter century, the Republican Party won four of the six presidential elections. Republicans controlled the Senate for the majority of this period and controlled both the Senate and the House of Representatives until 2006. The Republican Party, the religious right, the military, and the most powerful US-based multinational corporations are all white-controlled institutions. They, in concert, have orchestrated this shift to the right.

It is also true that being black and conservative is not exactly a newly paired description. A substantial portion of the black community—greatly influenced by their faith affiliations—has long held conservative beliefs, particularly on such social issues as the exclusivity of heterosexual marriage, Christian religious doctrine, male dominance, and self-reliance. While an overwhelming majority of black people have voted as Democrats since the 1960s, this reality reflects the ways that economic priorities (regarding education, health care, and public services) have trumped social positions (on heterosexual marriage, family, and religion).

What makes the importance of black conservatives over the last quarter century unprecedented is that although the actual number of black conservative leaders is small, the political presence and the power they are being afforded to undermine racial justice have been substantial. Some of them have been encouraged to run against more progressive black politicians and have taken high-profile positions in all branches of government. Others are granted legitimacy as pundits and "experts" who uphold the notion that race is no longer an issue in the United States. And this trend is growing to include a small group of strategically placed conservative Latinos, who, with the exception of Cubans, have historically supported a liberal agenda in US politics.[5] To a large extent, the Republican Party has orchestrated this trend by aggressively courting and nurturing black and Latino conservative voices.

While there has been much helpful writing about the economic and political factors underlying this trend, little has been written about what is happening at the level of black consciousness.[6] To address this question, we turn to W. E. B. Du Bois and his work on double consciousness in particular.[7] Might Du Bois—who seemed to say everything about anything that applied to black people in his ninety-five years—have identified a racial dynamic that is still relevant in this post–civil rights era?[8] To what extent is double consciousness, first articulated in 1903, relevant in helping us understand black conservative leadership now? Might Du Bois show us how the individualism espoused by black conservatives of the post–civil rights era maintains white supremacy? While the Bush administration and others tried to cover up the racism and classism at the foundation of the response to Katrina, the victims of the hurricane spoke in multiple ways about the injustice aimed at entire groups and about survival based on group recognition. Their responses reveal how historical memory about the Middle Passage, slavery, and land remains with us, informing consciousness, whether named or not, across time.

## COLOR BLINDNESS AND CONDOLEEZZA RICE

While there is a range of black conservatives in the post–civil rights era, for multiple reasons we decided to focus our attention primarily on Secretary of State Condoleezza Rice.[9] First, she is the highest-ranking black woman in the history of US politics, in a position that has largely been considered the domain of men. She may well be the highest-ranking black woman ever to have considerable influence on military operations (if you don't count Harriet Tubman, who led the largest military operation by a black woman in US history, freeing more than 750 slaves in the process).[10] Second, there is already substantial writing about Rice's life—both autobiographical and by commentators from various political persuasions. Such writing enables us to analyze her emerging identity as a child growing up in the South and then the West, and her developing consciousness in academic and then governmental settings. Third, the ways she has been represented in the media and how she portrays herself reveal how race, class, gender, and sexuality collectively inform consciousness. Rice's politics cannot be conflated with those of other black conservatives; they are not a monolithic category. However, Rice's longevity in positions of substantial power reveals much about racism in the post–civil rights era.

One of the most graphic examples of how racism and sexism are reflected in portrayals of Rice appeared in a 2005 article from the *Washington Post*. The article announces:

> Secretary of State Condoleezza Rice arrived at the Wiesbaden Army Airfield on Wednesday, dressed all in black. She was wearing a black skirt that hit just above the knee, and it was topped with a black coat that fell to mid-calf. The coat, with its seven gold buttons running down the front and its band collar, called to mind a Marine's dress uniform or the "save humanity" ensemble worn by Keanu Reeves in "The Matrix."
>
> As Rice walked out to greet the troops, the coat blew open in a rather swashbuckling way to reveal the top of a pair of knee-high boots. The boots had a high, slender heel that is not particularly practical. But it is a popular silhouette because it tends to elongate and flatter the leg. In short, the boots are sexy. . . .
>
> Rice's appearance at Wiesbaden—a military base with all of its attendant images of machismo, strength and power—was striking because she walked out draped in a banner of authority, power and toughness. She was not hiding behind matronliness, androgyny or the stereotype of the steel magnolia. Rice brought her full self to the world stage—and that

included her sexuality. It was not overt or inappropriate. If it was distract-
ing, it is only because it is so rare.[11]

What is so striking about the above account is that it contains no men-
tion of Rice's race. On the surface it is simply a description of a powerful
woman's clothes. Few would see it as racist or sexist. Many, in fact, would
laud it as evidence that racism is waning because Rice's race, while visible
to anyone who looks at the photograph, is never mentioned in the text.
What is insidious, however, is that much is being said about her race and
gender in code. Implicit in the passage is a portrayal of Rice as an updated
version of Sapphire, a character from the *Amos 'n' Andy* radio program of
the 1950s, a black woman who was more masculine than feminine and who
challenged authority. Sapphire became a signifier of sinister and dangerous
forces attributed to black women. We doubt that any white woman of equal
status would be described in such a manner.

Racism in the twenty-first century is being reproduced in such a way
that it is hard to locate and even harder to cite. As the conditions for many
black people have worsened—rates of poverty, unemployment, incarceration, and disease are as bad as or worse than they were prior to the civil
rights movement—there was little collective outcry until Katrina. Racism's
cool sophistication and the way it is embedded in other narratives make
it hard to counteract. Now it is difficult to recognize that the description
of the first black female secretary of state reads as a cross between a fashion magazine and a pornography magazine—rendering her, essentially, a
"rare" and exotic black body. At the same time, the elusiveness of racism
has contributed to the lack of mobilization in the black community as well
as the rise of the race-neutral individual who has little, if any, accountability to black people. These individuals are characterized by their com-
petence, intelligence, loyalty, and American identity, which, of course, is
purported to have nothing to do with their blackness or the black community. The damaging effects of this racism expand as these representations
gain increasing international visibility.

That Rice could be described in highly racialized ways without race
being mentioned is a powerful example of color blindness, the dominant
racial ideology in the post–civil rights era. Color blindness was first cham-
pioned in the United States by liberals in the 1960s who saw it as a crucial
response to segregationist politics. Color blindness reflected an integrationist strategy of considering everybody equal under the law. Liberals
believed that the passage of the Civil Rights Act, the Voting Rights Act,
and other key legislation would eliminate the need for color-coded, color-

conscious policies. Legal equality would be sufficient to eradicate centuries of racism. Many people saw color blindness as an avenue for integration. Color blindness asked that people, in the famed words of Martin Luther King Jr., "not be judged by the color of their skin but by the content of their character."[12] Color blindness appeared to be a way to erase years of negative stereotypes by asking people to see color differences as irrelevant. It also dovetailed with American individualism—judging each person as an individual, separate from his or her group affiliation.

While this political strategy was initially intended to resist legal segregation, beginning in the 1970s conservatives began to twist it as part of the backlash against the gains of the civil rights movement. What began as an integrationist method aimed at countering racism was distorted to the point that people who identified race or racism were, themselves, considered racist.[13] Programs intended to reduce discrimination, such as affirmative action, are considered inherently racist since they require the acknowledgment of the existence of racial categories. If racism no longer exists, then it is deemed illegitimate to bring it up in any serious context. Those who continue to name it are "beating a dead horse" or are accused of "playing the race card," which is seen as a poor excuse at best and more often as simply racist. They would argue that people who are poor or don't have health care are in that situation because of their own individual character flaws. It has nothing to do with their race, just as we are told that a successful black person like Rice became secretary of state solely on the basis of her individual talents. This new "raceless racism" seems more insidious than the Jim Crow that we fought.

The longevity of color blindness as an approach to race is partly a function of its ability to seduce. Color blindness trades on the invisibility of racism and the hypervisibility of individual successful people of color. It offers white people a way out from feeling guilty for past injustices, since their only job is to see the people of color they currently interact with as individuals. Color blindness is seductive for people of color in that it promises an escape from stigma, since the pact is that white people will ignore their color (and therefore will not discriminate). Color blindness is attractive because it gives people of color the illusion of a psychic space where they can flourish—in their careers, financially, and in their social lives. It professes a society where people can be free to be seen beyond their skin color. For years, in our classes we have seen students yearning to ignore color hierarchies—discussions seem more comfortable when guilt and stigma appear to be absent.

The essential problem with color blindness, however, is that it negates history and context, which makes it possible to ignore, minimize, and disguise people's real-life experience. Color blindness takes place when security guards consistently ask black male students (and not white students) for their identification cards but then, when confronted, say that they don't see color in how they interact with students. Color blindness among students of color occurs when they believe that racism has nothing to do with their lives. When asked why they sit only with black students at lunch, they will say, "It isn't because they are black. They are just my friends. I don't choose my friends based on color."

The ultimate seduction of color blindness is that both people of color and white people can end up buying into the logic—giving every explanation for inequalities other than racism, believing that the people of color who excel are not the exceptions, and asserting that identifying racism is an excuse for not facing one's own limitations. Color blindness binds white people together (by convincing them of their innocence) while blurring race consciousness among people of color.[14]

The new color blindness, with its attention to the hypervisible individual with his or her personal ambitions, does not give us space to hold people accountable. This political perspective is in stark contrast to conversations during the civil rights era, when it was possible to "call black people out" in the name of responsibility and accountability to the black community. People were castigated for not using their education and other cultural capital in service of black people. Now the focus on the individual-achieving black person makes it difficult to criticize the new black conservative friends of the right wing, particularly Rice. A critique of Rice that makes reference to her race is rarely seen as an informed analysis but rather is considered a "crabs in a barrel" maneuver: one black person trying to delegitimize another, successful black person out of envy or jealousy.

Are we in fact looking at a time when the black bourgeoisie have become the quintessential spokespeople for ruling-class ideas? How did we get to a point where Colin Powell, when he was secretary of state, decided not to attend the historic 2001 United Nations Conference against Racism, Racial Discrimination, Xenophobia, and Related Intolerance held in Durban, South Africa—in effect abandoning the five hundred African American delegates who were waiting for him? He appeared to have no regret. Since then, he commissioned a coat of arms from Scotland's heraldic authority that he was granted in a ceremony in 2004. He did not seek a parallel symbol of his lineage from Africa. Clarence Thomas performed a similar move by distancing himself horribly from his black background. It is common knowledge, however, that Thomas was put in that position—

that he had neither the credentials nor the experience to be an associate justice of the Supreme Court. Powell, on the other hand, is supremely qualified, a reality that makes his transcendence of blackness troubling. Did he, at some point, have to choose? Could he not be black to be deemed American?

While Rice, like Colin Powell, is typically portrayed simply as an American (but not black) in the United States, she strategically represents herself as a black person when she is abroad. Internationally, she uses the story of her upbringing in Birmingham, Alabama, the daughter of striving middle-class parents, as testimony to the power of democracy in the United States. Her presence symbolizes that black people are now full citizens in a way they had not been before. This blackness, which she understates in the United States, is brought front and center as she becomes a face of US military and strategic decisions around the world. Ironically, the scrupulously described clothes that she wore in Germany—a country with a recent history as both Christian dominated and white controlled—are eerily reminiscent of a Nazi uniform, complete with jackboots and shiny brass buttons running down the front of her tailored black coat.

While becoming the symbol of democracy in blackface internationally, back at home Rice supported the Bush administration's opposition to affirmative action even as she herself was a beneficiary of it, most directly when she was awarded a 1981 fellowship at the Stanford Center for International Security and Arms Control, with funding earmarked for faculty of color.[15] In addition, when she was hired to be an assistant professor at Stanford University, the position was created without a national search process, made possible through a "target of opportunity" policy.

Furthermore, what does it mean that Rice, who registered and voted for Jimmy Carter in 1976, who worked on the 1984 presidential campaign of Democratic senator Gary Hart, eventually became the cabinet member whom many believe to be closest to President George W. Bush?[16] What might her shifting party gears suggest about the Democrats' inability to recognize and reward her formidable political and intellectual abilities, to invite her into the higher party echelon in a way parallel to how she was promoted by the Republican Party? What does it mean that a woman widely known for her meticulous attention to political detail and daily intimate access to discussions among the president and other key advisers could, with a straight face, claim that there was little warning of the impending attacks on the World Trade Center? Are these seemingly schizophrenic positions twenty-first-century symptoms of the loss of what Du Bois referred to as "double consciousness"?

## W. E. B. DU BOIS

Rice's contradictory relationship to blackness takes us back to Du Bois's writing for insight. Du Bois and Rice were born almost one hundred years apart—Du Bois in 1868, Rice in 1954. Du Bois was raised by a single mother in a poor family in the North, Rice by two parents in a middle-class family in the South and then the West. Du Bois considered himself deeply spiritual and yet agnostic whereas Rice grew up as the daughter of a Presbyterian minister and still attends church regularly.

While differences between them are both obvious and influential, their similarities are in some ways more revealing: both were driven, working long hours each day with seemingly boundless energy. They both had access to elite educations, traveled all over the world (in positions of authority), were materially better off than most black people, were able to develop their unique talents (for her, ice skating and tennis; for him, cycling in Europe, writing novels and poems), and were respected in many white circles. And both lived most of their lives as "exceptional" black people.

How the two of them dealt with this exceptionalism may ultimately be what most separates them. In her case, Rice took her opportunities and ran with them to further her career, to become an extraordinary American, no longer responsible for reaching out to black people. By contrast, Du Bois took this exceptionalism to fuse his American identity with an African identity, allowing him to develop a world identity founded on the liberation of black people.

The extensive biographical work on Du Bois's life—including his three autobiographies, along with his almost century-long life, during which he packed more into a single year than many accomplish in a lifetime—makes any brief summary of his life daunting. Our attention to his background reveals how much his own life experience informed his responses to exceptionalism: he had an almost haunting sense of responsibility to find a way to live in a white-controlled world while never letting it get a complete hold on him. His biography also illuminates the ways he, unlike Rice, continually recreated himself to remain accountable to black people.

Du Bois was raised in Great Barrington, Massachusetts, a small town with very few black people. He never knew his father, who Du Bois surmised left Great Barrington in search of work not easily found by a black man in that region. His father, from black and French Huguenot ancestry, provided his French name. His mother came from people originally taken from the coast of West Africa. Du Bois's light skin revealed the mixing of slavery and migration, rape and consensual sex, that has been both untold and told in the history of African American heritage. Du Bois was devoted to his mother, who died soon after he graduated from high school, leaving him to travel to Fisk University alone with financial help from people in his community. While he had hoped to go to Harvard University, attending Fisk (1885–1888), the premier black institution of higher learning in the country at the time, exposed him to Southern black life, contact that had an indelible influence on the rest of his life.

About this period Du Bois wrote, "I was thrilled to be for the first time among so many people of my own color or rather such various and such extraordinary colors, which I had not seen before, but who seemed close bound to me by new and exciting ties. I had never seen such beautiful girls in my life or men who gave themselves such merited airs."[17] As a form of protection after being slapped by a white woman he accidentally bumped into, he made a decision to always present himself as a model gentleman—to be immaculately dressed and to speak in a highly proper and formal manner. He held to this decision for the rest of his life, as evident in his natty dress, perfectly coiffed hair, and requisite elegant tie. After graduating from Fisk, he attended Harvard, earning another BA before beginning graduate work. Again recognized as a star student, Du Bois studied history, philosophy, and what would have been social sciences had Harvard recognized such a field.[18]

Like the other top graduate students at Harvard, Du Bois intended to finish his doctoral work in Europe. Once in Germany, he studied economics, history, and sociology with a thrilling combination of theorists, including Max Weber, who in later years visited him in Atlanta and rallied for *The Souls of Black Folk* to be translated into German. In Germany, Du Bois lived with a German family and spent time with "gay young folk who made me realize that white folk were human."[19] Although he excelled in his academic work, he was not granted a PhD; the US philanthropic fund that had originally paid for his scholarship refused to grant him the final semester's finances he needed to finish his work. Nevertheless, his time in Germany, away from the particular racism of the United States from 1892 to 1894, helped him see racism as neither inevitable nor ahistorical in nature and course. As with Malcolm X, James Baldwin, Richard Wright, and so many other gifted black people, exile from the United States—whether forced or voluntary—had the paradoxical effect of giving Du Bois hope about the country. Exile assured through lived experience that racism had been mantled in specific ways in the United States and therefore, at least theoretically, could be dismantled there as well.

Du Bois returned to the United States, applying for multiple academic appointments while finishing his doctorate at Harvard. Despite his prodigious accomplishments, he received only one teaching offer, from Wilberforce College, a black school in Ohio. There Du Bois taught the classics until he moved to Philadelphia in 1896, where he launched and completed an exhaustive, four-hundred-page study on black life in the city.[20] This study was based on more than five thousand interviews he conducted personally, along with his participant observations made while living with his wife, Nina Gomer, in a one-bedroom apartment over a cafeteria in the Seventh Ward in Philadelphia, a historic black community. Du Bois was countering what he referred to as "car-window sociologists," those who, "while attempting to understand the South or black Americans, spent a few leisurely hours on holiday, riding in a Pullman car through the South, generally not venturing into communities."[21]

*The Philadelphia Negro* became the first urban sociology text in the country, predating the Chicago School's focus on ethnography by two decades. Capturing the complexity of his insider/outsider status as a black scholar studying the black community in Philadelphia, Du Bois wrote, "I did the work despite extraordinary difficulties both within and without the group. The Negroes resented being studied at all and especially by a colored stranger; the whites endured the study as a gesture toward an answer which they already knew."[22]

When Du Bois accepted the professorship at Atlanta University in economics and history (1897–1910), he still believed that scientific study of black life, history, and culture could turn racism around—that white ignorance of the contributions and ingenuity of black life was at the center of US racism. With this belief and ethic in hand, Du Bois launched a breathtaking range of sociological studies—of sharecroppers, health care, the black church, blacks in business—each intended to chronicle key aspects of black culture.[23]

During this period, two tragedies irrevocably shifted his worldview and vision about his life's work. The first was the death of his toddler son in 1899 from diphtheria. About the impact of this death on Du Bois's work, friend and biographer Herbert Aptheker wrote, "The loss of his son sensitized Du Bois and gave him a sense of the spiritual meaning that so many other blacks around him depended upon."[24] The second event took place that same year, when Du Bois, on his way to deliver a reasoned letter of protest about a trumped-up charge leveled against a man in the local area, learned that the man had been lynched. Du Bois wrote, "On the way the news met me: Sam Hose had been lynched and they said that his knuckles were on exhibition at a grocery store on Mitchell Street. I turned back to the university. I suddenly saw that complete scientific detachment in the midst of such a South was impossible."[25]

A third factor contributing to his decision to leave academia related to the mistreatment of many of his studies. After launching and completing many scientific studies contracted by the US government, Du Bois discovered that his most important work on sharecropping had been destroyed by the Department of Labor, an act reflecting governmental unwillingness to comprehend the complexity of his critique of race and class inequity. According to Aptheker, "This was one of the most devastating events in Du Bois's professional career—for years afterward, he did not even want to talk about it."[26] Du Bois wrote that, by 1910, "my work in Atlanta and my dream of the settlement of the Negro problem by science faded."[27] Soon after that, he left Atlanta University for New York City, where he became editor of the *Crisis*, a magazine affiliated with the National Association for the Advancement of Colored People (NAACP). Under Du Bois's tenure, it became the premier magazine of culture and politics, covering a wide range of domestic issues as well as foreign affairs in Europe, Asia, South America, and the Caribbean.

Amid these many commitments, Du Bois was constantly taking on conservative racial politics—whether initiated by black or white people. In his scholarship he consistently confronted the racist mores of the time. For example, his massive study, *Black Reconstruction in America, 1860–1880*, offered an economic, historical, and philosophical study of black people's work and lives during Reconstruction that overturned crude and dangerous ideas about black people espoused in most white historical material of the time.[28] His willingness to confront the accommodationist politics of Tuskegee Institute founder Booker T. Washington was a key factor in many potential funders' refusal to support his sociological studies while he was teaching at Atlanta University.[29] During both of his tenures at Atlanta University, Du Bois spoke out against white scholars and administrators who professed to support black people while patronizing them or espousing racist conceptions of intelligence. During his years working with the NAACP, his outspokenness was so troublesome to many members that he was constantly in battle. He allied himself with progressive black and white people while he confronted both individuals and institutions that double-crossed black causes.

While Du Bois's principles were sometimes costly, he did not let the obstacles he faced stop him from recreating himself and his approach to changing the world. This ability can be seen in his writing, his activism, and even his personal life. In terms of genre, his writing included historical treatises (for example, his dissertation on the suppression of the slave trade), dozens of sociological studies, a trilogy of novels, poetry, hundreds of articles for the *Crisis* and other magazines and newspapers, children's books, autobiographies, and comparative historical documents. In describing changes in his own autobiographical writing over the years, Du Bois explained, "I have essayed in a half century three sets of thoughts centering around the hurts and hesitancies that hem the black man in America. The first of these, *The Souls of Black Folk,* written thirty-seven years ago was a cry at midnight thick within the veil, when none rightly knew the coming day. The second, *Darkwater,* now twenty years old, was an exposition and militant challenge, defiant with dogged hope. This the third book [*Dusk of Dawn*] started to record dimly but consciously that subtle sense of coming day which one feels of early mornings even when mist and murk hang low."[30]

His activist commitments were equally astounding, shifting to keep up with the times. His work ranged from lobbying against legislation that would disenfranchise black people to organizing the Niagara Movement, an early civil rights organization that was a precursor to the NAACP; from becoming an internationally recognized leader in the Pan African Movement to campaigning against the persecution of Julius and Ethel Rosenberg.[31] In the five decades of his writing on Africa, Du Bois made significant conceptual changes in his thinking. Historian Eric Sundquist writes, "Beginning with an Afrocentric romanticism that was characteristic of his early essays and verse, Du Bois over time adopted a critique of colonialism grounded in a socialist interpretation of traditional African tribal communities."[32] Du Bois's longevity and his ability to rethink and refine his political positions revealed his changing understanding of what constitutes liberation, from a domestic focus to attention toward anticolonial struggles throughout the world.[33] His worldview became increasingly international as he saw the freedom of colonized people in Africa, Latin America, Asia, and the Caribbean as intimately tied to the liberation of black people in the United States.

Even in Du Bois's personal life, he was willing to recreate himself. Du Bois was a man of enormous self-discipline, who planned his life out with minutely detailed schedules and goals considered in decade blocks. He smoked three cigarettes a day for his entire adult life, one after each meal. He retired at ten each night, no matter what, even if it meant leaving a panel in the middle of a sentence.[34] He saw eating carefully, plenty of sleep, and discipline as keys to longevity. A man who may have invented the word "driven," he was also a lover of dance, music, and poetry. As Aptheker remembers, "Du Bois was a loner, a genius, and though he was a well-trained scholar and social scientist, he was at heart a poet."[35] At the age of eighty-three, a year after his wife of fifty-four years died, he married Shirley Graham, a writer, teacher, and civil rights activist who became his intellectual and political partner for the rest of his life.[36] At the end of his last autobiography, *Dusk of Dawn,* Du Bois wrote, "I am especially glad of the divine gift of laughter; it has made the world human and lovable, despite all its pain and wrong. I am glad that the partial Puritanism of my upbringing has never made me afraid of life. I have lived completely, testing every normal appetite, feasting on sunset, sea and hill, and enjoying wine, women, and song. I have seen the face of beauty from the Grand Canyon to the great Wall of China; from the Alps to Lake Baikal; from the African bush to the Venus of Milo."[37]

At no point did he recreate himself in a vacuum or within an insular space. He expanded his ideas about black needs based on historical and political changes among black people around the world. In his last major address to the nation before he was assassinated, Martin Luther King delivered a lengthy and passionate tribute to Du Bois at Carnegie Hall. The speech revealed King's deep study of and admiration for Du Bois. King described Du Bois as having had three careers: "Beginning as a pioneer sociologist he had become an activist to further mass organization. The activist had then transformed himself into a historian. By the middle of the twentieth century when imperialism and war arose once more to imperil humanity he became a peace leader."[38] As Du Bois was recreating himself, he was using history and his interactions with people globally as sources of inspiration.

The fact that he moved to Ghana in 1961 at the age of ninety-two (in large part because of support from Ghana's president Kwame Nkrumah to complete an encyclopedia of Africana, a project Du Bois had first conceptualized in Atlanta in 1909) speaks volumes to his ability to stay true to his scholarly and political priorities while remaining flexible about where he might need to go to bring his plans to fruition.[39] Ultimately, Du Bois was able to live and work amid many obstacles because of his expansive mind and his commitment to black people.

## DOUBLE CONSCIOUSNESS AND CONDOLEEZZA RICE

*The Souls of Black Folk,* Du Bois's most prophetic and poetic work, is widely considered among the foundational texts in the history of US letters.[40] Many consider it the "preeminent modern text of African American cultural consciousness."[41] The book opens with a rhetorical question: How does it feel to be a problem? This question situates the rest of the book that seeks to move away from the portrayal of blacks as problems to recognizing them as human beings with their own genius and contributions. This genius, Du Bois maintains, is soulfully expressed in black music, work, and families.[42] Du Bois professed that people need to reach back to their culture to move forward. They must reach back to their art, music, and religion in order to move forward as an authentic black people.

Du Bois conceives of double consciousness as resulting from a conflict between one's self-perception as a full human being and others' perceptions of that selfhood as inferior and forever an outsider: "The Negro is a sort of seventh son, born with a veil, and gifted with second-sight in this American world—a world which yields him no true self-consciousness, but only lets him see himself through the revelation of the other world. It is a peculiar sensation, this double-consciousness, this sense of always looking at one's self through the eyes of the others, of measuring one's soul by the tape of a world that looks on in an amused contempt and pity. One ever feels his two-ness—an American, a Negro; two souls, two thoughts, two unreconciled strivings; two warring ideals in one dark body, whose dogged strength alone keeps it from being torn asunder."[43] When Du Bois asked in 1903 what it means to be "looking at one's self through the eyes of the others," he spoke for aspiring black students who were not granted access to the best universities in the country. He spoke for the sharecropping farmer who had difficulty carving out an existence; for the washerwoman whose white employer couldn't seem to believe the clothes were clean enough; for the artisan whose creative blues contributions were never honored monetarily. He asked what it meant to be seen as a problem for black men whose lynchings often drew white crowds in the thousands.[44] Du Bois asked the question for his son, who died when two years old as Du Bois desperately sought medical help he never found.[45]

Du Bois opens with "The Negro is a sort of seventh son." Condoleezza Rice's heritage includes people of African descent, whom Du Bois referred to as a seventh people. She, like most African Americans in the United States, including Du Bois, came from a mixed people; all those with African heritage were labeled as black because of the "one-drop rule" in racial categorization. Though from a seventh people, she definitely was not a son. Rice was born a daughter in Birmingham, Alabama, in 1954. She was an only child, whose minister-and-football-coach father had wanted a boy. While other little girls rode horses and read books, Rice learned to love football.[46] She was socialized as a middle-class black girl, while allowed some of the knowledge typically granted only to boys if there are boys in the family. Rice was also a crossover child. She first lived in the segregated South; then, because of the civil rights movement and her family's move west, she lived in an integrated, mostly white community in Denver, Colorado.

Was she "born with a veil," the next phrase in Du Bois's passage? The "veil" is a recurrent theme in Du Bois's work, appearing from his early to his late scholarship. In places he uses it as a metaphor and in others as a historical reality. In a literal sense, he is making a biological connection to the caul, a thin membrane that covers the head of some newborns, and using it as a vivid description of segregation.[47] Du Bois was among the first to identify the ambiguity in his use of the term "veil." In his review of *The Souls of Black Folk,* he explains that the book has a clear message, a clear center, around which is a "penumbra of vagueness and half-veiled allusion. . . . How far this fault is in me and how far it is in the nature of the message I am not sure. It is difficult, strangely difficult, to translate the finer feelings of men into words."[48]

The "finer feelings" Du Bois refers to are what make *Souls* an intimate book. He writes, "Through all the book runs a personal and intimate tone of self-revelation. In each essay I sought to speak from within—to depict a world as we see it who dwell therein."[49] The veil, then, is a concept that Du Bois partly developed based on his own life experience, attending Harvard University but then eating meals by himself; becoming an intellectual steeped in European history, politics, and culture while finding scant and often damaging scholarship about African cultures; and seeing the impact of segregation on white people's inability to recognize the centrality of black labor in American identity. Du Bois also clarifies that the book was made possible because "the blood of my fathers spoke through me and cast off the English restraint of my training and surroundings."[50] This clarification signals Du Bois's incorporation of African as well as African American sources as a basis of knowledge, his use of written as well as oral knowledge, published work as well as work channeled from the ancestors.

In *Souls,* Du Bois writes of an invisible barrier between white and black people that keeps white people from being able to see black people. Black people are able to see beyond the veil to the world around them, but whites cannot see black humanity. The veil represents the separation between blacks and whites, enforced through segregation, which has physical, psychological, economic, and spiritual ramifications. The veil also separates people—both black and white—from their history and from their true selves.

Du Bois often refers to the veil as a social fact, a barrier from which all people need to be freed collectively, not just as individuals. Du Bois had great hopes for the black middle class (whom he referred to as the "talented tenth"); they would, as a group, help the black masses rise.[51] He saw the writing of *The Souls of Black Folk* as his attempt to lift the veil, to allow whites to see in. In his introduction to the text, Donald Gibson writes that Du Bois, "far from being held captive, has a sense of self and a self-possession so strong as to allow him to hold the world outside the veil in contempt and to live 'above it in a region of blue sky and great wandering shadows.'"[52] Du Bois believed that relieving all black people from a life behind the veil would reveal a wholeness of black life previously unrecognized and uncelebrated by black or white people.

The initial lines of Du Bois's passage appear to closely parallel Rice's trajectory. A belief in an individual's ability to step outside the veil (segregation) from which others can't escape seems entirely applicable to Rice, who from an early age was granted some protections from racism. Although Rice's education began in the Birmingham Public Schools, her parents enrolled her in a music conservatory when she was ten years old so she could continue to study piano and be exposed to flute, violin, and French. Rice describes her parents as strategic: "I was going to be so well prepared, and I was going to do all of these things that were revered in white society so well, that I would be armored somehow from racism. I would be able to confront society on its own terms."[53] In college and subsequently, Rice was mentored by a stunning array of white men in positions of considerable influence, each of whom sheltered her from racism by guiding her up the academic and then governmental ladder.[54] Her considerable intellectual abilities and drive, along with her white posse, lifted her from behind the veil. As Ivo Daalder, a former National Security Council member said, "She is a novel commodity. Here is a highly accomplished African American woman. . . . being part of what is and always has been [a] boys' club."[55]

While the ability to rise beyond the veil appears to hold for Rice, it is Du Bois's articulation of double consciousness that does not appear to pertain to her. For Du Bois, double consciousness is the ability to see multiple realities simultaneously, to see one's deep interdependence with human beings and other life forces, and to recognize one's spiritual accountability to end exploitation.[56] One of the ways in which Du Bois departed from late nineteenth-century US and European conceptualizations of consciousness is his rejection of consciousness as an individual process. Du Bois believed, according to historian Richard Cullen Rath, that "European-derived varieties of individualistic consciousness unmoored spiritual accountability and could justify exploitation."[57] The dominant notion of consciousness as a singular, unified, and individual state was insufficient to capture black reality, because black reality had demanded a deep understanding of interdependence and collective struggle.

For Du Bois, there is certainly such a thing as individuality, but that individuality is born from a collective consciousness—i.e., it cannot be separated from one's roots. For black people, double consciousness is a simultaneous sense of one's self as dynamic and evolving alongside the sense of being despised, guarding against the daily stereotypes projected onto one's humanity.[58] Double consciousness requires recognizing oneself as both African and American, as both denied fundamental rights and capable of seeing the pathology of such a denial, as both misinterpreted and misrepresented.

For Du Bois, double consciousness is both a burden and a gift. The burden comes from being behind the veil and knowing that much of the world on the other side is not accessible. The burden includes knowing that the people outside the veil have very little understanding of black people as individuals, as whole, as changing, as fully human. The burden also reflects having "two warring ideals in one dark body," having to translate others' perceptions while maintaining one's own. In his life, having to exist in this state of war meant struggling between his image of himself as a shining intellectual and the country's image of him as a man undeserving of intellectual resources and a revered place in the academy. It meant dreaming of editing an encyclopedia of black life across the diaspora and never being granted funding in the United States to bring this vital project to fruition. These two warring ideals manifested themselves in a personality that made it hard for him to work with others over extended periods and a deep frustration with compromises that he believed ultimately demeaned black people. The burden of double consciousness includes the need to build moats around oneself—to create defenses—in order not to internalize the barrage against one's sensibilities. The burden includes not knowing if those defenses are going to work or when new armor will be necessary. The burden involves living in the United States while not being granted fundamental rights, being asked to believe in patriotism and a sense of American belonging while being told, in ways both subtle and overt, that one does not belong.

The expansiveness and longevity of Du Bois's concept of double consciousness come partly from his unwillingness to see it only as a burden, an interpretation that would represent black people as forever crippled and without hope. Instead, Du Bois sees black people as "gifted with second sight"—the ability to recognize their alienation from the white world and develop a higher understanding, a transcendent awareness of political and social realities. "Second sight" is the ability to stand outside the stereotype, to see the projection as an illusion. It is a vital and essential form of protection, without which black people could lose track of their own gifts and contributions. As Karen Fields puts it, second sight "carried with it an ability to stand on the edge of that very world to which [black people] could not fully belong, and, from that vantage point, to see beyond its seemingly self-evident givens."[59]

Double consciousness offers people a rich inner life, since it requires that they be conversant with and literate in two worlds simultaneously. It makes it possible to see the world from more than one point of view, which can nurture capacities of empathy and understanding across difference. This consciousness opens space in people's psyches for movement, to embrace ambiguity, to find ways out of oppression that go beyond the visible doors. It enables people to make concrete, literal change as well as to find freedom in their imagination, to create worlds outside of oppression (to "think outside of the box"). Perhaps, most importantly, double consciousness offers people a direct link to the ancestors, since it rests upon a collective belonging. Du Bois considered *The Souls of Black Folk* a plea for black people to be taken on their own terms and to recognize that Africa means something powerful to them and to the world. Double consciousness provides a way for people to tap into the wisdom of the ancestors, a way to get through difficulty by drawing upon the struggles of previous generations.[60]

Du Bois believes that double consciousness is not only an elaborate consciousness for black people; it is also a gift for people across race and nation. Rath writes, "Double consciousness was not his own personal gift to scholarship, it was African America's contribution to the world. It provided a way of positively negotiating the stress, flux, and uncertainty of what we now call the postmodern world."[61] Scholars and activists around the globe have celebrated Du Bois's elaboration of black consciousness, from South Africa to Haiti, from Senegal to Trinidad, from Britain to the streets of Philadelphia.[62] Du Bois asserted that lifting the veil between white and black people would forever change both. In the process, it would rescue white people from the ignorance of humanity that is reflected in their telling of history and culture. Rath writes, "White folk could split off and insulate black folk, denying culture, history, and occasionally humanity itself to individual African Americans, but only by becoming unconscious of who and what 'black folk' were and losing consciousness of a part of their own America."[63] For Du Bois, the challenge and necessity were for all parties to lift the veil, an obstruction to a fully formed American identity.

## THE DIMMING OF DOUBLE CONSCIOUSNESS

While both Du Bois and Rice saw education as a means of lifting the veil, where they part company is in the accountability they demonstrate toward black people as a community. For Du Bois, consciousness cannot be separated from one's ancestors. This consciousness can certainly go beyond one's community, but it cannot ignore it. Double consciousness rests on seeing the world as a black person and as an American, simultaneously and synergistically. Based on biographies written about Rice, interviews she has granted, and her career trajectory, it appears that she had sidestepped the development of a double consciousness by the time she reached adulthood, opting instead to see the world through color-blind eyes. While she acknowledges that she was born in a black community, she has always been en route outside of that community, based on an individual model of success. Color blindness for Rice means privileging her ability to perform as an individual over group progress.

It appears that Rice avoided the "warring" experience of double consciousness by being steeped in and then embraced by white consciousness. For Rice, success pivoted upon becoming whiter than white people and, in the process, finding ways to beat them at their own game. In her biography Rice is quoted as saying, "I'm the one who speaks French. . . . I am the one who plays Beethoven. I'm better at your culture than you are. This can be taught!"[64] From childhood on, Rice assumed all the signifiers of whiteness that she could—ice skating, playing classical piano, speaking French, studying ballet, becoming an expert in Russian (not African) history, wearing her hair in a 1950s white woman's flip, and appearing to be almost sexless in a Waspy, polished, and forever coiffed kind of way. With these markers in place, she also learned the class-based art of putting people in their place, letting them know that her achievements separated her from working-class people across race and among black people in general.

Several years ago, upon being shown costume jewelry instead of the expensive brand at a reputable jewelry store, Rice said, "Let's get one thing straight. You're behind this counter because you have to work for six dollars an hour. I'm on this side asking to see the good jewelry because I make considerably more."[65] Rice met the clerk's race and class assumptions with class biases of her own, a reversal that is particularly troubling as class divides continue to deepen nationally and internationally.

Might this be a point in US racial history when the consciousness of certain black people in positions of substantial power and the consciousness of the white establishment have come together? Du Bois's double consciousness embodies an ability to bring complexity to a situation because of one's presence in two worlds. It appears that Rice's method of dealing with that complexity is to see herself as transcending her blackness, and racism. Rice is representing the United States in a world forum as an American while she considers her race irrelevant. She hardly considers herself facing "warring ideals in one dark body." She, in fact, sees the color of her skin as an insignificant marker—a biological fact not fraught with social and political meaning.

Given this reality, might Rice not only concur with but also be pleased by the way she is presented in the *Washington Post* article, a tribute to her fashion sense and her individuality? Does the color-blind point of view of the *Post* reporter actually parallel Rice's approach to negotiating amid white supremacy? Because Sapphire is a racialized stereotype—a white illusion projected onto black women—it is unclear whether Rice would recognize the way that depiction has been projected onto her own body. At the center of Rice's politics is a belief that the individual can triumph over any barrier. This triumph includes a black woman's ability to sidestep stereotypical portrayals of her body. For Rice, achievement is what matters most, a strategy that has clearly worked for her.[66] Lemann observes, "Rice believes so firmly that the individual (or, at least, the extraordinary individual, like herself) can triumph over imposed limitations that she is almost insulted by the idea that collective action and government intervention were essential to her own life. In Rice's rule book, you never, ever, complain personally about institutional racism or ask for things on explicitly racial grounds."[67]

### SBFF—SUPER BLACK FEMALE FRIEND

Painfully, we are left wondering about the consequences of Rice's visibility and her unwillingness to see racism's pervasive grip. First, Rice's visibility signals one of the many reasons the Republican Party has been so successful in recent years. Rice's approach to racism as a force that can be individually transcended mirrors Republican individualist rhetoric. The reality is that Republicans have made openings for individual African Americans and Latinos who are willing to espouse a conservative framework. Given the devastating history of lumping all black people into one derogatory category, African Americans have a tremendous desire to be recognized as individuals. By creating a space that allows individuality, the collective struggle against racism is robbed of people who might otherwise be among its most eloquent spokespeople.

Rice's approach to the power she is afforded also indicates new ways in which black people in general and black women in particular are being controlled in the post–civil rights era. In her brave and aptly titled chapter "The More Things Change, the More They Stay the Same," Patricia Hill Collins writes that since the civil rights movement African American women face "a new politics of containment" based on "increasingly sophisticated strategies of surveillance." Collins argues that prior to the gains of the 1960s, after more than two centuries of slavery that were followed by one hundred years of apartheid policies (including disenfranchisement, poverty, poor education, lack of health care, and denials of other fundamental resources), segregation was the primary mechanism designed to keep blacks from positions of power. Black struggle that made the civil rights movement possible eliminated the most egregious forms of disenfranchising people, an advancement that Collins believes has been met by new forms of control. Relying upon the "*visibility* of African American women to generate the *invisibility* of exclusionary practices of racial segregation," these forms of control produce "remarkably consistent Black female disadvantage while claiming to do the opposite."[68]

While Rice's highly visible approach to negotiating in the world is clearly providing her with an individual route to money, fame, and power, her visibility suggests that this route is available to others as well. The cruel reality is that those opportunities are foreclosed to most of the black community in general and to most black women in particular. Traditionally, the role of the black middle class was to use their resources—educational, cultural, and social—to "lift as we climb." This ethic included a collective understanding that those African Americans who obtained access to white spaces—both public and private spaces—had a responsibility to use their knowledge to educate other people in the community about how white supremacy worked.

With Rice, we see an example of a denial of this hand-up ethic to buffer against racism, while paradoxically her individual success is used as proof that discrimination no longer exists. Collins examines how African American women have historically used their positions as "outsiders within" white spaces to bring necessary information and other resources back to black communities.[69] This ranged from details about slave uprisings and slaveholders' plans to sell certain slaves to knowledge about hiring and firing within businesses and which employers could be trusted or not.[70]

Rice represents a small but growing number of politically conservative African Americans who see themselves charged with keeping white supremacy's secrets, rather than the opposite. Lemann writes, "In Washington, nothing matters more than closeness to the President, and she is evidently the person closest to the President, in terms of time logged in his presence. It isn't just that she briefs him every morning, attends several formal meetings with him every week, and sees or speaks to him several times in the course of a typical day; it's also that she spends many weekends as the Bushes' guest at Camp David or at the Presidential Ranch, in Crawford, Texas. Rice, who shares the President's passions for exercise and watching sports events, especially football, on television, will often spend hours with him during non-working time when other staff members never see him."[71] Rice is widely recognized as an adviser of unending loyalty who never, even to her closest personal friends, reveals information learned in the confidence of her relationship with the president. According to many accounts, Rice is anxious to "serve" the president and by extension the country, not only during the week but also on weekends. While willing to be his buddy, she drew the line only when he wanted her to cut brush with him, bowing out by saying it was not ladylike.

Her strategy is a stark reversal of the use of the "outsider-within" approach to provide information, resources, and safety to black communities. Rice seemed to willingly allow herself to be contained by her relationships with powerful white male mentors. And in the case of her work as provost at Stanford University, she was willing to be the school's hatchet man (laying off a well-respected Chicana administrator, denying funds to student-of-color cultural and political organizations).[72] At the same time, she certainly was under surveillance at every turn. Rice's extremely close relationship with President Bush, while easily interpreted as a sign of her power and influence, also indicates that she is under surveillance nearly round the clock. In this post–civil rights era, surveillance aimed at poor and working-class black people continues unabated (through police brutality, violations of women's reproductive freedom, institutionalized degradations of impoverishment, etc.), as does surveillance aimed at the minority of black individuals who have gained access to considerable institutional power. Racial segregation prior to the civil rights movement erased individuality. Black people were treated as interchangeable members of the subordinated group. In contrast, today's surveillance highlights individuality by making the individual hypervisible and on display. "Whereas racial segregation is designed to keep blacks as a group or class *outside* the center of power," Collins notes, "surveillance aims to control Black individuals who are *inside* centers of power."[73]

What makes surveillance work in the post–civil rights era is the ideology of color blindness—that race and racism no longer exist. Collins writes, "Overlaying this new politics of containment is a rhetoric of tolerance, claiming that race and other categories no longer matter."[74] Given this reality, it is imperative that Rice and the *Washington Post* reporter not signify Rice's race. The new politics of surveillance depends upon such erasure.

Nowhere is the cunning of this surveillance more obvious than in considering Rice's sexuality. In her twenties, she was engaged to be married and now is often escorted by a friend, ex–football player Gene Washington, to certain social events. But she has never been romantically involved with anyone since her association with the Bush family. In a gutsy column about why Rice "haunts most of us middle-class black women of a certain age," Patricia Williams writes about why this nagging persists. Describing the coverage of Rice the day after she was named the new secretary of state, Williams notes, "The day after her elevation was announced, the front page of the *New York Times* carried a photo of Rice gazing adoringly at Bush. It was quite a kittenish pose; she looked so young and coy one was compelled to imagine that her toes were pointed inward, like Minnie Mouse. All that was missing was a big bow in her hair. Indeed, no one seemed to know what to make of that conspicuously odd goof, when she said, 'My husb—— I mean the President.' There was genuine pathos in the moment, like she'd been drawing little hearts in her notebook, the silly thing, dreaming of the day she could grow up and marry her homeroom teacher. Or maybe she was more like the smartest kid in the class who slips the captain of the football team the answers to the test because it is her only route to recognition if not popularity. He's still going to marry the cheerleader; but she'll be shielded from the torment of loneliness that can sometimes follow the bookish and the brightest."[75]

In this era of the ascendancy of a few black women to positions of substantial power, it appears that sexuality is policed right out of existence. The *Washington Post* reporter portrays Rice as a Sapphire, while Rice is required to be a Mammy to President Bush. (Unless, of course, Rice and Bush really are intimate partners, making Laura Bush the desperate housewife she has, at least jokingly, claimed to be. While this scenario is certainly a possibility, the public imagery of Rice as Bush's confidante but not his lover, his best friend but not his mistress, his number one adviser but not his love object, keeps Rice contained in the decades-old, albeit updated, stereotype of Mammy.)

Given the brutal history of black women's exclusion from the centers of power, it is no surprise that on some level many black women, particularly dark-skinned black women, identify with Rice's success. She doesn't have to sing the blues. She doesn't have to be on welfare. She is not sick. She speaks many languages. She is smart. She doesn't have a man she is carrying around, who may be sleeping with her employees. She is a kind of warrior person and is attractive in many ways. This complication may be why Robin Givhan, the *Washington Post* reporter, herself an African American woman, is complicit in creating a new, twenty-first-century caricature of black women. This caricature rejects the welfare queen, twists the Mammy and Sapphire images, and then offers up to the world another caricature as deadly and disheartening as its predecessors. In her article Givhan clearly does not want to portray Rice as Mammy; she goes out of her way to say that Rice is not matronly or androgynous. While Rice does function as a Mammy for Bush in multiple ways and upholds the Mammy image as an asexual woman (who is too busy taking care of white men's interests to have time for a love life), the original Mammy figure was certainly not a world traveler, a cosmopolitan diner, and a speaker of multiple languages. Similarly, while Rice physically embodies aspects of Sapphire—with her severe, military attire mixed up with tall, shapely boots—ultimately Sapphire was tough and malelike, quite unsupportive of men.

The twenty-first-century caricature is an updated stereotype, with an appropriate cyber twist. When we think of Rice, what comes to mind is Halle Berry's character Storm in the three wildly popular x-Men action movies. In this series, Storm is a knock-down, drag-out gorgeous x-Man who, with her fellow mutant friends, is one of the leaders of the mutants. With her superpowers, she can both levitate and control the elements of nature, such as wind and rain. Unlike the black actresses of previous times—consistently killed off first, stuck in the role of a maid, or impassioned to the point of irrationality and hysteria—Storm is cool, calm, and steady. While this calm is a quality people come to count on, it also signals her lack of emotional depth.

Storm, unlike the other mutant leaders, rarely bonds with anyone. We get backstories for other key characters, but we have virtually no knowledge about Storm's past, her family, or her intimate involvements. Her personality is steady but not distinct; in fact it is quite ordinary. Although she doesn't get killed in the first scene, the audience gets little sense of her passions, personality, or attachments. Storm, like black female TV figures who get to play the sergeants, judges, doctors, and precinct officers, lives to help keep the team together while requiring little or nothing for herself. She is not Mammy or the welfare queen or Sapphire. She is, in this century, the SBFF—the Super Black Female Friend—a kind of global action figure able to leap tall buildings on behalf of the men, survive with no one to keep her warm at night, and be groomed for increasing positions of power as long as she controls the elements in a manner that meets her supervisor's approval.[76] She is equal to others in her staying power and abilities, but she does not have the soul or passion that would allow her to be whole. She is the modern black woman, having moved beyond the primitive state of Sapphire and Mammy to a machinelike, rationalized, plastic action figure—SBFF.

## HISTORY IN THE WATER

*The policeman takes dog*
*from young boy's hands*
Snowball *he cries*
*eyelashes rain*

*a man holds his wife and son*
*son and wife*
*water storms the steeples*
*she says:* let me go
*he does: grief streaming*

*woman with skin dressed in wrinkles*
*rocks on a superdome cot*
*people flood the stadium*
*three now beside her waiting*
*no blood between them*

*soldier calls home to Biloxi*
CNN *his only connection*
*water drowns phone lines*
*dust hijacks his memories of safety*
*he grounds the butt of his rifle in the sand*

*Bush views bottom of a slave ship*
*from his bubble in the sky*
*terrorists take notes*
*Black people still traveling*
*middle passage on buses*

*Rosa Parks stands up*
*her spoken word to the wind*
*blow to the middle of the sea*
*save these brave people from your moods*

*The next world war will be about water*

— BECKY THOMPSON

# TWO

# HURRICANE KATRINA AND
# HISTORICAL MEMORY

## HISTORY IN THE WATER

When warnings of Katrina's impending disaster reached the national news, President Bush was on his extended summer vacation in Crawford, Texas. Vice President Cheney was equally indisposed, and Condoleezza Rice was buying shoes in Manhattan. When asked about the possible racism in the government's handling of the disaster, Rice categorically denied it. "How can that be the case?" Rice said. "Americans don't want to see Americans suffer. Nobody, especially the president, would have left people unattended on the basis of race."[1] When asked to say a few words at a church service in Alabama, Rice said, "The Lord Jesus is going to come on time, if we just wait."[2]

When Katrina hit, people from around the world were horrified to see poor people who could not escape, wading in the water, beseeching others to help them, and then finally ending up in the overcrowded Superdome and Astrodome. In the subsequent year, as we traveled to Rio de Janeiro, Brazil, Tunis, Tunisia, and Montreal, Canada, giving talks and facilitating discussions on Katrina and its aftermath, we witnessed tremendous compassion on the part of the world community. In addition to direct aid offered by the governments of Venezuela, Cuba, Canada, and elsewhere, we saw people from a diverse range of countries whose political and economic analyses were typically more sophisticated than what the US government had to offer. They recognized the people of New Orleans as both American and homeless, as both citizens and unwelcome in their own country.

Katrina blew the roof off the rhetoric, both domestically and internationally, that racism no longer exists, exposing the price for the ticket of individualism as too high. The images of Katrina hurled us back into history in ways that tie us to group consciousness and an understanding of systematic racism and classism. As the rains began to flood the city and the winds began to blow off church steeples, the US public began to reel from the images—ghastly, ghostly, horrifying images of dead bodies floating in the streets; mothers on rooftops holding infants up to the sky, desperately waving signs in hopes of a rescue; thousands of people crammed into the New Orleans Superdome, their lives in shambles.

Several days after the levees broke, we began to notice that everyone around us seemed to be shouting, clearly disturbed on many levels by the unfolding death and destruction. Black people were shouting. Church people were shouting, students at our schools were shouting, homeless people on the streets were shouting. People with vastly different politics were shouting, because historical memory had been dredged up, had washed ashore, and was sitting on top of the Superdome, broadcasting very loud messages, a howl, a scream that Ginsberg wrote about, that Sethe lived in *Beloved,* that Pecola lost her mind over in *The Bluest Eye,* and that elderly people in Louisiana were asking us not to forget.[3]

As the crisis escalated and people across the political spectrum began to understand that the federal government had no systematic plan for protecting or helping residents of New Orleans, we began to see that we were living with at least two disasters at once—the current hurricane and its deadly aftermath, and memories of the Middle Passage, slavery, lynching, and imprisonment. Every black person we knew was distressed, some in ways they could talk about, others stunned into disbelieving silence.

They were disturbed because it reminded them of an earlier incredible loss of home, community, land, and sense of belonging. For many black people, witnessing Katrina meant reliving a deep and abiding fear that they were about to disappear, again. The parallels between these two disasters took on a menacing spin, affecting people on conscious and unconscious levels across the country. Historical memory was very much with us—on the news, on the streets, in people's body language, in the kind, vicious, confused, generous, immediate, and delayed ways that people were responding to each other.

Historical memory makes us aware that the past is with us in the present, that unresolved, complicated, and multilayered events from the past are replaying themselves in various forms in the present. Historical memory can be transmitted through tangible processes—song, art, dance, writing, media imagery, and photography. This memory can be imprinted on the body, on trees, in sound, taste, and smell. While it can be handed down directly, from one generation to the next, it can also skip generations. It is transmitted in dreams, rituals, and visions; in the water, buildings, and the air; through an ineffable awareness of a presence of ancestors and what has gone on in the past. Historical memory, while sometimes conscious, often exists in the realm of the unconscious; it is a mysterious knowledge that the past is affecting our actions in the present, that we are being followed, guided, and influenced by what was not solved in the past.

Historical memory, because it is often unconsciously held, can frequently take the form of a haunting experience that follows, confronts, and interrupts people's everyday actions even though it might not manifest itself in specific, identifiable memories. The haunting is a reminder that people have not yet come to terms with the initial trauma. This memory, in its physical manifestations, compels people to confront it, even as the haunting warns us to stay away. The haunting becomes a stand-in for the memory, which, when dealt with, promises to change people, often in ways both frightening and liberating.

### THE MIDDLE PASSAGE AND SLAVERY

As we watched the news and heard that a staggering number of people from Louisiana had no idea where they were going following the disaster, parallels between the current crisis and the Middle Passage began to haunt us. The images of water—the muddy water, the out-of-control water, the water in which people were drowning, the water carrying bodies, the water covering disappeared bodies—looked like the same water that the Africans saw while on ships from Africa. The Katrina disaster looked like another ocean of death right out of the centuries of the slave trade from Africa to the Americas. The Middle Passage, the transport of Africans from the west coast of Africa to the continent of the Americas across thousands of miles of open seas, has often been described as the most brutal of human atrocities toward other humans imaginable. This atrocity took between five weeks and three months, depending on the conditions and destination. Although statistics on the number of people who died while being transported vary, estimates range from forty to sixty million deaths.[4] An undocumented number of these deaths were a consequence of people jumping from the ships, an existential, symbolic, and literal protest against further enslavement. The ocean in this context is a metaphor that runs deep in black historical memory, a repository for countless untold stories.

For those who survived the Middle Passage, arrival in an unknown land typically added to, rather than alleviated, the terror they had suffered on the ships. The writer John Edgar Wideman suggests, "Imagine yourself disembarked on an alien shore after a long, painful voyage so harrowing you're not certain you survived it. You're sick, weak, profoundly disoriented. You fear you haven't actually arrived anywhere but are just slipping into another fold of a nightmare."[5] In both the Middle Passage and the aftermath of Katrina, people typically had no idea where they were going or where they were being taken. And they had little assurance that they would end up in a safe place. Media images following Katrina included children, adults, and elderly people wading and swimming against increasingly strong currents; people in water up to their shoulders, holding pets above the water so they would be able to breathe; speed limit and directional signs that were barely visible above the rising tides. The water flooding the streets, houses, and billboards made it impossible for people to keep their sense of direction, to know which way might bring them to safety. Water became their enemy, with no relief in sight. In one of the most disturbing front-page images in the *New York Times,* dozens of elderly people, many of them in critical condition, had been left strapped to stretchers, laid on and alongside baggage conveyer belts at the New Orleans airport.[6] The expressions on their faces revealed disorientation, numbness, and despair.

The more than two hundred people who were evacuated to Boston two weeks after the levees broke were not told their destination until midflight. They had just been rescued and taken directly to airplanes. Unlike people who had been staying in Houston, who resisted when they were told they were going to Boston, the newly evacuated did not have the wherewithal to refuse. This time, instead of permitting people a chance to think about the implications of such a dislocation, officials sent evacuees to Boston before they could get their bearings.[7] The powerlessness they faced was eerily reminiscent of Africans who were stolen from their communities, held in dungeons, and then marched to ships, en route to a place they knew nothing about and clearly did not want to go.

Another parallel between how officials handled the Katrina disaster and conditions under slavery was frighteningly visible in the breakup of families. The buying and selling of family members were key means of maintaining the institution of slavery by destabilizing the foundation of black culture. Mothers torn from their children, husbands sold far away from their wives, and extended families split among different plantations were common practices, often forcing people to carry on lifelong quests in search of their lost kin. Toni Morrison once said that, no matter the brutality and cruelty of the blurring of memory that takes place in the face of trauma, a mother will never forget the shape and feel of her baby's hand. Blood and belonging run deep, regardless of the state policies and punishments exacted to divide families.

When the levees in New Orleans broke and many people, mostly poor and black, could not get out, families scrambled as best they could to stay together. As people realized that no officials were going to protect them, they fled the city however they could, often on foot. In the process families were split up, and children wandered around without their parents; many kin did not have any idea where other family members were, or if they were still alive.

Some of the children who were separated from their family members were so traumatized that they could not speak their own names. Others were too young to speak at all. Many parents whose children were lost did not have photographs that might have helped them to locate their daughters and sons. The sorting processes orchestrated by some officials made matters worse. Patricia Williams reports, "The elderly were taken from their families, the sick from their caretakers, newborns from their mothers and, because men were apparently segregated from women, husbands from wives, mothers from sons."[8] FEMA, the Red Cross, and state agencies had no central registry of names and locations of those staying in shelters, leaving people to post makeshift signs with family members' names spelled out in longhand. At the Astrodome in Houston, officials rang a cowbell when a reunion took place—an ironic name for a bell announcing that people, not animals, had been found.[9]

Amid these images of the breakup of black families, the media also dredged up historical memories of black men being treated as bodies, not whole people. Less than two weeks after the hurricane hit, the sports section of the New York Times ran an article chronicling how two sixteen-year-old football players, stars in a New Orleans high school, had been recruited to play for a high school team in Texas that had not won any games the last season.[10] The article included nothing about the young men's family members. It did not address whether the athletes had been included in the decision about their move to the new high school or if their families would join them in the new town. It was hard not to miss the juxtaposition between FEMA's lack of a central registry of names of people in shelters—a registry that might have helped frantic people find their loved ones—and athletic coaches having enough information to know which athletes they might want to recruit to augment their team's power.

This current-day use of athletic black men by football coaches is painfully reminiscent of a practice under slavery of purchasing the black bodies that looked the strongest and could serve the master's purpose for hard labor. The young men recruited to play in Texas were serving the needs of the coaches in search of a strong football team. The *New York Times* article referenced several unverified reports of coaches contacting athletes still staying in the shelters, using the shelters as a location to find the best athletes, now available in ways they hadn't been prior to the hurricane.

Meanwhile, within ten days of the hurricane, Harvard Law School, the Massachusetts Institute of Technology, Yale University, Brown University, and other Ivy League schools began admitting students from Tulane University, a historically white, upper-middle-class school in New Orleans, to attend New England universities as special students. In the *Boston Globe* article about this educational exchange, the two photos accompanying the piece were of white students.[11] A graph that accompanied the article showed special admission standards used to accept the students. The graph was titled "Trading Up," a revealing title, given that special dispensation had been granted to elite (white) students in academic settings, while media attention to black students focused on athletic trading, from a winning team in New Orleans to a team that had yet to win a game in Houston. Seen together, one article played on trading down black bodies while the other played on trading up white minds, a juxtaposition conjuring a long history of slavery and subsequent educational apartheid.

In another brutal image, a photographer for the *New York Times* captured the moment when an emaciated black man was carried out of his house by three white officials.[12] The man was stark naked, except for a very small cloth that he clutched to cover his loins. There was no accompanying text. The photo was forced to do all of the explaining, betraying an extraordinary lack of respect for his body. The image of a stripped-naked, bone-thin, black man was chillingly reminiscent of scantily clad black men in lynching photographs. In the past, the lynch mob had left its victims hanging. Now the man was being carried naked for the world to see. The elderly man was carried out of his house as if he were property, robbed of even the dignity of having his body covered.

In this photo, aggressiveness had been replaced by a neglect that has never been benign. In 1970, Daniel Patrick Moynihan, the urban affairs counselor for President Nixon, wrote a memo to the president that stated that the issue of race could benefit from a period of "benign neglect."[13] Benign neglect has always been an oxymoron. During the decades when lynching was a highly publicized method of maintaining white supremacy, it served its function of policing every black person, regardless of whether they knew someone personally who had been lynched or not. In writing about the history of lynching, the historian and social critic Manning

Marable explains, "Terror is not the product of violence alone, but is created only by the *random, senseless and even bestial use of coercion against an entire population.*"[14] Marable's definition makes clear that an entire community is affected by the mistreatment of one individual.

In addition to the photo reminiscent of lynching, the *New York Times* ran an article entitled "'Prison City' Shows a Hospitable Face to Refugees from New Orleans." The text informed the reader that three hundred people who had survived the flood in New Orleans had been turned down when they sought shelter at the Astrodome. Aboard eight buses, they kept driving, eighty miles north, until they reached the First Baptist Church in Huntsville, Texas. This church butts right up against the Huntsville prison, which executes more prisoners than any other prison in the country. The article reported—as if it were shocking news—that some of hurricane survivors said they "felt blessed and had no fear of the inmates." Given the number of poor, disproportionately black people who have family members in the prison system, it is not surprising that "many called it heaven" upon arriving in Huntsville. Alongside the article was a large photo of an eight-year-old black girl who, with carefully combed hair and an open, curious face, held a neon green tank top she had pulled from a box of donated clothes for evacuees. The young girl was photographed standing alone, leaving the reader to wonder if she had family close by or if she were there by herself, searching for clothes. In the text and photo, the overwhelming message was of black people being turned away, left alone, in prison, making do, finding refuge in a church next to an execution chamber, or finding clothes in a box labeled "moving and storage."[15]

### DOUBLE CONSCIOUSNESS: COLLECTIVE TIES TO THE LAND

While much of the imagery after Katrina captured the historic and current victimization of black people, Du Bois's double consciousness could be seen in media representations as well. A vivid example of this consciousness involved a national network news program that was broadcast several days after the levees broke. This program included shots of a group of elderly black men sitting on their rickety lawn chairs in front of their small houses. They were, according to the commentators, refusing to move. The elders continued to sit as officials threatened them that the area was unsafe, that there was no food available, and that they would eventually be forcibly removed. The elders were not defiant or rude, simply resolved. Through their embodied presence, they were speaking for and from two times. We can imagine they were speaking from ancient sources of knowledge, as Yoruba and Benin (from what we now know as Nigeria) and Ndongo and Malembo (from what we now know as Angola), as men who did whatever was needed to protect and guide their communities against slave catchers.[16] They were being resourceful, helping those around them, and waiting out the crisis. These elderly men were refusing to leave their communities because they knew that, as free human beings, they had a right to determine their own lives and deaths. They were demonstrating that if they were going to die, they would rather do so in their own homes than in a stranger's land.

Historically, black people have done whatever they can to avoid dying in hospitals, prisons, or anything resembling a closed container. Given this historical reality, it is completely understandable that these men did not want to leave. Instead of providing them with basic supplies, the officials lectured and threatened them, even though they were clearly finding ways to survive on their own. Once the elderly men had obviously survived the storm, with no help from the government, they were trying to stay where they had been raised, lived, and planned to die. With their bodies they were communicating that the officials were not recognizing them, could not see their ties to their past or their resourcefulness in the present.

This wanting, this need, this understanding of home, resonates with the spirituality that Du Bois embedded in his concept of double consciousness. The kind of individualism that says—I must save my individual life and leave this place—is not the consciousness that the elderly men were demonstrating. They were demonstrating a consciousness that told them they could not be happy without the land they knew. A life with strangers was not a life for them. When he wrote *The Souls of Black Folk,* Du Bois tapped into a consciousness that is connected to land and ancestors. He tapped into black souls—the collective, intimate, historical, and spiritual connections that tie black people to each other across oceans, rivers, and levees—a connection that has been frayed by individualism. Individual pursuits trade on a profound loss of consciousness. These elders were reminding people about how crucial the connections to land and the ancestors' presence can be.

The elders were speaking to those who have lost a sense of connectedness to black people and black land. They were also telling the officials that relocation was another word for not seeing them. Gil Scott-Heron sings, "You're my lawyer, you are my doctor, yeah, but somehow you forgot about me."[17] With Katrina, the elders knew there was a possibility of a new generation of lost children who would not know their names or where they came from. They would not necessarily be able to count on black people elsewhere to know their names either. An ethic of individualism and the rhetoric of color blindness had whittled away at black people's sense of themselves as connected to a larger historical process. The elderly men on lawn chairs remained a witness to this process.

Another image that appeared one year after the hurricane also provides a quintessential example of double consciousness and its link to historical memory. This image is in the form of a mural adorning the exterior of the Ernie K-Doe Mother-in-Law Lounge, a beloved club scheduled to reopen around the first anniversary of the hurricane. Painted in vibrant colors, the mural shows two men and a woman, all from the African diaspora, wearing clothes befitting a tropical climate. The men's hands are extended around each other and the woman in a circular embrace that also includes a large egg, a parrot, and a handkerchief with a peacock design. The mural, like double consciousness, is reaching back and forward at the same time, back to the Caribbean and other stops along the slave trade route and to people whose blood has been mixed on more than one continent, and forward to adorn a jazz club in its latest incarnation. Historical memory is communicated in song, as a medium that got people through in the fields, at the washboard, in their runs for freedom, and in the haunting look in one of the men's eyes—a soulful yearning, an intensity and a relaxation, a wondering and immediate presence. A mural of an elderly woman stands above this one on the wall of the connected building, watching over the mural below, keeping watch on the neighborhood in its current transition. There is an interconnectedness to the images, even though they are on different walls, perhaps painted at different times. Meanwhile, a man on the second rung of a ladder is working on a new mural on another side of the building, painting into concrete, new memory.

Although it will take a long time, maybe years, to begin to make sense out of the images that captured the attention of the nation and much of the world following Katrina, the catastrophe certainly offered a cautionary tale to those who have thought Du Bois's reference to "the problem of the color line" was outdated.[18] Katrina asked the nation and the world to think about how historical memory continues to be embedded in consciousness, how healing from Katrina will require coming to terms with the Middle Passage and slavery—all catastrophes surrounded by murky water. Katrina asks us to consider the consequences when black conservatives, from Rice on down the line, are willing to trade accountability to black people for a ticket to the White House.

*The murals at the Ernie K-Doe Mother-in-Law Lounge capture the African influence, vitality, and regenerative energy of people in New Orleans following Hurricane Katrina of 2005. "New Orleans Faces One Year Anniversary of Hurricane Katrina." Photograph by Mario Tama. Getty Images News, 71726166.*

### EXPANDING CONSCIOUSNESS

We are grateful to Du Bois for his understanding of consciousness as both a material and spiritual entity, his unwavering commitment to racial justice, his willingness to channel ancestral knowledge into his rigorous intellectual treatises, and his ability, more than one hundred years ago, to explain and predict many of the dynamics now evident in black consciousness in this century. Yet, understanding the Katrina disaster left us reaching beyond his work, primarily because of the racial binary embedded in his thinking and his underdeveloped conceptualization of gender and patriarchy. For Du Bois, double consciousness is based on a black/white dichotomy, on two warring souls, a duality born from the history of slavery that he conceptualized based primarily on the experiences of black men.[19] What Du Bois was not able to do, in the words of historian Darlene Clark Hine, was account for black women's "'fiveness': Negro, American, woman, poor, black woman."[20] It is this fiveness that we need to comprehend in order to understand the impact of Katrina.

Through the Katrina catastrophe, women faced many of the same hardships men faced: losing their houses, being separated from their children, and witnessing the government's disregard for their humanity. But women were vulnerable to additional dangers as well. Women were vastly overrepresented in the shelters, locations that put them at risk of many hazards, including rape and other sexual assault. Without the protection of family and community, women were especially at risk of sexual exploitation. To make matters worse, amid these and other dangers, the women had no privacy that would give them a chance to pull away from the crowd, regroup, make sense out of their own reality, and begin to recover so that they could put on a brave face for their children again.

Thrown into public space, black women were exposed emotionally, physically, and sexually in ways largely undocumented. In overcrowded shelters, black women had to tap into their deepest resources to simply function in those environments. They had few, if any, economic resources to aid them in this process. Since so many women were forced to depend upon men—who have the power to both protect and exploit—we can imagine that some faced compromised relationships in the aftermath of Katrina in ways reminiscent of how they were cornered on slave ships, in auctions, and on plantations.

The frightening parallel to the vulnerability women faced post-Katrina is the danger that black women faced historically when they had to develop both a private and a public persona so that they could function. Katrina recreated a southern history of black women without access to property, women who were themselves property, at the mercy of men willing to further exploit them. Black women were, again, in situations where men could exploit the only property black women had—their bodies. As feminist Zillah Eisenstein observes, "It is important to name and see women—particularly women of color—and their gendered lives at this moment. We see the narrative of slavery quietly reproduced [in New Orleans]: slaves are said to be blacks defined by a system of racism even though slavery was a sexual AND racial system of oppression. . . . There are continued silences that need to be spoken here."[21]

Darlene Clark Hine identified a coping strategy that black women have historically adopted as a "culture of dissemblance" that includes "behavior and attitudes . . . that created the appearance of openness and disclosure, but actually shielded the truth of their inner lives and selves from their oppressors."[22] One of the characteristics of the culture of dissemblance is that black women are silent about much of what they endure. We may see black women telling their stories on television and read about them in the papers, but a haunting silence about the depth of their experiences still exists. This dynamic is why literary scholar Ann duCille refers to black women in the post–civil rights era as simultaneously hypervisible and super-isolated.[23] Their resistance to telling the totality of their experience stems from their concern about being further stigmatized or associated with long-standing demeaning stereotypes of black women. This concern only adds to the silences about racialized sexual abuse and other injuries that they are especially vulnerable to during crises. We need to envision a time when black women do not need to dissemble in order to make it through their days.

An understanding of consciousness that accounts for race and gender is one that refuses to trump exploitation primarily aimed at women with terror aimed primarily at men. African American studies scholar Hazel Carby has documented that "the institutionalization of rape of black women has never been as powerful a symbol of black oppression as the spectacle of lynching."[24] Katrina underscores why we need to recognize race and gender and poverty as equally powerful factors in twenty-first-century disempowerment. The realities of black women's lives, including the multiple enforced silences about privatized domination, mean that journalistic accounts of the aftermath of Katrina tend to focus on black men's vulnerabilities while sidelining black women. For example, while Cornel West was one of the only writers who alerted us to the rape of black women in the Superdome, he did so by calling our attention to the husbands who had to watch: "There is the danger of nihilism and in the Superdome around the fourth day, there it was—husbands held at gunpoint while their wives were raped, someone stomped to death, people throwing themselves off the mezzanine floor, dozens of bodies."[25] West's portrayal focused on the husbands' inability to protect their wives, while the rape itself became a secondary concern. In that, and many other instances, the woman's inability to protect herself and the telling of the rape from the point of view of the man were taken as a given. The Katrina disaster amplifies why double consciousness needs to be expanded to account for multiple traumas that black women faced historically—and face currently. We also need to highlight the strategies of resiliency black women have developed.

The disaster also asks us to expand consciousness beyond the black/white dichotomy that is the foundation of Du Bois's conceptualization of "double consciousness." Just as an analysis of race without gender is insufficient to understand the dynamics of disempowerment after Katrina, a black/white analysis of race in New Orleans is unable to fully identify who was victimized by the storm and how the federal government proceeded following the disaster. The historical roots of New Orleans have always been multiracial. Before and during the colonization by the French and Spanish, Louisiana was home to many indigenous people, including the Chitimacha and the Houma.[26] As a major port of the slave trade, New Orleans has also long had the feel of a city of the African diaspora. As is true of much of the diaspora, the multiracial culture reflects layers of slavery, colonialism, and immigration.[27] The Creole population of Louisiana is a blending of French, Spanish, African, and Caribbean people (reflecting consensual relations between free blacks, Spanish, African, French, and Caribbean people as well as a history of rape under slavery). Creole, a language spoken by many people of African and Caribbean descent, is a blending of French, African, and Caribbean languages that has been spoken in the region for centuries.

In the twenty-first century, Louisiana is the home to Houma, Biloxi-Chitimacha, and Choctaw Indians; people of African descent, many of whose families have been in the area since the slave trade; white people of European descent (German, Spanish, French, English, Irish, etc.); and many recent immigrants (primarily communities of color). These immigrants include Hondurans, who first immigrated to the area in the twentieth century to work in the ports and fisheries; Vietnamese, who immigrated to the area in the 1970s following the Vietnam War; and Jamaican immigrants.

One reason that the media representation after the hurricane portrayed a city in black-and-white terms is that many other people of color (Native Americans, Hondurans, Vietnamese, and Jamaicans) had little or no contact with mainstream media or state and federal emergency agencies. The situation of the Honduran community provides a useful case in point. Approximately 120,000 Hondurans lived in the New Orleans area at the time of the crisis.[28] Many of the Hondurans were legal residents and have been in the United States for a long time, some for generations. Some Hondurans came to New Orleans in 1998 after Hurricane Mitch, which left 10,000 people dead and many more homeless.[29] Those who were not legal residents had no access to resources from FEMA. Many without residency were afraid to seek help—either to be evacuated or after the hurricane—for fear that the border patrol or immigration services might turn them over for deportation. Even those who were residents were afraid, many of them unable to get access to documents that would prove their residency. A similar scenario of vulnerability existed for Jamaican immigrants; many did not seek help with evacuation or food and shelter following the disaster for fear that they might be deported. For both the Honduran and Jamaican communities, the suffering they experienced reflected a combination of barriers to emergency help.

The reporting on recent immigrants and Native people by alternative media sources documented their ingenious methods of helping themselves through the crisis. Five hundred members of the Tunica-Biloxi tribe in central Louisiana took refuge at a casino in the region; nearly 20,000 Vietnamese fled to the Hong Kong strip mall in Houston, where Vietnamese charity groups provided shelter, food, and clothing; Koreans found refuge in family-run Korean stores in Houston; and Hondurans sought out a Honduran restaurant in Houston's mostly Latino neighborhood.[30] All of these groups avoided the Superdome, seeking community-controlled networks instead.

While Hine's analysis adds gender to Du Bois's conceptualization of double consciousness, she, like Du Bois, assumes "American citizen" in her framework. The Jamaicans, Hondurans, and Vietnamese in New Orleans ask us to include nation and citizenship in the framework as well. Their realities ask us to account for how immigration—often a response to colonization in a country that leaves few options for people other than to flee their homes in search of work—shapes consciousness as well.

For this multidimensional conceptualization, we turn to the work of Gloria Anzaldúa, a Chicana theorist whose book *Borderlands/La Frontera* offers a multilayered analysis of the culture, history, and politics of people living in the Southwest of the United States.[31] Much of what she examines in relation to that border resonates with the realities facing immigrants living in New Orleans. Anzaldúa describes the border between the United States and Mexico as "*una herida abierta* [an open wound] where the Third World grates against the first and bleeds."[32] The immigrants living in and around New Orleans, who came to the United States in large part because of First World colonization of their lands, give example to Anzaldúa's reference to the bleeding of Third World people. For the immigrants without documentation, bleeding after the hurricane came from knowing that they had contributed much labor to the United States, many of them for years, and yet did not see US services as an option in a time of crisis.

Anzaldúa asserts that the psychic, linguistic, and geographical location of those who are sandwiched between cultures nourishes what she has named "*mestiza* consciousness": "From this racial, ideological, cultural and biological cross-pollinization, an 'alien' consciousness is presently in the making—a new *mestiza* consciousness, *una consciencia de mujer*. It is a consciousness of the Borderlands."[33] This consciousness comes from a melding of two realities—in this case the reality of one's country of origin and the reality of the new country—into another that is larger than the sum of its parts. Like Du Bois's double consciousness, mestiza consciousness recognizes a clashing of cultures and power inequities.

To the equation of slavery and racism, Anzaldúa adds the history of colonialism, which creates internal struggles within people's psyches. Du Bois referred to this state as "two warring ideals." For Anzaldúa, signs of this inner war are manifested in what she has named "psychic restlessness." This state is characterized by "mental and emotional states of perplexity" as well as "insecurity and indecisiveness." Psychic restlessness comes from the willingness and sometimes the necessity to juggle multiple worldviews simultaneously.[34]

Anzaldúa's mestiza consciousness has vertical and horizontal dimensions not developed in Du Bois's work, dimensions made possible by living a multicultural reality.[35] While Du Bois assumed a dichotomy between black and white and a linear relationship between two warring poles, Anzaldúa's mestiza consciousness is more like a balloon that has been inflated by wind coming from many directions. For Anzaldúa, who recognizes herself as a creation of indigenous, white, and Mexican blood, linear conceptualizations were not big enough to describe her consciousness.

Because mestiza consciousness takes into account identities that cross borders and are not solely determined by one national belonging, Anzaldúa's conceptualization allows us to think about how—in a disaster—people remember themselves as connected historically, emotionally, and psychically. For example, following Katrina, Jamaican workers faced fears of deportation if they sought services, yet returning to Jamaica was no real option, given the grinding unemployment in that country (largely due to foreign capital intervention). A long British colonial presence in Jamaica, followed by multiple invasions and interventions by the United States and increasing exploitation by foreign corporations in recent years, has left Jamaica vulnerable to losing its citizens to the United States and other countries in search of jobs. The US war in Vietnam resulted in the immigration of South Vietnamese to many communities in the United States. The settlement of Vietnamese refugees in Louisiana began after the fall of Saigon in 1975, facilitated by Catholic charities in the region.

There is also a long history of connection between people of African descent in New Orleans and Haiti. Haiti and Louisiana were both French colonies until the Haitians defeated the French in 1804. Haiti became the first free black republic in the Western Hemisphere. The Louisiana Purchase was a result of Napoleon's need to make money by selling a big chunk of southern territory, in part due to the expense of the Haitian revolution. A vertical interpretation of New Orleans is one that looks at the relationship between white and black people. A vertical and horizontal interpretation allows us to see the multilingual, multicultural history of New Orleans and demands that we think beyond national borders.

After Katrina, Haitian American writer Edwidge Danticat raised questions about the many political and media pundits who expressed shock at the devastation after the levees broke by saying that New Orleans looked more like Haiti than the United States. Danticat observes, "It's hard for those of us who are from places like Freetown or Port-au-Prince not to wonder why the so-called developed world needs so desperately to distance itself from us, especially at a time when an unimaginable tragedy shows exactly how much alike we are." Danticat continues, "We do share a planet that is gradually being warmed by mismanagement, unbalanced exploration, and dismal environmental policies that might one day render us all, First World and Third World residents alike, helpless to more disasters like Hurricane Katrina."[36]

Mestiza consciousness is also a crucial concept for understanding the political dynamics of rebuilding New Orleans. In 2004, Bush proposed his "compassionate immigration plan," which included a three-year "guest worker policy" aimed particularly at Mexican immigrants. Anti-immigration activists opposed this policy because of their long-standing opposition to immigration from countries with brown and black people. Progressives opposed Bush's plan, seeing it as a way to introduce a labor force that could be easily exploited and used to undermine union safeguards. Given the opposition from at least two directions, Bush tabled this proposal until after Katrina, when he announced that Congress should pass the previously tangled bill. His logic was that the rebuilding of New Orleans would require labor far surpassing what was currently available from domestic workers.[37]

Mestiza consciousness becomes an important vantage point from which to view Bush's plan, since it recognizes connections among and between communities that often get pitted against each other in political wars. As most of the large-scale contracts for rebuilding were quickly granted to companies outside the region, working-class communities, mostly communities of color, were forced to compete against each other for jobs, housing, and other fundamental resources. Double consciousness runs the risk of missing the nuanced, historical relationships between and among communities of color. The recent transnational history of New Orleans reflects layers of colonialism, war, and natural disasters. The multilingual, multiracial, multiethnic composition of the city, and the uneven and complicated story of how various communities fared following Katrina, give compelling example to the consciousness Anzaldúa describes.

### MULTIPLYING CONSCIOUSNESS

The seduction of color blindness and the pathways to financial and political success offered up to individual conservative people of color make it hard to imagine that Katrina, as horrible as it has been, will lead to an awakening. While it is not surprising that many people have been convinced that the Republican Party and its focus on individualism are the way to go, we would like to believe that such an upheaval as Katrina would enable the Rices, Powells, Thomases, and Gonzaleses of the world to feel an accountability to people of color.

There have, in fact, been a few sightings that might suggest such a reawakening. At the height of the 2006 Israeli bombing of Lebanon, after weeks of US support for the Israeli assault, Rice finally tried to push for a cease-fire. Israeli prime minister Ehud Olmert argued that Lebanese civilians had been adequately warned to leave the regions Israel was bombing. According to two US officials, when Olmert made this proclamation, Rice shook her head and said, "Look, we've had this experience with Katrina, and we thought we were doing it right. . . . But we learned that many people who want to leave can't leave."[38] While double consciousness would require that Rice keep holding herself accountable, to see her fate as intimately connected to the people of New Orleans, there was a glimmer of consciousness in her statement. And the fact that she was making a transnational connection—that the poverty of many people in Lebanon was creating a vulnerability similar to that experienced by people in New Orleans—speaks to Anzaldúa's vision of a consciousness that rises above nationalist divides.

Trauma does and can awaken historical memory. It may not awaken it among black conservatives and others who have bought into an individualistic framework for living their lives, but they, in fact, remain among the few. When Clarence Thomas became an associate justice on the Supreme Court, Leon Higginbotham, a renowned black judge and scholar, wrote an open letter to Thomas, following protests from many directions regarding Thomas's lack of qualifications and his sexual harassment of lawyer Anita Hill. In the letter, Higginbotham urged Thomas to "recognize what James

Baldwin called the 'force of history' within you. You will need to recognize that both your public life and your private life reflect this country's history in the area of racial discrimination and civil rights. And, while much has been said about your admirable determination to overcome terrible obstacles, it is also important to remember how you arrived where you are now, because you did not get there by yourself."[39] Although Thomas has done little to suggest he listened to his elder, Higginbotham's widely read letter was a resounding reminder of the import of historical memory, particularly in times of retreat from racial justice. The trauma of black women all over the country as they witnessed the Senate Judiciary Committee's attempt to undermine and humiliate Anita Hill led to the formation of Black Women in Defense of Ourselves, a network of women who waged highly visible protests of Hill's mistreatment.

Meanwhile, in New Orleans, people are living with exhaustion. Few who have remained there can get through their days without showing signs of post-traumatic stress—numbness, disorientation, crying, depression, despair, disembodiment. Somehow, though, amid this collective trauma, a vision is emerging that starts with recognizing New Orleans as a diaspora, an African city embellished by a Caribbean, Mexican, and Central American presence. People are working in multiple ways to reclaim the St. Bernard Public Housing Development by organizing the "Survivors Village" across from their old homes. People are reopening jazz and dancing clubs all over the city. Over 4,500 public school teachers in New Orleans lost their jobs after Katrina.[40] The reinstitution of their jobs is key now. Education in the hands of black people has always been the cornerstone of a liberatory ethic. These teachers are not looking to Condoleezza Rice or Mayor Ray Nagin—or even to Jesse Jackson or Al Sharpton—to reclaim their schools. Just as they did during the nineteenth-century Reconstruction, the people of New Orleans know that self-determination is the alphabet they need to teach.

# PART TWO

# SPIRIT

*The 9/11 Attacks*

## BEIRUT 2006

*My Israeli friend Nachum who is blind*
*and an expert stone mason tells me*
*he carries a pistol when he goes back to Nahariya*
*I'll shoot them all before they kill me*
*I look at him speechless*
*cite the lopsided numbers*
*his face goes blank*
*he feels my silence*
*reminds me*
*I am here, not there,*
*trying to make peace with the stone*

—BECKY THOMPSON

# THREE

# THE 9/11 ATTACKS AND MAX WEBER

*Five mysteries hold the keys to the unseen: the act of love, and the birth of a baby, and the contemplation of great art, and being in the presence of death or disaster, and hearing the human voice lifted in song. These are the occasions when the bolts of the universe fly open and we are given a glimpse of what is hidden, an eff of the ineffable.*

— SALMAN RUSHDIE, *THE GROUND BENEATH HER FEET*

Diane first learned about the attack on the World Trade Center when she turned on her television on the morning of 9/11. At the time, no one knew what was going on at the Pentagon. Her immediate thought was that another Timothy McVeigh-white-supremacist type had planned an attack against a well-known public space. When she heard that the Pentagon had been hit, she couldn't understand why a plane flying over it hadn't been immediately shot down, since it is illegal for planes to use that route. By midafternoon, she had begun to brace herself, as several of her colleagues made derogatory comments about Muslims and acted incredulous about why anyone might want to do anything to harm "Americans." No amount of reason seemed to deter their blanket statements. As one colleague after the next expressed a fear of feeling unsafe in the United States for the first time ever, Diane kept thinking about how odd that response was. For as long as she could remember, she had known that at any moment some unpredictable force could do her harm. Just driving down the Taconic Parkway from Vassar College to New York City reminded her that she was not safe traveling through an area where few black people live who could offer her witness or refuge if the police or white people accosted her.

Becky first heard about the attack while talking on the telephone with her activist friend Bonnie Kerness, who has worked in the criminal justice division of the American Friends Service Committee in Newark, New Jersey, for thirty years. Several minutes into the conversation, Bonnie interrupted to say that a plane had just flown into one of the World Trade Center towers. One of Bonnie's first comments was, "This is going to be terrible news for prisoners across the country, especially the political prisoners." She knew, without even taking a breath, that no matter who was responsible for the attack, political prisoners would be blamed, and there was nothing she could do in any immediate way to protect them. Bonnie and Becky hung up quickly. Becky's mind reeled, trying to integrate the enormity of this information.

Becky and other colleagues frantically ran around the college where she teaches, trying to find a television set that would broadcast any channel other than the college's announcement of daily events. Fully twenty-five minutes into their frenzy, they located a television that could receive network stations; after being hauled into the middle of the main campus building, it was watched continuously for days. Three days later one of Becky's students came to her, worried about another of the students in their class—a Saudi student related to Osama bin Laden—who, Becky learned, had not come out of her room once, afraid that she would be attacked.

We begin with these stories, not because they are special or extraordinary, but because everyone has a story about where they were and what they were doing when cataclysmic events took place: when World War II ended, when the Rosenbergs were executed, when Malcolm X was assassinated—and when the Towers and the Pentagon were attacked, killing more than three thousand people. In the moments following a tragedy, time often seems to take on a slowed-down, amplified dimension, a shift that compels people to register their witnessing. These stories are ways that people attach themselves to history by adding their piece of memory to the event's collective life.

Like many other people's stories about the aftermath of 9/11, ours reveal both logical and magical thinking, both rational and irrational thought. For Diane, rational thought included her caution against colleagues' unbridled scapegoating and her awareness that 9/11 was not the first and foremost example of danger facing African Americans in US history. For Becky, rationality came in the form of learning that certain people would be instantly vulnerable after the attacks in ways others would not. Arab and Muslim Americans (and anyone looking like those perceived to be Arab or Muslim) could be in danger.

Alongside these methodical and reasoned responses, we had reactions that, retrospectively, revealed a type of thinking that is characteristic of trauma. For Becky, irrationality was evident in her almost obsessive search for a television, a search coming from an unnamed belief that watching the television would somehow contain the event, would connect her to the people of New York. As political scientist James Der Derian explains, "In our public culture, the media networks rather than the family, the community, or the government provide the first, and by their very speed and pervasiveness, the most powerful response to a crisis."[1] In moments of crisis, the television has become a sort of talisman to keep the evil spirits away, to keep us emotionally safe by not having to be alone with the terror, a gesture in search of community at a moment when community has been threatened. For Diane, the logic that the attack wouldn't include the Pentagon came from some deep belief that rules would keep the building safe from attack. Rules would stop such an action; either people would know not to fly over the Pentagon, or US regulations would ensure that they would be shot down. Either way, rules would protect against disaster.

We were not alone in having irrational reactions to the attacks, in trying to rely on totems and magic to help us deal with 9/11. In fact, one of the most stunning and revealing characteristics of the national response to the attack was reliance on what can only be seen as irrationality. What makes the national response to 9/11 instructive is the extent to which irrational behavior became dominant, while being identified as rational. From our perspective, naming this irrationality is a crucial step toward an effective response to the attack, a giant step beyond tactics of retaliation based on fear and a desire for revenge.

### IT'S NOT EASY BEING MAX WEBER: LIVING THE PROTESTANT ETHIC

Trying to make sense out of 9/11 led us careening back to the work on rationality and irrationality done by the German sociologist Max Weber, one of the most prolific and expansive social theorists of the nineteenth and twentieth centuries. Weber, who was born in 1864, was raised in mid-nineteenth-century Berlin in a prosperous family. His father was a politician, and his mother was a devout Protestant. Family life for Max Weber was perennially tense. Because he was sickly, his mother tried to draw him out and provide him with as much intellectual stimulation as possible.

His father, who was domineering and bombastic, controlled his wife's and children's every move. As Weber grew up, he resented his father's patriarchal ways, including his treatment of Weber's mother, and yet he identified deeply with his father's public recognition and authority. This early ambivalence, which reverberated later in his life, seems to have been linked to his emotional struggles. The complicated dynamics Weber experienced as a child also gave him a window into seeing contradictory, multilayered social tensions. One striking characteristic emblematic of all of Weber's work is his ability to see how one factor and its opposite can simultaneously be true.

As a young scholar, Weber was trained as a lawyer, served in the military, and then earned his doctorate, writing a dissertation that made links between economic and legal history. Early in his career, he was identified as a formidable talent, learning both Spanish and Italian to complete his thesis (and later intensively studying Hebrew and Russian for subsequent research).[2] He was a voracious reader with an encyclopedic knowledge of several disciplines. At the age of thirty, he accepted a full professorship in economics at the University of Freiburg, an appointment that would suggest he could begin to slow his pace as he settled into a lifelong academic career. Instead, Weber threw himself even more intensely into his work, believing that he had no choice but to work around the clock. Again, Weber was embodying ideas that would later manifest themselves in his scholarship, specifically his writing on the Protestant work ethic. He felt pressured to maintain an ever more demanding level of productivity, even though that productivity came at the expense of his health. He was trying to rationalize (control, measure, and maintain) his workload despite his body's seemingly irrational needs.

Weber spiraled into a depression in 1897 that was several years in duration. Its timing has led scholars to surmise that his breakdown was, at least in part, related to his relationship with his father.[3] Just two months before Weber's father died unexpectedly, they had a terrible fight; for the first time, Weber had stood up against his father's attempt to control Weber's mother. He did not see his father again. This connection speaks to another of many times in Weber's life when the rational and irrational reckoned with each other. Death may be one of the most irrational aspects of the human condition. It cannot be controlled, it is rarely predicted, and we have little information about where people go psychically and spiritually after they die. The fact that Weber could no longer keep his breakneck work pace following his father's death—that he could no longer embody the Protestant ethic that became the focus of his most famous work—provides a powerful example of his acknowledgment of the contest between rationality and irrationality. In Weber's life, irrationality often won, as it frequently does in contemporary society as well.

The paradoxes in Weber's personal life were multiple, each signaling contradictions and complexities that he drew upon in his long list of expansive scholarly projects. As Gerth and Mills observe, "A number of contradictory elements stood in tension with one another and made up the life and views of Max Weber. If, as he wrote, 'men are not open books,' we should certainly not expect to find even an easy index to his many-sided existence. To understand him, we have to grasp a series of irrational half-paradoxes."[4] Although Weber was not religious—in his words "religiously unmusical"—he devoted much of his scholarly work to studying the impact of religion on people's lives throughout the world.[5] He was a nationalist early on, very much an advocate of a strong German state, and yet, in his scholarly work, he treated nationalism as antithetical to individual rights and a tool of the owning class. He wrote "Science as a Vocation," one of the most cited and influential essays on the need for objectivity in the study of society, and yet his scholarly pursuits revealed, and were deeply influenced by, his own personal struggles.[6] As Gerth and Mills note, "What was most personal to him is accessible and at the same time hidden by the objectification of his work. By interpreting the prophets of disaster and doom, Weber illuminated his own personal and public experiences."[7] Both the life he led and his prolific writing were multilayered and complex, riddled with contradiction, ambiguity, and nuance.

Although the possible applications of Weber's work to 9/11 are wide-ranging, our emphasis is on his understanding of rationality and irrationality, arguably among his most ambitious and influential concepts.[8] His work on the two can be found in multiple sources, including his most famous collection of essays, *The Protestant Ethic and the Spirit of Capitalism*.[9] His early interest in the Protestant ethic was partially influenced by his own compulsive work habits and deep fear of any enjoyment beyond the productivity of work. Understanding the foundations of Protestant values emerging from sixteenth- and seventeenth-century Puritan churches and their relation to capitalism might help him grasp the underpinnings of his own problems.[10]

Weber saw Protestantism as a wellspring for capitalism. In this way he took issue with Karl Marx, who saw religion as an impediment to a modernizing society, keeping people tied to traditional values rather than to those necessary for industrialization (such as individualism and rationality). Drawing upon comparisons between Catholic and Protestant countries in Europe, Weber contended that, in areas that included both, Protestants were more economically successful. Internationally, capitalism was thriving in Protestant countries in Europe (the home of the Reformation) but not in India, the Middle East, China, and Catholic-based nations in Europe.[11] Weber asserted that Buddhism, Islam, Hinduism, and Catholicism all made room for beliefs and rituals that support magical, mystical thought; this Weber believed undercut a capitalist emphasis on formal rationalization. Early Protestantism was one of the few religions that squelched magic and the realm of the inexplicable.[12]

Although Weber wrote the first essay of *The Protestant Ethic* in Germany, his 1904 trip to the United States gave him the insights he used for the subsequent chapters, drawing upon firsthand knowledge of the astounding capitalist growth he had witnessed there. As an eleven-year-old, he had been given Ben Franklin's autobiography, which became a central touchstone in *The Protestant Ethic*.[13] Franklin, Weber believed, embodied in his work several adages illustrating the Protestant ethic. "Time is money" spoke to a value system founded on an individual denial of enjoyment and an emphasis on productivity.

Based on his travels through New England, the South, and the Midwest, Weber was struck by how an emphasis on work and economic productivity trumped all other social values. This reality both ensured capitalist production and stifled virtually all emotions, activity, and thought that were not in the direct service of amassing wealth. Weber also took note of how the work required of common laborers under capitalism wasted many of their talents, making them beholden to job descriptions that often truncated their abilities. His interest was in understanding the value system that led people to work long and hard hours even when they were miserable. From his perspective, it was possible to address this question by analyzing the rise of a Protestant value system and its influence on—in fact, support of—capitalist growth.[14]

According to Weber, the Protestant ethic came from a religious assertion in predestination. In Weber's own family (particularly his devoutly religious mother), and through his travels in the United States, Weber had seen how the Protestant belief in predestination was consonant with the needs of capitalism. Whether someone would get to heaven after death was determined before birth, a decision never revealed during one's lifetime. Given the enormous insecurity of this unknowing status, people spent their lives seeking signs for themselves and those around them, the most tangible of which was economic success. Spending time outside work to enjoy life was seen as antithetical to productivity, a sign that people did not see themselves as "heaven material."

Because Protestants believed that they had their own private relationship to God, and that they would not know until they died if the relationship had been successful, the only way they could measure whether they had "done good" was to demonstrate a life of quantifiable, tangible, good works. In this system, it is not enough to make money; it must be saved as proof of productivity. Stockpiling wealth, avoiding all pleasures, and refusing to be distracted by the power of the flesh were all mandates of the Protestant ethic. Enjoying one's wealth was unacceptable, since any short-term gratification might be interpreted as a sign that one was not devoted to one's calling. Leaving a grand inheritance for one's children, however, was a sign of pleasure deferred, money saved for reinvestment in the future. Weber wrote of this agreement that a person "gets nothing out of his wealth for himself, except the irrational sense of having done his job well."[15]

The link that Weber made between the Protestant ethic and what he called the "spirit of capitalism" is that capitalist productivity became its own religion—the pursuit of profit became an end in itself. The spirit of capitalism was reflected in the belief that people had a duty to increase their profit and consider work a calling. According to Weber, in a society where work had become a calling, "man is dominated by the making of money, by acquisition as the ultimate purpose of his life."[16] In this way, a particular religious system (Protestantism) went hand in glove with an economic system (capitalism) by rendering people, first and foremost, as productive agents.

The dominance of Protestantism in US society means that people of all other religions are also influenced by its ethic—its drive to produce wealth at the center of what it means to be American. Because a belief that has religious origins has become incorporated into the values of the economic system, all people living in this society are socialized to embody this drive. Jews, Catholics, Muslims, atheists, and people of other religious callings are as susceptible as Protestants to upholding this calling. (In fact, in a Protestant-dominated society, many who are not raised Protestant may do the work of upholding this calling even more rigidly than Protestants do, as a consequence of the pressures of assimilation and the demands of uniformity, felt especially by those who do not fit the mold.)

## WEBER'S RATIONALITY AND IRRATIONALITY

Weber's central worry about the rise of capitalism was that its investment in legality, bureaucracy, and universal regulations (what he called rationalization) left little room for the heart, individual personality, deviation, creativity, and innovation. He referred to this trap as the "iron cage."[17] Weber believed that people living in the iron cage ran the risk of developing a deep "disenchantment of the world."[18] He asserted that although people in early Protestant sects saw round-the-clock work as a calling, over time choice had merged into an imperative, trapping everyone in society. Disenchantment with the world was an inevitable consequence of a society that eliminated magical thought and practice and cordoned off romantic love, creativity and unpredictability. Of course, Weber's worry about what it meant to live in an iron cage, separated from one's creativity and the chance to enjoy one's life and the world, resonated deeply with Karl Marx's work on alienation: both men were lamenting intrusions on what makes people fully human.

According to Weber, rationalization is an organizing principle that links the Protestant ethic to the spirit of capitalism. Rationalization, the logical and mechanized parceling of activity to achieve measurable ends, makes trains run on time and enables hospitals to keep track of dead bodies in a morgue. It makes it possible to find cereal in the same grocery aisle every week and allows people to go through a green light at least fairly certain that there won't be oncoming traffic. Rationalization also makes Muzak out of jazz, Tater Tots out of potatoes, SAT scores out of intelligence, and following orders more important than breaking rank. Rationalization in religion is the systematizing of belief—specifying that there is just one God, assigning uniform meaning to individual symbols, and creating job descriptions for religious leaders.[19] Rationalization in the academy is the emphasis on specialized and compartmentalized knowledge, on strict and hierarchical divisions between disciplines.

The more rationalized a society, the less magic is tolerated; the more bureaucracy is enforced, the less individual creativity is nourished; the more regimented our activity, the less spontaneous joy is possible; the more efficient our work becomes, the less it means to us; the more rigid the work, the more mind-numbing it is. Weber saw bureaucracies as a particular case of rationality. As the most common method of organizing work in the United States, bureaucracies are characterized by a hierarchy of authority (with most of the power lodged at the top), impersonality, written rules of conduct, efficiency, and a specialized division of labor.

Weber's worry was that increased rationalization would reduce, if not eliminate entirely, the quirky, spontaneous, ineffable, and mysterious in society. Increased rationality would create "specialists without spirit, sensualists without heart; this nullity imagines that it has attained a level of civilization never before achieved."[20] Unlike many of his contemporaries, who saw the emergence of rationally driven economic, political, and military institutions as signs of human progress, Weber worried about the cost to humanity caused by systems based on calculation and quantification. For Weber, "life and the world are fundamentally irrational," a reality that is ignored at our peril in a society where rationality trumps irrationality at seemingly every turn.[21]

Weber rooted the cultural sources of irrationality in a bygone era, in traditional societies where religion held sway over all other ethical frameworks, before capitalism cemented technical rationality into the foundation of modern society. In traditional societies, irrationality could be seen in the many rituals that surrounded birth, ascension to adulthood, marriage, becoming an elder, and death. Birth and death rituals served to make people feel safe. The rituals tied them to each other and to their ancestors and made them less afraid of death. Cultural anthropologist Ernest Becker notes that premodern people believed that "death is the ultimate promotion, the final ritual elevation to a higher form of life, to the enjoyment of eternity in some form."[22] The talisman that people in many traditional societies wore to ward off evil spirits, the dances people performed to make it rain, were among the rituals that gave life meaning. All these acts were symbols of irrationality. Rituals gave people a way to express their hopes and fears and to deal with change.[23]

Weber rooted the psychological source of irrationality in romantic love, which he believed carries a passion and power no society can ultimately contain. The magical, mystical experience of romantic love that he treated as the heart of irrationality resonates with the truth of Adam and Eve, Romeo and Juliet, Chloe and Olivia, and many other iconic love partners. In a brilliant essay on the sphere of the erotic in world religions, Weber wrote that "the erotic relation seems to offer the unsurpassable peak of the fulfillment of the request for love in the direct fusion of the souls of one to the other. This boundless giving of oneself is as radical as possible in its opposition to all functionality, rationality, and generality."[24]

For Weber, the union between two lovers could be so complete, so overpowering, and so transformative that the connection itself might be a sacrament: "The lover realizes himself to be rooted in the kernel of the truly living, which is eternally inaccessible to any rational endeavor. He knows himself to be freed from the cold skeleton hands of rational orders, just as completely as from the banality of everyday routine. This consciousness of the lover rests upon the ineffaceability and inexhaustibleness of his own experience."[25] For Weber, the capacity to experience this boundless connection was a way of knowing life itself. While the irrationality of this love freed people from rational order, by its very nature it remained ineffable.

Again, as is true for many of Weber's most profound insights, he was overtly drawing upon his scholarly knowledge of a topic—in this case how the erotic is interpreted in multiple religious systems. But his own personal knowledge of the subject comes through as well in his eloquent and soulful writing. As a young man, Weber had been in love with a woman who had been institutionalized. Eventually, he broke the relationship off, racked with guilt and ambivalence about his decision. Then, in 1893, he married Marianne Schnitger. She became an influential feminist and intellectual, writing extensively on women and gender.[26] She remained devoted to Weber throughout his life, even during the many years of his debilitating depression.[27] They shared a life of the mind, creating a home that became an intellectual hub in Germany. Max Weber also had at least one passionate extramarital affair. This relationship may have given him an embodied experience of the erotic as an inexplicable, life-affirming power.

In this instance and others, there is a fascinating interplay between Weber's personal life and his theoretical interests. His own nervous breakdown, which he said freed him from the "icy hand" of all work and no play, seemed to encourage his own break from asceticism (the renouncing of the comforts of society in order to lead an austere life of self-discipline) and his theoretical critique of asceticism as well. His increasing interest in the arts, Eastern mysticism, and avant-garde literature paralleled his personal and sociological inquisitiveness about the erotic. His fascination with charisma (which reflects a magical, transcendent means of leadership) dovetailed with his work on the concept of *verstehen* (intuitional understanding) and his recognition of the erotic sphere in culture (and his own life).[28]

Among Weber's concerns was what happens to irrationality in a highly bureaucratic society, where little is left to chance, where rituals that might celebrate the mysterious in life are denuded of their poetry. Many of the rituals people in the United States commonly practice are rational practices—applying for jobs based on technically worded job descriptions, getting married (a ritual that is often preceded by legally drawn-up prenuptial arrangements and followed by a legal-rational process of divorce in 50 percent of the cases), and attending funerals. Weber rooted this avoidance or fear of the spectacular in the making of Puritan traditions. A Puritan, he explained, "even rejected all signs of religious ceremony at the grave and buried his nearest and dearest without song or ritual in order that no superstition, no trust in the effects of magical and sacramental forces on salvation, should creep in."[29] Even the few rituals that tapped into the most irrational of sources—the miracle of birth, the mystery of love, the magic of prophesy, and the finality of death—were socially sanctioned with deeply rational elements that often left people feeling empty and alone rather than assured and connected.

Weber asserted that in modern society the rise of rituals based on rationality means that eventually the irrational—the spontaneous, the magical, and the surprising—will bubble up and assert itself, requiring society's complete attention. While rationality promises efficiency and uniformity, it deadens creativity and wipes away charm. Rationality relegates emotions to a time clock and renders love and spontaneity superfluous acts rather than essential to what makes us human. Given this reality, according to Weber, even the most rationalized societies cannot fully protect against irrationality. As rationalization increases, irrationality intensifies.[30] There is a paradox—bureaucracies, the epitome of rationalization, can act in irrational ways. Bureaucracies can employ irrational actors who do not follow the rules. This irrationality can take the form of whistle-blowers and dissidents unwilling to go along with the status quo in organizations. It can also manifest itself when people in bureaucracies use the letter, not the spirit, of policies to justify horrendous cruelty. During the Holocaust, to call up one of the most devastating of examples, Bayer, Ford, and many other corporations used their rationalized systems to back the highly irrational, charismatic leadership of Hitler.

State-sponsored bureaucracies that are organized around rationality can act irrationally. Rationality and irrationality work dialectically with each other, a relationship that is often most evident in times of great stress and upheaval. Explaining Weber's work on this reality, Gerth and Mills state: "[The] process of rationalization is punctured, however, by certain discontinuities of history. Hardened institutional fabrics may thus disintegrate and routine forms of life prove insufficient for mastering a growing state of tension, stress, and suffering."[31] The 9/11 attacks were such a puncture.

QUESTIONS

What is it like, salat in the city?

*Five times a day, the muezzin's voice*
        *fog horn the color of sand*
*calls the men to prayer*
        *knees leading toward Mecca*
*the city breathes mosques*


What is it like to stand during prayer?

*My mind bows with the men*
        *stays with the women*
*I want to cover my head*
        *bend away from the West*


What was it like when you died?

*My mother calls me home*
        *come lamb, he is going*
*her flute singing psalms*
        *you open your eyes*
*we are with you, there are circles*
        *surrounding your bed*
*rocking we are rocking*
        *your eyes as big as the sea*
*you ride smoke rings to the sky*
        *Arab father now sand*


Is there a prayer
        that is upright and kneeling?
Is there a home
        that is not made of glass?

—BECKY THOMPSON

# FOUR

# MOMENTS OF GRACE/
# GRACE UNDERMINED

### THE PEOPLE'S IRRATIONALITY

Following 9/11 there was nothing about people's days that could have been, or should have been, considered business as usual. Jobs did not matter. Attending college lectures did not matter. Even news of a potentially lethal anthrax scare did not matter in comparison with the devastation at the World Trade Center and the loss of so many lives. This is why people skipped work for days on end to hand out food at ground zero. This is why so many of the people who worked in high-tech, corporate, and financial jobs at the World Trade Center never returned to that line of work, to that high-powered life. This is why people from all over the world sent money, gifts, and cards in many languages to the families of those who died, even though many of them had never seen the towers, had never met the people, and did not look for thank-you cards in return for their acts of kindness.

In the initial weeks following the disaster, many behaviors long associated with an advanced capitalist society were thrown aside, replaced, even if momentarily, by different ways of being. Weber asserted that a society based on the Protestant ethic requires insularity—contact restricted to people whose values mirror one's own—and a stoic approach to birth, death, and all social processes in between. The characteristics of this stoicism in US society include keeping a stiff upper lip, refusing to let your enemy know you have been hurt, valuing toughness, circling the wagons, and isolating from anybody and anything (individuals, governments, or international policies) that offer even faint criticism. Weber argued that this mentality was encoded into the frontier, the pioneering way of life; it has become a worldview that both hinders and justifies silence about traumatic events. Immediately following 9/11, this ethic was interrupted, at least momentarily.

One of the beauties of the weeks immediately following the attacks was that people could not retreat into their own isolated spaces to try to cope with the disaster.[1] Everybody was out in the streets—going to spontaneously held community meetings, creating makeshift altars, making murals of hundreds of photos of lost loved ones, and talking with everybody and anybody about the disaster. Thousands of mourners traveled to Union Square each day to pay their respects and serve as witnesses. As sociologist and New York resident Janet Abu-Lughod wrote, "Union Square became a magnet for thousands of pedestrians who felt the need to gather, to mourn, and to dissent. (Not since the 1960s have I seen such voices for peace. . . .) . . . Ceremonies, both spontaneous and planned (the latter widely shown on TV) were generated, often featuring pictures of the missing. Memorial altars were adorned with lit candles, flowers, and poems. Secular spaces were transformed into sacred places, suggesting that the yearning to draw sustenance from a collective place of worship and supplication was deep."[2] Moustafa Bayoumi, a professor of English and a New York resident, noted, "For a moment it felt that the trauma of suffering—not the exercise of reason, not the belief in any God, not the universal consumption of a fizzy drink, but the simple and tragic reality that it hurts when we feel pain—was understood as the thread that connects all of humanity."[3] People desperately needed to come together collectively, in unorganized, spontaneous, and emotionally rich ways; there was simply no systematic, calculated way to understand or deal with the reality of people jumping out of windows to save—to end—their lives.

People from all over the country told their stories about where they were when they heard the news, what they thought, whom they called, and how they explained it to themselves at the time and later. After 9/11, many people rejected individualism and keeping to oneself and one's community—values that run deep in US society. After 9/11, there was little room for individualism. The collective was essential. People talked with neighbors for the first time about real issues of death, dying, and loss. Family members who hadn't talked for years with estranged relatives living in Manhattan made calls to inquire about their safety. Children in Idaho wrote letters to children in New York whom they had never met. Trauma initially broke the US habit of retreating from public life in search of individual modes of grieving, coping, and moving on after death.

The events of 9/11 also showed that no amount of medical or scientific technology could protect people from sudden and brutal mass murder. Over the last several decades, many people in the United States had come to believe that they were gaining some control over death. The elongation of the life span, astounding medical contributions in diagnosing and treating illnesses that used to be fatal, the capacity to harvest organs, and cryogenic techniques that enable bodies to be preserved after death are all highly publicized examples of how technology and medical science were outsmarting death. After 9/11, people saw the limits of science as a protection against death and came to feel that death of that magnitude needed to be dealt with collectively.

Millions of people became devoted to reading the profiles of each and every person whose lives were honored in the New York Times. People who had never read the Times bought it every day, unwilling—unable—to separate themselves from those who had died. People thought that if they read the profiles, they might somehow know all those who had died. Such a witnessing might counteract each person's worry about being alone, forgotten, and anonymous in death. Unlike many obituaries that are written in methodical, chronological, and formulaic ways, these profiles were full of personality. They were idiosyncratic, surprising, and intimate. While they often included traditionally recognized accomplishments (degrees, marriages, occupations) of those who had died, the profiles also incorporated many details that celebrated their originality, their unique lives. In her essay "Wounded New York," comparative literary scholar Judith Greenberg wrote, "The intimacy produced by the 'Portraits of Grief' section in the New York Times and the 'family album' quality of the missing person fliers publicly attempted to bring the grief of the broken private home to the broken public home."[4] These profiles made people who had died real for the readers, a gift that countered the anonymity characteristic of an advanced capitalist society and accentuated in urban metropolises.

A society built on long-term gratification and the postponement of enjoyment became one with intense focus on the immediate—the immediate grief of the families who had lost loved ones; the current needs of the firefighters and rescue workers; the overwhelming craving for families and friends to be together across the country; and the compelling impulse of many people who had once lived in New York to return there, even if only for a few days, as a kind of witnessing and as an act of solidarity. There was a transnational love fest for New York. People felt compelled to put their bodies right back in the city, in the midst of the devastating, marvelous, incredible, inexpressible pain that the city felt. It is no surprise that some of the earliest writing to emerge after 9/11 was in the form of poetry—the most immediate, visceral, and intimate of written arts.[5]

The events of 9/11 also invited people to reconsider their relationship to money. During the first weeks after the attack, the bedrock value of creating and preserving personal wealth was, at least momentarily, replaced by a sense that holding on to one's money did not matter. Money was no protection. In fact, some of the wealthiest people in the world worked at the World Trade Center, and yet no amount of money could have saved them. After 9/11 people gave huge amounts of money in all directions, by phone, on the Internet, through charities, in individual envelopes, and in collection plates. This giving flew in the face of a common practice in a country built on the ethic that all profit must be reinvested to make more profit. One of the most striking aspects of the marriage between rationalization and the Protestant ethic is the removal of sacrament as a means of showing one's faith in God. With predestination, there is no need for sacraments. There is no need to give money during one's lifetime. Rather, giving is reserved, in the form of inheritance, until after one's death.

Immediately following 9/11, people did not hesitate to give freely. Money became an immediate sacrament—not just for the people in one's immediate circle but for all of the people who had lost family members in the attack. The capitalist ethic of keeping money in the family, and deferring enjoyment of that money until after one's death, was momentarily replaced by a wide distribution of the wealth—across generation, race, language, and ethnicity—with few, if any, earmarks on how the money should be spent.

People's responses after 9/11 demonstrated that suffering needed to be understood as its own experience. It could not be cordoned off, ignored, or reduced to greeting-card sentiment. Suffering needed to be honored. In one of his many profound essays on religion and society, Weber observed, "The ethically unmotivated inequality in the distribution of happiness and misery, for which compensation has seemed conceivable, has remained irrational; and so has the brute fact that suffering exists."[6] In this passage, Weber makes clear that suffering lies in the realm of the irrational. Injustice often lies in the realm of the irrational too. It is indeed irrational to think that injustice can be simply compensated for or eliminated. Suffering—the acknowledgment of it, the rituals created to honor it, the depth of it, the universality of it—is what makes us human and brings out our humanity. The 9/11 attacks were themselves irrational; the suffering was the genuine, understandable, and unavoidable consequence of the attacks.

Everyday people's actions showed us that trauma could not be controlled through calculated, systematic means. People could not cope with it by working extra hard, saving extra money, making extra investments, stifling extra emotions, saving up for extra mean times. September 11 *was* the mean time, a devastating reality that enabled the precious, unpredictable, vulnerable, and unmediated aspects of irrationality to flower in people's hearts and minds.

Although it is logical to think that people responded to 9/11 by becoming more what Weber described as "disenchanted of the world," at least initially—and ironically—the opposite took place.[7] Philosopher David Loy notes, "The 'disenchantment of the world' means not so much the debunking of magic and superstition as the tendency to devalue all mysterious and incalculable forces in favor of the knowledge 'that one can, in principle, master all things by calculation.'"[8] People knew that there was no way to fix the devastation of the attacks through calculation. Honoring all those who had died had to come first. In one of her poetic essays, Toni Morrison professes, "Some have God's words; others have songs of comfort for the bereaved. If I can pluck courage here, I would like to speak directly to the dead—the September dead. . . . First I would freshen my tongue, abandon sentences crafted to know evil—wanton or studied; explosive or quietly sinister; whether born of sated appetite or hunger; of vengeance or the simple compulsion to stand up before falling down. I would purge my language of hyperbole; of its eagerness to analyze the levels of wickedness; ranking them; calculating their higher or lower status among others of its kind."[9]

Many of the poems, essays, songs, and prayers written immediately following 9/11 revealed that no authentic response could be "seduced by blitz."[10] There was no quick, easy, or measurable way to bind up and fix the trauma. There was entirely too much missing to respond through calculation. The 9/11 attacks had blown up New Yorkers' private and public understandings of home. The public and private emblems people created illuminated how much was missing, haunting, inexplicable, and certainly unmanageable. This is the nature of trauma and grief: unassimilated absence.[11]

The events of 9/11 gave people a chance to adorn themselves in empathy for all those victimized by the attack, to embrace all those who could not, should not, have gone back to work and conducted business as usual. Although the period right after 9/11 was one of the most devastating times in US history, it was also a liberatory moment, a temporary relief from the "iron cage" of capitalism.[12] The problem, however, is that a certain irrationality—mainly that espoused and supported by the state—trumped the irrationality born of suffering and humility.

## THE POLITICS OF RETALIATION

While the attacks on 9/11 brought forth ineffable, mysterious, and precious manifestations of human kindness, a simultaneous upsurge of hate and violence against people of Muslim, Middle Eastern, and South Asian descent emerged from multiple directions. For many of us, the grief of witnessing the attacks on the World Trade Center towers was hideously multiplied by a bold reassertion of the United States as a nation based on white and Christian control of schools, streets, playgrounds, neighborhoods, and airwaves. One of the most profound problems following 9/11 was how quickly the irrationality of love was sidetracked, sidestepped, and realigned into the irrationality of hate.

Soon after the attacks, in preparation for doing an interview on Voice of America about anti-Arab, anti-Muslim violence taking place across the country, Becky spoke at length with one of her colleagues, an activist friend of Arab and Jewish descent. As they spoke, it became clear that Becky's colleague, who had long worked in antidefamation organizations, was much more qualified to do the interview than Becky was. However, Becky's friend believed she would be putting herself and her family at risk if she did the interview. In this and many other instances, white privilege protected Becky, while people of Arab descent living in the United States were quickly being racialized as potential terrorists.

This reality was powerfully portrayed in the title of Tram Nguyen's book *We Are All Suspects Now: Untold Stories from Immigrant Communities after 9/11,* which documents widespread assaults on immigrant rights following the attacks.[13] South Asian and African colleagues of Becky's and Diane's, with long-standing green cards and years of teaching at universities in the United States, began to worry that their permanent residence status would be revoked. Taxi drivers were threatened, harassed, detained, and physically injured.[14] Middle Eastern and South Asian immigrants across the country faced great worry and fear about the possible retaliatory responses the US military might aim at their countries of origin. Sociologist Monisha Das Gupta writes, "Most of my family lives in India, and in the days that immediately followed 9/11, the thought of a war in Afghanistan and its impact politically and economically on the region brought back panic-stricken memories of strife and insecurity. I remembered the blackouts, sirens, and the deafening sound of fighter planes in my Kolkata neighborhood during the 1971 freedom struggle that gave birth to Bangladesh, at which time I was ten years old; the flood of refugees in Delhi following the 1979 Soviet invasion of Afghanistan when that word 'mujahideen' entered our vocabulary; and the 1984 assassination of then prime minister of India Indira Gandhi, which was avenged by taking thousands of Sikh lives—a time when it seemed as if everything associated with the word 'human' was suspended."[15] Rightfully, Das Gupta was worried that her students and colleagues in the United States had little "inkling of this history of political turmoil that I carry in my body."[16]

Communities across the country also faced the threat that people in their neighborhoods would be taken away unannounced to unspecified detention centers, with no grounds stated, with no due process. Interviews with Afghan and Pakistani Americans underscored the double trauma that many faced—first the trauma of the attack itself, and then "being subject to racist backlash and constructed as the enemy."[17]

In many ways, this upsurge of racism qualifies as irrational in the Weberian sense of the word—spontaneous, unpredictable, unmanageable, illogical, and driven by passion. A white driver impulsively spitting on and assaulting an olive-skinned passenger in the next car; a woman tearing at another woman's head scarf as she walks down the street; a schoolteacher patrolling the US-Mexico border for "terrorists"—all of these acts qualify as irrational, as the antithesis of the acts of love and generosity cited above. Hate crimes—including the murders of a South Asian convenience store owner, a Sikh gas station owner, and a Pakistani market owner—were aimed at such an extraordinary range of people that their selection could be seen only as irrational—both illogical and unpredictable.[18] Their unpredictability only fueled the terror that many people experienced following 9/11; the random acts of violence served to curtail and contain entire groups. The irrationality was evident in the illogical assumption that the acts of nineteen men could be generalized to indict millions of people internationally. As the young Palestinian American poet Suheir Hammad wrote soon after 9/11:

> we did not vilify all white men when mcveigh bombed oklahoma.
> america did not give out his family's addresses or where he went to
> church. or blame the bible or pat robertson.[19]

That the irrationality was institutionalized—backed by the state—helps explain why the irrationality of love immediately following 9/11 could not overpower the irrationality of hate. More than 1,200 Muslim, Arab, and South Asian men were detained and held indefinitely following 9/11, and 11,000 individuals of Muslim, Arab, and South Asian descent were interviewed by the FBI following the attacks.[20] Four years later, more than one-quarter of the 500 prisoners still incarcerated at Guantánamo Bay in Cuba organized one of the longest hunger strikes in recent history.[21] The strike reflected both the men's desperation and their unified resistance against the injustice of imprisonment without representation. Covert actions by the FBI, the newly created Department of Homeland Security, the Federal Aviation Administration, and other government-sponsored enforcement agencies all trampled the rights of thousands of Arabs, Muslims, and others.

While there is some precedent in the United States for retroactively recognizing racial and ethnic scapegoating as both antidemocratic and unjust (with regard to the Palmer Raids of 1919–1920 of "suspected" communists and the imprisonment of Japanese Americans during World War II), the widespread discrimination against people perceived to be Arab or Muslim following 9/11 inscribed stark notions of who belongs in America and who is afforded citizenship rights as Americans.[22] The Patriot Act, passed in October 2001 and then renewed in 2006, gave the FBI extraordinary power to monitor people's lives, including their most private records and accounts. Severe restrictions on refugees, extensive plans to further militarize border patrols, massive deportations, assaults on educators' academic freedom, and the well-orchestrated shift in Hollywood to favor shoot-'em-up, John-Wayne-takes-over-the-world films are but a few of the many institutionalized strategies (i.e., rationalized and backed by bureaucracies) following 9/11.

That is racism's essential rub. It is both highly irrational (since race is a concept with no scientific basis, and racism is often perpetrated in random and illogical ways that reflect the mysteries of individual paranoia) and profoundly rational (because it is state sanctioned, institutionally supported, and legitimized through a stunning coordination of historical lies).

The military response to 9/11—first in a war waged against Afghanistan and then against Iraq—also reflected a pairing of irrationality and rationality. Weber showed that a highly rationalized society—which, in many ways, the US models for the rest of the world—takes many steps to guard against, block, deny, ignore, and contain irrationality. As a consequence, when irrationality does manifest itself, its characteristics are often distorted, manipulated, and damaged almost beyond recognition. Weber's work teaches us that irrationality can go seriously awry, can be mismanaged, misdirected, and underestimated, to the point that it can transmute into war, violence, and further destruction. In "If You Have Tears," literary scholar Peter Brooks points out that "our mourning was hijacked by a simplistically militaristic response, a knee-jerk jingoism that substituted for any reflexive policy."[23] This is, at its core, the problem with the politics of retaliation that have dominated US consciousness since the attacks.

The politics of retaliation distracted us from thinking deeply about what motivated the people who used their bodies and those of the airplane passengers as human bombs. The retaliation stopped us from being both self-reflective and expansive in our response to 9/11. The military, one of the most rationalized institutions that currently exists, took over as the principle means of handling the attacks, bombing children's birthday parties in Afghanistan and sending young men and women who were just beginning to live their lives to fight in wars most of them could not begin to understand.

This response was carried out in the name of nationalism, which, as sociologist Jyoti Puri explains, has the power to "unify people and provide a sense of belonging to a community that takes precedence over all else, whether family, or ethnic or local group."[24] To be an American, to reaffirm one's devotion to America, following 9/11 required that one support the politics of retaliation, despite its irrationality. The power of nationalism is its ability to convince people to die and kill for their nation, even if they don't understand the causes or consequences of the war.[25] Meanwhile, the US retaliation sidetracked us from reckoning with how capitalist rationality—run by bureaucracies that are increasingly devoid of spiritual depth and human accountability—was a key aspect of the terrorists' motivation for attacking the World Trade Center to begin with.

Such a reckoning might start with acknowledging the legitimate concerns that many people in the Middle East have with the history of imperialism in the region.[26] During World War I, the division of the Ottoman Empire through a series of agreements, including the Sykes-Picot Agreement of 1916, gave Britain and France control over land that is now Syria, Iraq, Jordan, Lebanon, and parts of Turkey.[27] The British-sponsored 1917 Balfour Declaration provided the rationale for the Zionist request for a Jewish state on land that was occupied by several groups of people at the time, including Palestinians and Jews. The stage was then set for the Western-orchestrated establishment of the state of Israel in 1948 that was spearheaded by Britain, further complicating regional politics, since Palestine was partitioned off without regard for the wishes of Palestinians.

Following World War II, the United States became the preeminent world power. By the late 1950s, after the Suez Crisis of 1956, Israel became the strongest ally of the United States in the Middle East. The other countries were identified as US allies based, not on whether they were democracies, but on whether they supported US economic and military priorities.[28] So, for example, while Saudi Arabia is one of the most repressive societies in the world (in terms of the domination of women, violation of human rights, and so forth), it has long been an ally of the United States (with 25 percent of the region's oil located in that one country).[29] Until the 1979 Iranian revolution, Iran was the United States' strongest ally in the region (other than Israel), despite the Pahlavi regime's record of human rights abuses. The United States supported Saddam Hussein's one-party military dictatorship for many years, even as it systematically slaughtered Kurds, until Hussein asserted increasing independence from US direction, leading to plans to invade Iraq that long predated 9/11.[30]

The history of US imperialism in the Middle East makes clear that the growth of Islamic militancy over the last twenty years has a materialist base. This militancy is a direct response to decades-long actions by the United States and western European countries to control Middle Eastern oil supplies, national governments, and land divisions. In an attempt to explain the rise of terrorism among Islamic fundamentalists, political scientist Michael Parenti suggests, "We must try to look at the larger conditional causes of terrorism. The terrorist groups that have arisen in the Middle East and Central Asia have emerged from societies in which all popular coalitions and democratic movements have been destroyed by US intervention: Turkey, Yemen, Egypt, Iran, Iraq, Afghanistan, Syria, Saudi Arabia, Pakistan and others." Drawing connections between national attempts at democracy and US repression of those movements, Parenti explains, "In country after country where democratic forces have tried to mobilize for political and economic democracy, where student leaders, labor union leaders, farm and peasant communal collective leaders, independent journalists, liberal clergy, women's rights advocates . . . have fought for social change in a democratic direction, these reformist democratic forces have been the object of the worst sort of oppression over the last half century."[31]

US military aggression since 9/11 has fueled an explosion of militant groups that consider the United States their enemy, only some of whom hold themselves accountable to al-Qaeda. Among militant leaders, Osama bin Laden is probably the most well-known in the United States, but he is certainly not the only one. If bin Laden were assassinated today, the threat of militant Islamic attacks would not be eliminated; al-Qaeda is only one of many transnational networks.[32] The US wars against Afghanistan and Iraq, and the 2006 Israeli war against Lebanon, have fueled militancy far beyond what al-Qaeda could have done on its own. This is why many commentators assert that "Islam has become the vocabulary of nationalism in much of the Middle East."[33] Islamic militancy is not isolated to one country, to one ethnicity, to one political perspective, or to a single method of responding to US imperialism.

Al-Qaeda and other groups are protesting the Israeli occupation and assaults against Palestinians; attacks on Muslims in Somalia, Chechnya, Lebanon, Kashmir, and elsewhere; and the spread of US military bases around the globe. The attacks waged by militant groups on the symbolic power centers of Western culture—a tourist area in Bali, the subways of London, the World Trade Center and the Pentagon in the United States, malls in Israel—are a response to decades of abuse. They are outcries against underdevelopment resulting from globalization, which has left many young people unemployed or underemployed, without access to quality schooling, jobs, and cultural opportunities. They are protests against dictatorships sponsored by the West that have allowed corrupt leaders to loot their countries' most fundamental resources.[34] These are real political and economic injustices, and they have left an increasing number of people willing to put their lives on the line in protest.

While these materialist realities are a consequence of the highly rationalized government and military in the United States, it was people's yearning for—need for—irrationality that helped legitimate US aggression in the Middle East after 9/11. One of the most visual irrational responses following 9/11 was the use of flags in every form imaginable—plastic sticky-on-one-side flags, flags pitched at the top of construction sites, and flags woven into children's underwear. They were plastered, draped, and hung all across the United States. The patriotism sparked by 9/11 enabled the flag to become the symbol raised to both heal the nation's wounds and stop further attacks. The flag-waving also reflected magical thinking that such an emblem might ward off further aggression from al-Qaeda.

Meanwhile, many Arab Americans, Muslim Americans, and South-Asian Americans who saw their citizenship become provisional following the attacks used flags as symbolic shields to guard against discrimination from fellow Americans.[35] Puri concludes, "What complicated the positions of these groups is that anything less than unequivocal support for American nationalism and American foreign policy was considered akin to sedition and, moreover, support for the terrorists."[36] Once the flag was lifted in the name of war, anyone who dared to stand against it ran the risk of being portrayed as failing to support all those who had died on 9/11.[37]

*After the attacks on September 11, 2001, the flag became a fetish imbued with qualities of protection and unity across the United States. "Attack on World Trade Center." Photograph by Spencer Platt. Getty Images News, 1163814.*

The irrational imbuing of a piece of cloth with properties that could heal a country, that could unite people in support of those who died, was portrayed as a rational, nation-loving response to 9/11.

The particular rational/irrational nexus following 9/11—the way the two sidled up to each other—meant that people bought into plans to retaliate, even though that meant sidelining the actual long-term effects of the suffering. People accepted military aggression, even though it required disregarding international laws and sentiment, even though they still wanted rules that would protect them. People wanted rules to be the magic bullet, an understandable reality that left congressional members and senators willing to accept the extremes of the Patriot Act and other legislation that undermined fundamental civil rights.

People also wanted to be able to rely on the military's rules and procedures to get the job done. This made the abuses at Abu Ghraib prison in Iraq and Guantánamo Bay in Cuba particularly troubling, since they revealed the absence of discernible, predictable laws of governance. The

Protestant ethic (evident in the need to respond immediately and produce tangible results) teamed up with a spirit of capitalism bent on ensuring US aggression. The people of Afghanistan and Iraq, and all the men and women sent to fight in those countries, became the victims of this plan.

Although the US war against Iraq launched in 2003 was billed by the Bush administration as a response to the terrorist attacks, it is now widely accepted that Saddam Hussein and the Iraqi government had no ties to al-Qaeda. The 9/11 attacks became a well-orchestrated excuse used to achieve interlocking goals: to assert US power to initiate preemptive wars; to remove a country's leadership, without the support of the country's people or the international community; and to extend US control over oil-producing nations.[38] The justifications used for the war were multiple. The administration fanned Americans' fears following 9/11 and launched a massive propaganda campaign professing Iraq's weapons of mass destruction and Hussein's history of brutality against Iraq's citizens.

The US also broadcast Orientalist portrayals of Iraqi society as patriarchal, "sick," and "backward."[39] All these justifications were used to bolster US attempts to exert military and political control over the region decades before 9/11. The mass media, US leaders, and other influential bodies collectively portrayed the people responsible for the attacks as irrational murderers. The reality that a group of highly educated men in the prime of their lives—fathers, brothers, husbands, and sons—would willingly spend what appeared to be years planning to blow themselves up easily qualified as one of the most irrational acts in recent history. Osama bin Laden was also portrayed as highly irrational. He was represented as a man who saw no wrong in plotting the destruction of thousands of unknowing, innocent people, and who willingly sent some of his most trusted people to their deaths with his assignment. Against the backdrop of these acts as ultimate examples of irrationality, the United States was portrayed as the opposite—a highly rational society (law-abiding, rule oriented, and predictable in its principles of governance) that had been held at the mercy of irrational terrorists.

One problem with this equation is that the irrationality at the foundation of many US responses to 9/11 either went unnamed or was misnamed as rational. Rationality ensured the quick and efficient deployment of military troops with various specialties to Afghanistan, utilizing the most technologically sophisticated military equipment in the world. But, as Weber's work predicted, the height of this rationality was met by an equally intense irrationality. Julien Freund, a Weber scholar, observes, "Rationality and intellectualization have made no inroads on the empire of the irrational."[40]

While the war against Afghanistan was cloaked in a veil of rationality, irrationality was abundantly evident in the Bush administration's retaliation against an entire country—although bin Laden was neither part of the government nor supported by it. Since al-Qaeda is a transnational organization, attacking Afghanistan was like bombing a school because drug dealers once did their business there. When Bush declared war on Iraq based on his claim that its government had weapons of mass destruction, he attempted to make a link between al-Qaeda and Saddam Hussein, despite the overwhelming lack of credible evidence of either weapons or an alliance between Hussein and bin Laden.

When people pointed out that Iraq had a secular government, Bush claimed that Muslims all stick together, and therefore attacking Muslims in Iraq would bring the United States a step closer to finding bin Laden. This logic was akin to drilling for oil in Alaska in hopes that it would open up reserves in a country that had no oil. The justification for the wars was wrapped in the language of efficiency and professionalism that reflected the rhetoric of retaliation in order to avenge an injury. This language deluded much of the American public into the illogical notion that such an approach would broker safety.

After the Bush administration was denied support by virtually every country other than Great Britain, the administration decided to take a go-it-alone tactic to further its goals anyway. Immediately after 9/11, support for the United States soared to what may have been an all-time high in recent history. The world community—including, and perhaps most especially, the vast majority of Muslims—abhorred the violence of 9/11, according the United States tremendous leeway and respect. Bush disregarded and, worse, trampled on this response, rejecting this window of opportunity in alliance building and failing to capitalize on the support of the international community.

Again, the Bush administration's response linked rationality and irrationality. In fact, while Bush was utilizing the most highly rationalized military in the world, he justified waging war by saying he was called to do so as a Christian. His irrational logic was that, he, as an individual, had been called to do God's work by spreading rational American values worldwide. The Palestinian foreign minister Nabil Shaath reported that, in his meeting with Bush in 2003, "Bush said that God guided him in what he should do, and this guidance led him to go to Afghanistan to rid it of terrorism after 9/11 and led him to Iraq to fight tyranny."[41]

Ironically, that irrationality humanized Bush to many people in the United States because his conviction appeared to be passionate and deeply felt. In a highly rationalized society, such passion can be attractive, especially as an antidote to the overwhelming numbness the country experienced following 9/11. At the same time, Bush's justification was unsettling, since there is virtually no way to counter conviction born of religious righteousness (which became a basis for opposition to bin Laden's religious righteousness).

It might be comforting to chalk up Bush's irrationality to the private predicament of a son trying to work out conflicts with his father, former president George H. W. Bush, who had unsuccessfully attempted to remove Saddam Hussein from power. It might be a relief to see the younger Bush as a singular, religiously motivated man.[42] The truth, however, is that much of the American public initially went along with his strategies. Certainly the fact that the general populace was never permitted a vote on whether to go to war made compliance easier. There was, in fact, an international outcry against the wars in Afghanistan and Iraq that included hundreds of thousands of peace activists. But the reality was that the irrationality of supporting the wars did not stop with the Bush administration. Both houses of Congress also voted overwhelmingly in support of the war against Iraq.

While thousands of people were labeled as threats domestically, the highly bureaucratic military was called upon as the most efficient way to save those deemed fully American from external threats. This approach actually further endangered countless people in the United States and in the war zones. The image of this bureaucracy in the form of the military, along with images of the flag, became modern people's magic, which, in reality, backfired.

### HUNGER FOR THE SACRED

For Osama bin Laden and many other Islamic militants, US imperialism has not only caused economic damage (by trying to control the region's oil supply and support corrupt governments). It has also posed a massive threat to Islam.[43] A revealing example of this point is that although bin Laden's writing includes detailed critiques of US militarism, economic control, and suppression of Arab and Muslim countries, the "word 'imperialism' did not occur once in any of the messages he had sent out. He defines the enemy differently. For him, *jihad* is aimed not at an imperium, but at 'global unbelief.'"[44] For al-Qaeda, US imperialism includes the export of many values that are antithetical to Islamic fundamentalism: homosexuality, promiscuity, gambling, drugs, the degradation of nature, and violations of international laws and human rights.[45] Islamic funda-mentalists, like Christian and Jewish fundamentalists, are concerned about the practicalities of being religious in a modern world, about how to keep God at the center of decisions in an increasingly secular environment. For many fundamentalists, the pervasiveness of secular society has eroded private life, sacred spaces, and values that don't revolve around competi-tion and the production of wealth. Secular society has taken people away from knowing, consulting, and being guided by sacred texts. It has moved people away from a divine presence, from basing their beliefs on system-atic religious values. Across fundamentalisms, religious texts are treated as ahistorical documents requiring literal interpretations that may stand above and beyond secular law.

In general, fundamentalists see secular society as attempting to destroy God and God-loving people. In response, fundamentalists often withdraw from mainstream society, where money has become many people's only God, to form "sacred enclaves" where faithful people can focus on living a sacred life. Examples of this pattern of retreat include Lubavitch com-munities in New York and Minnesota for Orthodox Jews, Bob Jones Uni-versity in South Carolina, Promise Keepers meetings for fundamentalist Christians, and training camps for Islamic fundamentalists.[46]

Although the Western media consistently treat the Middle East as the primary source of religious fundamentalism, it is on the rise in the West too. It can be seen in the astounding growth of Evangelical Protestantism, the spread of Mormonism, and the popularity of other proselytizing faiths. Despite US attempts to separate these Western and Eastern fundamental-isms—by positing the conflict as one of a region that loves democratic freedom against a region unable and unwilling to accept democracy—the truth is that these fundamentalisms have much in common. All are raising legitimate concerns about an emptiness in secular society. They are be-moaning an emphasis on wealth and accumulation that is devoid of ethics. They are searching for a sense of belonging and meaning often missing in consumer-based cultures. They are rallying for ritual to be attended to and honored, for rituals that give people a sense of order and connection to one another.

What primarily distinguishes Christian fundamentalists from Islamic fundamentalists is that millions of Muslims have had to maintain their religious ties in countries that have been colonized and/or controlled by external economic and political forces. This reality does not justify al-Qaeda's methods of opposing US imperialism and threats against Islam. Those methods are abhorrent. It is also impossible for us to understand how a militant group that justifies its work with a religious text could believe it is protecting the sacred by murdering thousands of people. The problem is that while anyone of conscience can categorically reject bin Laden's aggression and take legitimate issue with violent fundamentalists' interpretations of the Qur'an, US politics of retaliation have hindered people from really hearing the concerns of Muslims who do not embrace violence.

Immediately following 9/11, many of the impulses of those mourning the attacks mirrored concerns voiced by Muslims about the impact of modernity on the sacred. In fact, both parties were protesting the "disenchantment of the world" that Weber warned us about. In his quest to understand what happens to enchantment in modern society, Weber intensively studied several world religions. Despite the significant limitations in his work on Islam, part of what continues to make it relevant is that many of the dynamics he named one hundred years ago can help us understand connections between bin Laden's worldview and Western culture's response to 9/11.[47] While the growth of Islamic militancy since the late 1960s clearly has a materialist basis, that militancy also has a religious base. As Islamic scholar Bassam Tibi notes, "The view that September 11 is nothing more than a revolt against US globalization demonstrates crude reductionist thinking that reduces religiously motivated upheaval to a response to social injustice while overlooking the meaning of religion involved."[48] Tibi asserts that to understand 9/11 we need to recognize two crises at work simultaneously. Whereas one is structural, the other is a crisis of meaning that is a response to modernity itself, including values imposed on Middle Eastern countries by the West.

In Weberian terms, what we are witnessing is a reach toward the sacred, a response that stands in sharp contrast to the dominant archetype of Western society—ascetic Protestantism (which is based on productivity, frugality, deferred gratification, rigidity, and a fear of joy). While the sacred is founded on contemplation and the search for illumination in this lifetime, the ascetic sidesteps questions of meaning by focusing on self-denial and productivity. The mystic sees contemplation as necessary for its own sake, but the ascetic regards this attitude as reprehensible. Calvinists believe in a "remote God whose motives were impenetrable to mere human cognition."[49] This means that there is no need for contemplation. In fact, it is a big waste of time. Immediately following 9/11, people were so stunned, caught off guard, and grief-stricken that they could not move into the space of the ascetic right away. Questions of the meaning of the attack, the meaning of life and death, and the relationship of individuals to a larger, loving community were paramount in people's minds. People were granted an example of the spontaneous creation of the sacred, even as that energy was diverted to reject similar pleas by many Muslims wishing to keep the sacred in their lives as well.

For people who have not grown up in Egypt, Syria, Tunisia, or Iran, it may be hard to imagine living in cultures where manifestations of the sacred are embedded in everyday life in tangible, predictable, and concrete ways. It may be difficult to comprehend the impact of thousands and thousands of people praying together, in public spaces, five times a day;[50] to picture what it means to live in a culture where people stop and pray in the park, out loud, but do not run the risk of being labeled crazy or treated as if they had run out of their medication; to feel what it is like to step off an airplane and see people, everyday people, praying in an airport.[51] This prayerfulness invites a daily celebration of the sacred. It nurtures a collective humility, since everybody is praying to a higher power, acknowledging that the highest power does not rest with a government, with an individual religious leader, or with the patriarch of a family. The higher power is a God that no one person can control. Praying five times a day is the embodiment of what Weber identifies as a ritual of contemplation. Anyone who was brought to her knees after 9/11, who sought to make meaning that could not be satisfied by shopping, or who felt the trembling of total strangers knows the power of the sacred in life.

Of course, a yearning for the sacred can be distorted, manipulated, and mauled to the point of being unrecognizable. Certainly, fundamentalist support of violence or patriarchal control over women's sexuality and fertility is antithetical to the sacred.[52] Certainly, a fundamentalism that mandates particular rituals that all people must follow, no matter what, is a twisting of the sacred. Likewise, citation of the Qur'an, the Bible, the Torah, or any other religious text does not, by definition, make the interpretation sacred. US slaveholders' use of the Bible to justify slavery and bin Laden's quoting from the Qur'an to justify militant retaliation are examples of the distortion of sacred writings by textual interpretation.

The events surrounding 9/11 revealed how both Islamic militants and the US politics of retaliation twisted people's yearning for the sacred to justify war. Weber teaches us that war and violence mimic a hunger for the sacred. It is revealing how closely the feeling in the air, on the streets, and in people's homes in the United States approximated Weber's description of how people feel during war. According to Weber, "Warfare releases a devotion and an unconditional community of sacrifice on the warring sides; moreover it unleashes, as a mass phenomenon, a labor of compassion and a love for the needy which explodes the boundaries of natural associations. In general, religions can achieve similar results only in heroic communities based on an ethic of brotherhood."[53] Immediately following 9/11 we saw an "unconditional community of sacrifice," "a labor of compassion and a love for the needy" that did, indeed, explode the boundaries of natural association. Many people responding to 9/11 experienced the camaraderie, community, and compassion that war veterans have spoken about as having no bounds on the battlefield. The authenticity, profundity, and singularity of this experience of communion, prior to the retaliation for 9/11, meant that when war was initiated, it was a cheap substitute for what had preceded it. Weber observes, "From this merely unavoidable dying [during war], death in the field is distinguished by the fact that here, and in this massiveness *only* here, the individual can *believe* that he knows he is dying 'for' something."[54] The experience of war provides a competitor to the sacred. War has become modern people's pilgrimage in search of the sacred. This reality is frightening for all living and breathing beings. Bush capitalizes on this yearning with his calls for patriotism in the form of wars of aggression.

So does Osama bin Laden. Of course, the terror of the US military's aggression is only heightened once it is clear that "the other side," in this case al-Qaeda and bin Laden, is running on potent, destructive powers as well. While the rational authority of US society and al-Qaeda are both driven by bureaucracy (which does its best to wipe out the mystical), the authority upon which bin Laden draws has another power too. Weber identifies three major types of authority in the world: traditional, rational, and charismatic. Traditional authority is assigned through family power and is associated with feudalism and rural society. Rational authority is based on obeying laws that are upheld through bureaucratic systems. Charismatic authority rests on an individual's powers of persuasion and tends to emerge during periods of turmoil—political, spiritual, and/or economic. Like many of the most influential and world-changing leaders in human history, bin Laden has charisma—that magical, irrational, and magnetic personal power that makes people listen even when they don't want to. Bruce Lawrence, in his introduction to bin Laden's speeches and essays, writes, "For millions of Muslims around the world, including many who have no sympathy with terrorism, bin Laden is an heroic figure. His worldwide charisma is based not just on his success in so far eluding Americans and their allies, exhilarating as that may be for many ordinary Muslims. It is because his personal reputation for probity, austerity, dignity, and courage contrasts so starkly with the mismanagement, bordering on incompetence, of most Arab regimes. Unlike the latter, bin Laden has demonstrated that he can forgo the temptations of wealth, that he dares to strike powerful wrongdoers, and that he refuses to bend to superior might."[55]

Bin Laden is well educated and worldly, a talented writer and polemicist, a wealthy and successful businessman, a master at using the media to get his message out, and a brilliant image-crafter (staging his press conferences in caves, wearing religious robes, and growing a beard that makes him look much older than he is). The image he has created both fuels his mystique and is used by Western authorities to portray him as representing an inferior, barbaric, uncivilized, and premodern culture. The power of al-Qaeda comes from the combination of bin Laden's charisma, the organization's highly rationalized military operations, and its ability to create spectacle through the media. As a complex transnational network, al-Qaeda has its own bureaucratic logic and depends upon a sophisticated use of the Internet for much of its communication and growth.

But just as the irrationality of the United States' retaliatory war is a cheap substitute for the mysticism felt immediately following 9/11, bin Laden and al-Qaeda embody a fatal contradiction as well. While consistently framing his goals as religious and not political, as based in Islam and not a military quest, Bin Laden is in fact using his charisma to further the politics of retaliation, not a politics of peace.[56] Bin Laden has taken on many of the characteristics of the ascetic while battling against asceticism. The tactics of austerity, self-denial, withdrawal from the world, and secrecy that bin Laden has adopted (all of which became necessary for his survival since 9/11 but were practiced by him previously) embody the very value system at the heart of American society that he is seeking to destroy.

By using his charisma to further the warrior way of being in the world rather than the saintly way, bin Laden becomes a competitor of the Bush administration. Of course, the brutality of the two warriors is not comparable. Bush's agenda has led to the deaths of many, many more than has al-Qaeda. That discrepancy is not inconsequential. The United States continues to maintain itself as the biggest war machine in the world. The permanent war economy we are now witnessing in the United States is built on a history of manifest destiny that ran out of new territory on this continent and metastasized in its drive to take over the world. Our point here, however, is that the politics of retaliation on both sides has succeeded in diverting us from the mystical. War will forever be an inauthentic version of the sacred.

# PART THREE

# LABOR

## *The Abu Ghraib Prison Abuses*

# FIVE

# KARL MARX AND ALIENATION

A few years ago, we went to a three-week yoga retreat on the Atlantic coast of Costa Rica. The Atlantic and Pacific coasts of that Central American country are quite different ethnically, linguistically, and culturally, and in terms of vegetation and land use. The Pacific coast is Spanish speaking, with an ethnic mix linked to indigenous and Spanish intermarriage. The Atlantic coast is English speaking, more black than Hispanic, with ties to Jamaica. The Pacific coast has been developed by many multinational corporations, with high-rise and fancy hotels for tourists who visit from all over the hemisphere. The Atlantic-coast topography is rain forests, with vegetation that grows so fast and furiously that it is almost impossible to build expensive hotels there. The torrential rains also keep many tourists away.

We share all these details because it was thrilling for us to see a part of the world where nature—in the form of weather and kudzu vines—has been able to stave off multinational-outsider investment and control of a local economy. Most people who live in this area don't have much in the way of land and savings. Salaries are low, subsistence farming is still a key way families keep themselves going, and people work hard, often seven days a week, to feed their families. We were aware that struggle was a daily part of the people's lives and that we as tourists were not part of that reality, yet the struggle did not seem to overwhelm the residents' sense of connection to each other and to the earth. At night, there was joy in the air—fabulous dancing, a deep connection to Jamaican and Latino cultural and aesthetic roots, and a pride in living in tune with and next to the sea. Three weeks in this environment—where people switch between English, Spanish, and Patois with amazing fluency, where "rush" is not a word people use when they are enjoying each other, where the local economy is still, for the most part, controlled by the locals—can do wonders for anyone's soul.

It was when we returned to the United States, by way of Orlando International Airport, that we turned to each other and noted that everyone we saw looked angry. Everyone seemed rushed. Everyone seemed aggressive. No one seemed to be looking at anyone else, to be experiencing each other's presence in the coming and going of the day. The contrast between the feel on the streets, the pace of the life, the connection to the ocean and land in Costa Rica, and the hostility, anger, and stress we felt once we touched down in the United States encouraged us to ask a number of questions: Why such apparent unhappiness and stress in the wealthiest nation in the world? Why such seeming loneliness and separation? What kind of numbing, blocking, and denial must we have been doing to live in the United States? Why was the only thing we wanted to do was reverse our tickets and fly back to a country we had just left?

Three years after returning from Costa Rica, we were reminded again, in a way even more painful than before, of the importance of trying to understand the anger we were witnessing among people in the United States. During the spring of 2004 a story broke about cruelty being committed by US military members toward people incarcerated at Abu Ghraib prison in Iraq—a prison formerly controlled by Saddam Hussein and repurposed for use by the US military. A series of photos became this war's version of the photo of a naked child running from a napalm bomb in Vietnam. Splashed across the pages of national and international newspapers and televised programs was a photo of an army private, Lynndie England, holding a leash strapped around the neck of a naked Iraqi man. In another photo, England is smiling and smoking while giving a thumbs-up sign and pointing at the genitals of an Iraqi prisoner who is naked, except for a sandbag over his head, and he appears to be masturbating. In another photo, England is embracing Specialist Charles Graner. Both of them are smiling and giving a thumbs-up sign behind a pyramid of naked Iraqi men forced to climb on top of each other.

In a country where many Muslims consider nudity the most private of conditions, regard explicit Western displays of the body as immoral and corrupt, and consider homosexual acts a violation of Islamic law, these photographs could not have been a more explicit commentary on US disregard for Muslim culture and values. It wasn't only the humiliation of Iraqi men (whose Muslim faith considers it degrading for men to be seen naked by other men), but it was a woman doing the humiliation in a culture that maintains strict hierarchical divides between men and women. It is hard to imagine a parallel act aimed at a Christian or Jewish man's body that could be as symbolically degrading.

The racial dynamics of the scene—a white woman leashing a darker-skinned man—give visual representation of continued white domination. The smile on the guard's face, her willingness to mug for the camera, the fact that she is a white woman humiliating an Iraqi man, left us asking many troubling questions. What kind of disembodiment was required by the female guard to be able to leash a fellow human being and then smile about it, seemingly shamelessly? Cruelty during war is not new or unexpected, and white domination of the colored "other" has been with us since the fifteenth century. However, at least three factors distinguish this cruelty from earlier examples. First, these are the first war abuse photos that feature women as active participants. Women were now perpetrating abuse during war that historically men committed. Second, England and the rest were posing for photographs that were transmitted worldwide by digital technology and the Internet. The photographs of these particular scenes were joined by dozens of other photos of nude Iraqis forced into countless demeaning sexual acts and poses. The photos advertised transnationally an atrocity that seemed to be business as usual, permitted at multiple levels within the military hierarchy.[1]

A third distinction between these photos and images from previous generations of war atrocities is that, in the past, photojournalists were the ones who took the images that were released and imprinted on the collective conscience. Philosopher and cultural theorist Douglas Kellner writes, "Wars are often defined in the public mind by negative images of atrocity, such as the naked young girl fleeing in Vietnam, with her body scarred by napalm, or the image of a young US soldier lighting a peasant hut on fire with his cigarette lighter. Iraq, too, may be remembered by horrific images, in this case taken by the US troops themselves."[2] Sontag notes that, until this war, it was exceedingly rare for perpetrators of abuse to place themselves among their victims in photographs.[3] That England and Graner placed themselves in the photos implicated them in the atrocity in a way that a journalist positioned as the outside observer does not. The border between the photographer and the perpetrator has been blurred, even obliterated. At the same time, the digital age that makes it possible for images to be sent instantaneously all over the world has eliminated the lag time afforded to previous generations that might have enabled judgment to step in and stop the snowballing dissemination of the photos.

In this moment of horror we found ourselves willing to turn in multiple directions to understand what happened. Of theologians we asked, is there a religion, a worldview, a prayer that could protect us from this inhumanity? Of psychologists we asked, are there books, studies, and experiments that can help us explain wartime behavior to ensure it will not be repeated? Of lawyers we asked, do laws exist, nationally or internationally, that could stop such madness? Of activists we asked, what steps, strategies, and tools of social change are necessary to eliminate violence sanctioned by the state and perpetuated with seeming impunity in prisons in the US and by the military throughout the world? This, we knew, was not an isolated case. Could sociology show us a way out of the madness? Of Karl Marx we asked, can your ideas help us? In fact, our need to understand the Abu Ghraib prison abuses led us to look both to Marx's theory of labor and alienation and to contemporary psychoanalytical work on trauma, a combination of theories that shows a dialectical (reciprocal, ongoing, and interconnected) relationship between the social and the psychological, between structure and consciousness, between the seen and those seeing.

### KARL MARX

Calling upon Marx is no small task. He wrote on a thrilling range of subjects, from political economy to state power, from class structures to revolutionary change. In the academy, Marx is claimed as a philosopher, a historian, an economist, and a sociologist. His academic versatility speaks to his enormous gifts as an intellectual. For activists, Marx is often identified as the most influential thinker on world politics in the twentieth century. Our main interest in Marx lies in his early philosophical work. Like the surrealists of the 1920s and the leftist activists of the 1960s, we have worried that Marx's "original emancipatory thrust had been abandoned or diluted by most of his followers, who had reduced the complexity of his thought to a crudely mechanistic economic or sociological determinism."[4] The liberatory message we are interested in revolves around Marx's exploration of the dialectical relationship between economic change and shifts in consciousness; one cannot occur without the other. For us, the most poetic, compelling, and enduring of Marx's works is *The Economic and Philosophic Manuscripts of 1844,* in which he details the psychic, emotional, and physical consequences of working in a capitalist society. Although Marx did not intend the manuscripts to be published when he wrote them—in fact he saw them more as notes—much of what he developed in *Capital* and in other works is first sketched out in the manuscripts. There is an originality, clarity, and elegant simplicity in the manuscripts that have kept this work central to Marx's oeuvre. It was to this early creation—in particular to Marx's writing on alienation—that we returned following the Abu Ghraib prison abuses.

Marx (1818–1883) wrote these essays when he was only twenty-six years old, while living in Paris. He had moved to France from Germany for several reasons, not least of which was the German government's closure of the daily paper he had been editing because it published critiques of government censorship, poverty among rural workers, and laws against the poor. By then, having recently completed his dissertation in philosophy at the University of Jena, he had already become frustrated with those who were satisfied with philosophy for philosophy's sake. Marx had studied Hegel, Germany's most famous philosopher, and was introduced to communist activists and writers who considered private property the primary source of misery in modern societies. Hegelians believed that reasoned arguments would, in and of themselves, be enough to change society. While initially attractive to Marx, this idea was soon amply contradicted by personal experience. When the government blacklisted Marx, effectively blocking his chance to find a teaching job at a university, he and his long-time sweetheart, Jenny von Westphalen, decided to move to Paris. Unable to find an academic job despite his fierce intellectual abilities, Marx was less willing, by the time they left Germany, to see scholarly ideas as capable of eliminating inequalities without being coupled with activist change.

In Paris, Marx saw firsthand the inequities between rich Parisians and workers in the city. In Paris he began to develop a more comparative, international perspective than he might have attained had he stayed in Germany. He became close friends with Friedrich Engels, who described for him in detail the misery of workers in England, drawing on what he had seen among those working in a cotton mill his father owned. Engels also reported workers' struggles and organizing within Britain's industries. Throwing himself into intensive study of British political economics, Marx learned about the contrast between working conditions in urban factories and working conditions for people in small businesses in Paris and peasants working in vineyards in rural Germany. Amid these variations, he identified a conflictual relationship between those who owned the means of production and those whose contribution was their labor.

There are myriad life experiences that Marx may have drawn from to conceptualize class conflict and alienation. Certainly, his early life with Jenny and their financial struggles while seeing wealth all around them (a reality that would follow them all of their lives, contributing to the ill health of Marx and his family) influenced his focus on class inequalities. Living in Paris, he witnessed a freedom of speech and protest by working-class people on a scale unheard of in Germany. His own situation as a thinker and activist whose talents did not easily translate to a routinized occupation, and his wide-ranging intellectual interests, may have also contributed to his ability to imagine a world that did not center on paid work.

By the time Marx wrote *The Economic and Philosophic Manuscripts of 1844* he was already firmly convinced that a society's economic system shaped the nature of work. By then he knew from personal experience the thrill of getting lost in ideas—in the life of the mind. This experience fed his awareness that people have creative potentials that reach beyond the labor they do for money. When he wrote *The Economic and Philosophic Manuscripts,* he already knew how to write about people's labor and political economy with a poetic touch, having spent time in college and graduate school writing poetry, a comic novel, a tragic play, and a philosophical dialogue.[5]

Using a combination of poetic flair and philosophical reasoning, Marx asserts that people are basically productive beings. He argues that we need the opportunity to create—with our hands, our minds, *and* our imaginations. Confinement to narrow and fragmented spheres of activity enslaves workers to the task, rather than allowing them to control their own productivity.[6] In Marx's worldview, human nature requires us to use all of our senses, not to be beholden to work that narrows our abilities and imagination. Marx's passion for learning and his deep engagement with life may well have been his inspiration for one of the most quoted passages in his oeuvre, in which he dreams of a world that "makes it possible for me to do one thing today and another tomorrow, to hunt in the morning, fish in the afternoon, rear cattle in the evening, criticize after dinner, just as I have a mind, without ever becoming hunter, fisherman, shepherd or critic."[7]

The problem, Marx reasoned, is that in an economy in which most people need to work for wages in order to survive, they have neither the types of jobs nor the time they need to hunt, fish, think, critique, and breathe in a given day. Capitalism hijacks the need to be creative by separating us from each other (mandating competition) and giving us little control over what we create. This is what Marx means by alienation. The people who have time to do all of those things are the few that own private property and sufficient capital to control the kind of work they do, hire others to do the labor they don't want to do, and ensure for themselves "free" time that allows them to be creative.

Marx was not the first theorist to write about alienation. In fact it was his dialogue with Hegel and Ludwig Feuerbach that led Marx to his contributions on the subject. Unlike Hegel and Feuerbach, Marx asserts that alienation is neither an inevitable characteristic of the labor process (as

Hegel suggested) nor a concept primarily embedded in people's relation to God. Instead, Marx asserts that alienation is historically specific (i.e., not inevitable) and the product of a social order based on class inequities. Marx was documenting a transition from one economic system—feudalism—to capitalism, identifying how industrialization would systematically increase workers' alienation from the product of their labor and, in the process, enforce their privation.

Under capitalism, there is an inevitable conflict between the owners of the means of production and the laborers. If we take present-day examples to explicate Marx's work, we would say that the owners (of companies that make the iPods, cell phones, CDs, Timberland shoes, Frappuccinos, pillowcases, and dog food) own not only the materials that are used to make the product but also the products themselves. In Marx's conceptualization, when products are sold on the market, they become commodities (products intended to be for use and for exchange).[8] Once a product becomes a commodity (i.e., it is bought and sold), workers lose control over it and ultimately over themselves. The workers (the people who assemble the iPods, make the Frappuccinos, and distribute the dog food to grocery chains) sell their labor time but have little control over the price of the item, how it will be marketed, how it might be redesigned, or whether they can make enough money to buy the item they have produced. Their relationship to their work and its products is fragmented.

Under this system, Marx argues that the workers are alienated in four ways—from the products they create, from the process of production, from themselves (their nature), and from their community.[9] To earn a living, workers must make products, but in doing so, they become alienated from the product because the product is not theirs. They might make a Frappuccino for an eagerly waiting customer but have no say in deciding the proportions of milk to syrup to coffee or whether only fair-trade coffee beans should be used. In the process, the commodities that workers produce are treated as more valuable than the workers themselves. At the local Starbucks, the uniformity of the Frappuccinos and the rapidity with which each worker can make the frothy drink are more important than the worker. The worker will, in fact, be replaced by another equally poorly paid worker if he or she doesn't make the drinks to the company's specifications. The workers' value lies not in their individuality or creative imagination as workers but in their ability to do the work that will create profit.

Whatever the workers produce beyond their wages is what Marx refers to as surplus value—which, in Marx's view is the source of exploitation, since the owners, not the workers, control the profit.[10] Since workers are typically paid by the hour, a speedup in their labor actually lessens, not heightens, their value, making more profit for the company owners and lowering the workers' economic worth on the market. The more drinks the worker makes, the more profits the owners realize, but the worker's hourly wage will not rise in any way commensurate with the profit. The more profit the owners make, the less control the workers have, since the profit provides more resources to expand, contract, relocate, and hire and fire workers. The profit rarely translates to a higher wage for the worker. In fact, the opposite is typically true.

At the same time, workers have little control over the production process. They know little about the people who planted and picked the coffee beans, the marketers who decided that Starbucks should sell Ray Charles's CD *Genius Loves Company* alongside the coffee, and the truck drivers who load and unload the Frappuccino syrup. The "Frap" maker's role is restricted to frothing the milk and cleaning up the spills. The Frap maker is also essentially separated from other workers, since they are in effect competing with each other for who can froth the fastest, stay the calmest amid demanding customers, and show the least boredom on the job. This process leaves the Frap makers alienated from themselves (their nature), since they are always aware that they are more than Frap workers, that they can do, think, and jump higher than they are allowed to. They know on many levels that their jobs are not giving them the chance to live up to their own human potential, their own nature. At the same time, they are separated from their community, since membership in a community is based on working in collaboration (not in competition) and in a fully creative way.

The interrelated components of the alienation process led Marx to believe that, under capitalism, the more that a worker produces, the more of a thing the worker becomes. The more powerful the objects become, "the poorer he himself—his inner world—becomes, the less belongs to him as his own."[11] Since, under capitalism, workers need to work in order to survive, they end up working against themselves (against their creative potential, against their interest in knowing the entirety of the production process, against their need to apply their passions in multiple ways and in collaboration with others). Marx explains, "It is true that labor produces for the rich wonderful things—but for the worker it produces privation. It produces palaces—but for the worker, hovels. It produces beauty—but for the worker, deformity. It replaces labor by machines, but it throws a section of the workers back to the barbarous types of labor, and it turns other workers into machines. It produces intelligence—but for the worker stupidity, cretinism."[12] Finally, workers are always in competition with other workers, trying to make sure they keep their jobs, which makes them competitive and distrustful of fellow workers. As the sociologist George Ritzer notes, "Alienation, then, is the structurally imposed breakdown of the interconnectedness, that is, to Marx, an essential part of life."[13]

When Marx wrote about alienation from the product, he was referring to products such as textiles, wine, furniture, and shoes. He was writing during the time of industrialization, when most of people's paid labor involved the production of tangible products. In the last thirty years, we have witnessed massive shifts in labor around the world. Globalization—the political, economic, and cultural shifts in which activity in the world is increasingly taking place between people who live in different countries— has ushered in the internationalization of production, distribution, and marketing of goods and services. As a response to the job vacuum created when companies leave metropolitan countries in search of higher profits, postindustrial countries have witnessed a dramatic rise in service jobs. Many of these jobs have no tangible product. In postindustrial contexts, a service economy is a primary source of working- and middle-class jobs, providing employment that, in an earlier era, might have been available through industry.

Given this dramatic shift, we find ourselves asking if Marx's concept of alienation also applies to postindustrial contexts where the labor of an increasing number of people appears to be missing a product. Part of the genius of Marx's work is that the characteristics of alienation he named in relation to concrete products also apply in postindustrial societies—in which more and more people are involved in work that produces not a thing but a service. Nurses, flight attendants, nannies, sex workers, tour guides, and elder-care workers all perform service labor that is intangible, not tangible. Flight attendants smile and assure passengers that the flight will take off and end safely while they serve meals and coddle infants. Nannies protect and nurture other people's children, letting their charges know they are loved even if their parents are not present. Sex workers use their bodies in ways that attend to people's sexual and emotional needs.

Sociologist Arlie Hochschild asserts that much of this service work involves what she calls "emotional labor," which is "the management of feeling to create a publicly observable facial and bodily display; emotional labor is sold for a wage and therefore has exchange value."[14] Much of this work, formerly performed in private spaces and by family members for free, is now performed in public settings by strangers. This newly paid labor often provides services that are essential to keep people alive. Much of this work has the capacity to be regenerative, since it involves taking care of others, providing intimacy, nurturance, and sustenance for human life. This emotional labor is fundamental in many ways, whether it be rocking a child to sleep, assuring passengers that turbulence is not the same as the end of the world, or holding the phone up to a grandmother's ear when her granddaughter calls to say she loves her.

The essential, regenerative nature of this work does not, however, eliminate alienation. It simply gives alienation a different shape. The regenerative nature of the work also shapes the types of organizing that people do to counteract the alienation.[15] While being paid for the work gives it a value (in a society where an act's importance is largely judged by the money it garners), it also reduces regenerative work to "fee for service." Alienation from the process of production in service jobs takes place when workers are sent to care for and wait on people who often treat them poorly, who have little regard for their humanity.[16] People who provide this service become alienated from themselves because their emotional lives are no longer reserved for themselves. This work is regulated by the needs of the employer. Nannies may try to love other people's children while their own children may be home alone, wondering where their mothers are.[17] Sex workers must pretend to enjoy the sex even as they often have to dissociate to provide that labor.[18] Flight attendants are taught to smile and stay calm, even if they know the plane is going down. These examples all show how people become alienated from themselves, since they are essentially manufacturing their feelings, a most intimate betrayal.

Service labor in a capitalist society alienates people from the community because distinguishing between what is genuine and heartfelt and what has been bought and sold on the market is no longer possible. In a service economy, the alienating components of the emotional labor often trump its regenerative value, yet people are often stuck, needing their jobs in order to support themselves and their families. In a service economy, emotional labor is often the most important work done and yet the least well paid, an irony that Marx did not explicitly predict but seems to have somehow anticipated. It is both stunning and frightening to see how closely Marx's multitiered illumination of alienation applies to what we are witnessing now on a global scale.

## LYNNDIE ENGLAND AND THE LEASH:
### ALIENATION FROM THE PRODUCT

Flash forward 150 years to Fort Ashby, a small town in West Virginia where Lynndie England grew up in a trailer park with her mother, father, and two siblings. England once worked in a chicken-processing plant, a job that, in a quintessential way, fits the model on which Marx based his concept of alienation. Neither England nor the other chicken-processing workers had any control over the low wages, few benefits, poor working conditions, and products of the plant. To England and many other residents of her small town (which had no mayor, no town council, and no incorporation), joining the military must have seemed like a huge step up. She joined the Army Reserve in high school to make money for college. For many working-class young people, the military promises financial security, steady employment, help with a college education, health benefits, and the beginnings of a retirement account. Lynndie England entered an economy in which service jobs have largely taken the place of jobs available through industrial production. In this context, the military provides some of the benefits and security that industrial jobs used to provide, jobs that are now open to women as well as men. Once England was in Iraq, her labor was no longer the production of chicken fingers, nuggets, and thighs. Instead, it was the guarding of people—the systematic humiliation of people, actually.

By now, the reader might rightfully be asking, have we already veered off course from the Marxist conceptualization of alienation? After all, at Abu Ghraib there is neither a tangible product nor service labor that is, in any way, regenerative. What exactly is the product or the service performed when one's job centers on degrading other people? What is revealing about the Abu Ghraib story is that, in the face of work that had no tangible product nor provided any form of a regenerative service, the prison guards reverted to a pre-service-economy means of doing labor. The twist in the Abu Ghraib story is that they *did* find a product. In a situation of hyperalienation, they created one. Their product was the photos made available for the world to see.

In sworn testimony, England told investigators that the photo in which she is seen holding a leash tied around the neck of a naked and crawling detainee was the first one Graner took. After that, sometimes she was the photographer, sometimes he was, and sometimes others were.[19] With each photo taken, there was another product that stood outside England, with a power that confronted her. Marx writes, "The *alienation* of the worker in his product means not only that his labor becomes an object, an *external* existence, but that it exists *outside him,* independently, as something alien to him, and that it becomes a power on its own confronting him. It means that the life which he has conferred on the object confronts him as something hostile and alien."[20] The worker, in effect, must give a part of herself or himself away to the product—in this case, the photographs.

In this instance, the power was conferred by the media as the photos were displayed worldwide, each time exposing both those being abused in the photos and the military members who were present. Continuing to explicate the worker's alienation from the product, Marx writes, "The height of this bondage is that it is only as a *worker* that he continues to maintain himself as a *physical subject,* and that it is only as a *physical subject* that he is a *worker.*"[21] So what does it mean that, at the opening of this century, England's means of maintaining herself as a physical subject required her to be forever bound to images of her work torturing others? It is hard to imagine any act England could perform in the future that will grant her more visibility, more fame, than the acts she has already performed. She, and those she was abusing, will remain forever encased in those images.

### ALIENATION FROM SPECIES BEING

Marx conceptualized another step in alienation: alienation from one's species being. Species being is the human capacity to know oneself and others as free beings, the awareness that one's "physical and spiritual life is linked to nature." An individual is part of nature; nature is "his *body,* with which he must remain in continuous interchange if he is not to die."[22] Species being is the capacity to know that all of nature informs human consciousness. One must be able to practice, to constantly experience one's connection to human life, human activity, and nature. From Marx's perspective, what separates us from other animals is our conscious understanding of this need to see ourselves as connected to every species. Insects, plants, stones, and birds are all part of nature and live within an interconnected web. Humans, unlike stones, plants, birds, and insects, are able to conceptualize this interrelation. We have the capacity to see the big picture (what Buddhists may refer to as enlightenment). Species being, because it centers on this knowledge of humans as free beings, is at the center of human ability to make culture, art, and music—to externalize this freedom in tangible and imaginative ways.

According to Marx, when people are estranged from their labor—from their ability to be productive, imaginative, and expansive beings—they are estranged from their species being. They are separated from mental nourishment, their conscious life activity, their sense of themselves as connected to nature, a product and process of continuous interchange. Because alienation is a historical process—determined by specific economic relations—its form shifts in relation to particular economic conditions. The Abu Ghraib prison abuses are a frightening example of what happens to one's species being when the product of one's labor involves abusing others. As Marx puts it, "Estranged labor estranges the *species* from man. It changes for him the *life of the species* into a means of individual life."[23]

To be estranged from one's species being means losing one's touchstone, one's sense of connection and belonging to one's humanity and community. Alienation from one's species being means losing the ability to see oneself as connected in physical, spiritual, and artistic ways to other human beings. In this void, the photos from Abu Ghraib became a mirror of disconnection. In her article about the photos, Sontag states, "For the meaning of these pictures is not just that these acts were performed, but that their perpetrators apparently had no sense that there was anything wrong in what the pictures show."[24] Fatalism, nihilism, and the loss of any moral compass become three glaring symptoms of alienation from one's species being.

In this case of alienation, reality turned in on itself, creating multiple paradoxes. Kellner cites the Abu Ghraib photos as an example of "immanent reversal," which he describes as a "flip-flop or reversed direction of meaning and effects, in which things turn into their opposite."[25] Abu Ghraib prison is the location Saddam Hussein used during his reign to incarcerate more than fifty thousand men and women, subsequently and supposedly liberated by the United States. The United States then used Abu Ghraib as a military prison to incarcerate thousands of Iraqis, including women and children.[26] The prison offers employment billed as a step up for a young woman seeking a way out of a chicken-processing plant. She then finds herself being taught to humiliate and torture people who, months earlier, she had never met. Months earlier she would not have known them as either friend or foe. In these and many other instances, much has turned into its opposite. Might, in this context, the product of the military's labor—the photographs—have become a mirror, an inverted record, an image of these many reversals?

Marx, who believed that individual identity is itself both vulnerable and fragile and is typically overpowered by institutions, shows us how incredibly vulnerable species being is in the face of exploitation. The photos taken at Abu Ghraib became a witness, for the entire world to see, of the depravity people are capable of when put in inhumane conditions. In this case, England, Graner, and the other military personnel involved were simultaneously the workers (the low-level military, who either taught others or were taught to humiliate the prisoners) and the owners (the ones in charge of the torture), whose work determined the conditions, the possibilities, and the realities of the prisoners. All of the "actors" were tainted by these conditions. None could leave unscathed. The photographs documented the reduction of human community to individuals, accessing their humanity only through depravity. At Abu Ghraib, species being was seen as its inverse, a reversal that could, in no way, be considered an isolated incident, either cordoned off or rendered an exception.

While it might be convenient to assume that damage done to species being was isolated to the individual military personnel involved in the abuse, much research reveals the limits of this "few bad apples" approach to understanding violence. Two famous psychological studies, the Milgram experiment conducted at Yale University and the Zimbardo experiment at Stanford University, taught us that ordinary people who simply were willing to participate in a scientific study on conformity were capable, within a matter of a few sessions of explicit instruction, to humiliate and torture other people.[27] In the Milgram experiment, participants were instructed to deliver progressively severe electric shocks every time the subject got an answer wrong. Two-thirds of the participants continued to follow the instructions, administering increasingly powerful shocks, even as the subjects showed debilitating signs of distress. In the Zimbardo experiment, twenty-one male college students were divided into two groups — the guards and the prisoners — and instructed to maintain their responsibilities for two weeks. The abuse by those asked to be the guards became so extreme that the experiment was canceled after only six days. Some of the participants, in fact, stayed beyond the required sessions, on their own volition, to perfect their tactics of torture.[28] Both experiments underscored ways that institutions — the academy, science, religion — can overpower an individual's sense of right and wrong, one's connection to a larger collective. Certainly, we can add the military to the list of institutions that can severely compromise species being.

For Marx, the deepest meaning of the impact of alienation on species being can be found in the German word he originally used — *entäussern* — that was then translated into the English word "alienation." Dirk Struik, a Marx scholar, explains that translators chose the term "alienate" because it "is the only English word which combines, in much the same way as *entäussern*, the ideas of 'losing' something which nevertheless remains in existence over-against one, of something passing from one's own into another's hands, as a result of one's own act, with the idea of 'selling' something." Struik continues: "Both 'alienate' and *entäussern* have at least one possible meaning, the idea of a sale, a transference of ownership, which is simultaneously a renunciation."[29]

The photos are the objects the soldiers and the Iraqi detainees lost to the world that remain in control of both the tortured and the torturers. The photos were passed from the soldiers' own hands into another's as a result of their own act, with the idea of "selling something" that they would never be able to buy back. In this instance, the renunciation—a term meaning a formal announcement of relinquishment that is often associated with a religious giving up of one's sexual pleasure in the world—brings us full circle to Marx's understanding of species being as rooted in one's sexual and sensual nature. For Marx, the "epitome of the alienated worker under capitalism was not so much the unhappy worker as those who were happy with their work, for they were really suffering from the ultimate illusion if they could find satisfaction in such a wretched existence."[30] When asked why she participated in the photos, England replied, "We just wanted to have fun." Certainly, things have turned into their opposite, have turned in on themselves, when torturing others becomes a method of having fun, when denying one's own and others' humanity becomes a source of individual entertainment.

### COLLECTIVE ALIENATION

For Marx, alienation from one's species being inevitably leads to an additional component of alienation—estrangement of "man from man"—from the human community: "In fact, the proposition that man's species nature is estranged from him means that one man is estranged from the other, as each of them is from man's essential nature."[31] The photographs at Abu Ghraib reveal that England, Graner, and the others had lost their ability to recognize the Iraqi men as human. History has long taught us that, in a situation of oppression, the first thing that oppressors must do is take steps to make those they are abusing appear to be less than human. Taking away people's names, separating people from their families, forcing them to cut their hair, starving them, and compelling them to treat each other with cruelty are all steps in the process. The oppressors develop these tactics to deny humanity—to see those they are abusing, not themselves, as less than human, based on the idea that humanity is a scarce commodity.

Marx predicts that in a situation of alienation, which we believe is in its most extreme form when the process of production centers on abusing fellow human beings, "man (the worker) only feels himself freely active in his animal functions—eating, drinking, procreating, or at most in his dwelling and in dressing-up, etc.; and in his human functions he no longer feels himself to be anything but an animal. What is animal becomes human and what is human becomes animal."[32] Dressed up in their army fatigues, in a dwelling not of their making but certainly one they became a part of, the soldiers attempted to reduce the Iraqi detainees and, in so doing, reduced themselves. About the process of man's separation from man, Marx observes, "Just as he estranges his own activity from himself, so he confers to the stranger an activity which is not his own."[33] The image meant to capture the Iraqis' humiliation only superficially obscures the humiliation that the soldiers brought upon themselves. Both the military and prisons, as institutions, severely limit work that is either productive or regenerative, a reality that compromises species being.

That those serving in the military both documented and disseminated evidence of the abuse raises questions about whether the photos serve as a sort of collective witness about their alienation from themselves and others. In an economic system in which an increasing number of people have jobs that produce no tangible product, might the photos be a form of witnessing one's presence, one's existence at that job? What might it mean that the military, not just one or two bad apples but many camera-toting soldiers, are seeking that kind of witness? Photographs of US military personnel torturing Iraqis have not stopped appearing since the Abu Ghraib abuses. They have continued. Have people come to feel so invisible, so insignificant, that documenting their existence—even by means of an image of devastation and destruction—has become necessary?

Given his ability to predict, apparently far into the future, the myriad layers of destruction done in the process of alienation, it is no wonder that Marx, early in his career while working on *Rheinische Zeitung*, a daily paper in Germany, included an allegorical rendering of the banning of the paper with a drawing of himself as the "Greek God, Prometheus, who defied Zeus and stole the sacred fire (of civilization) from Mt Olympus. Because of this he was regarded as the 'preserver' of humanity. He was also punished by being chained to a rock, where an eagle continually devoured his (immortal) liver."[34] In Western medicine, the liver is known as the organ that metabolizes carbohydrates, fats, and proteins, the sustenance that keeps us alive. In Chinese medicine, the liver ensures that energy and blood flow smoothly; it is the organ associated with fear and anger; the stagnation of the liver brings irritability, depression, and frustration. In both worldviews, the devouring of human liver remains a powerful symbol for the Abu Ghraib photos—what they have already and will continue to reflect back to us as people who are clearly still searching for Marx's species being.

## POST-ATTICA VISIT

*I dreamed there was a jungle gym*
*in your cell, we*
*trapezed from side to side*
*limber and flying*
*the guards heard laughter*
*and came running*
*we made ourselves tiny birds*
*on the metal tree top*
*our wings small enough to squeeze*
*through the bars*
*into the meadow the sky so blue*
*you lost your breath*
*we flew until just before count*
*squeezed back in*
*I see blue birds now and yearn, I*
*sleep sitting up*

—BECKY THOMPSON

# SIX

# LOOKING FOR SPECIES BEING

*Trauma and Its Consequences*

## ALIENATION FROM THE PROCESS: TWENTY-FIRST-CENTURY FETISHES

In Marx's conceptualization of alienation, people lose control over the product and themselves through the process of production. Graner and England made a commodity that they both used and exchanged, gaining attention that perhaps neither of them fathomed before. Once the photos were distributed, they became commodities that could be downloaded and reproduced on the Internet. They could be bought and sold, consumed individually or communally, and then quickly become valuable politically. In the process they also became fetishes, Marx's term for commodities that are imbued with all kinds of social and sometimes religious significance that the items themselves could not possibly hold.[1] Fetishes are commodities that have spun out of control, both holding and zapping meaning at the same time. The Abu Ghraib photos became fetishes that gained multiple social meanings. They became icons for the Iraq War; a representation of the consequences of an empire that was running out of control; pornographic images on a worldwide scale; a twenty-first-century reenactment of lynching and white supremacist terror; and a symbol and a reminder for people who have been traumatized that socially sanctioned terror continues.

Although the applicability of Marx's discussion of alienation from the product, one's species being, and the collective is more than sufficient to underscore the continued relevance of his work, it is his identification of a fourth characteristic of alienation—estrangement from the process of production—that reveals the most complicated aspects of the Abu Ghraib abuse. About this process of estrangement, Marx writes, "How could the worker come to face the product of his activity as a stranger, were it not that in the very act of production he was estranging himself from himself? . . . Labor is *external* to the worker, i.e., it does not belong to his essential being.

... In his work, therefore, he does not affirm himself but denies himself, does not feel content but unhappy, does not develop freely his physical and mental energy but mortifies his body and ruins his mind."[2]

Marx is teaching us that being alienated from the process of production requires a dissociation of one's mind from one's body, a formation of a false self. What Marx identifies in sociological terms as estrangement from the process of production, psychological theorists have identified in terms of dissociation—the separation of the self into parts that occurs in the face of exploitation. Psychiatrist Robert Jay Lifton suggests that in an "atrocity-producing situation," dissociation or doubling—the formation of a second self—is required for the psyche to survive.[3] At Abu Ghraib, being alienated from the process of production—making, viewing, and appearing in the photos—involves three inevitably interconnected groups: those who perpetrated the abuse, those who were abused, and those involved in the process of the photo dissemination—the world audience.

### THE MILITARY MEMBERS TAKING THE PHOTOS

On first reading, it appears that England and Graner were not alienated from the process of production. They both actively participated in the process of taking the photos. Yet the story of how England became involved in the torture helps explain the dynamics of participating in the abuse. As a private in the 372nd Military Police Company, an Army Reserve unit based in Cresaptown, Maryland, England first met then-private Charlie Graner, a former prison guard and marine who had rejoined the military after the 9/11 attacks. Soon after they were notified that they were going to be shipped to Iraq in February 2003, they attended a party in Virginia Beach where they drank heavily. When one of their friends passed out, Graner and England exposed themselves on top of the unconscious man while they took turns photographing each other.[4] While still in Maryland, they made videos of themselves having sex together. After that, Graner kept upping the ante on the sexual requests he made of England.

Once they were shipped to Iraq and assigned to work in the prison, England and other less-experienced soldiers looked to Graner as an authority on how to act and work at the prison. England, who was twenty-one at the time, said she listened to Graner, fifteen years her senior, since he had experience working in a prison in the United States and was an MP.[5] At night, after finishing her shift as a clerk in another area of the prison, she began visiting him on the cellblock where he worked and having sex with him there (the same location where Graner eventually had sex with Megan Ambuhl, another private whom he later married).[6]

In October 2003, Graner told England to pose with naked and abused men. When he asked her to hold the leash in the first photo taken, England initially refused, but when he asked again, she consented.[7] In her testimony England said that when Graner handed her the leash, he told her to hold it since he thought "it would look more humiliating if a female my size would hold it."[8] They then took many more photos. Graner e-mailed one of the photos home with the caption: "Look what I made Lynndie do." He wrote that the pictures of detainees masturbating were a birthday gift for her.[9] In early March, Graner e-mailed home the news that England was two-months pregnant with his child.[10] In this email, he misspelled her name.

We can't know without England's words, of which there are few, whether she left a part of herself behind or created a second self in order to participate in the photos. We can, however, make an intelligent guess. While Graner had a history of acting abusively before working at Abu Ghraib,[11] England had no known history of such brutality. By the time she had become pregnant and participated in the torture of Iraqis, it would be hard to imagine that her sexual boundaries were still intact. That she was vulnerable to Graner's requests suggests to us that, before meeting him, she may have had a history of, at the least, deferring to older male authority. While the media and her legal team focused on England's cognitive deficits as a means of explaining her willingness to participate in the abuse, the fact that no reporters or investigators seem to have pursued a possible abuse history speaks to the continued taboo of seriously dealing with widespread abuse of girls in US culture.

The probability that Graner took the lead in torturing the prisoners, preying on England's vulnerabilities in the process, does not make England any less accountable for the torture itself. England is an adult who could have made crucial choices along the way that might have extricated her from her eventual participation in the abuse. Women have in fact used their membership in dominant groups (as whites, as military officers, as heads of state, as prime ministers, as slaveholders, and the list goes on) to keep up with male violence, and then some. Identifying "women's active participation in this current phase of US imperialism through violence and torture" has been a challenge for feminists.[12] Feminists work both to reveal the forms of violence aimed at women that have remained privatized—perpetrated behind closed doors and steeped in shame and secrecy—and to articulate how some women have internalized the culture of violence and used their femininity to abuse others.

Understanding England's position requires looking at multiple ways in which violence affects women. As Aihwa Ong and other feminist theorists have noted, social regulation for women in public spaces exploits many contradictions and polarities. Drawing upon Foucault's work on discipline and punishment, Ong asserts, "Disciplinary procedures seek to induce 'docile bodies' without resorting to 'brutal' forms of control in the workaday life."[13] Graner's disciplinary procedures appear to have induced a docility in England without his ever having lifted a hand to abuse her. At the same time, he was inflicting brutal forms of control on men he saw as his inferiors. During her trial, England said she had been drawn to Graner because "he showered her with attention and made her feel safe." She added, "He was very charming, funny and at the time it looked to me like he was interested in the same things I was. Now I know it was all an act, to lure me in, I guess."[14]

It is painful to grapple with the psychological defenses that Graner himself must have developed in order to be actively involved in the process of torturing prisoners and then documenting the abuse. His training to be a prison guard in the United States would certainly have been preparation for the abuse he inflicted at Abu Ghraib. Investigative reporter Anne-Marie Cusac notes that the *New York Times* described Graner as one of the "most feared and loathed of the American guards." Before working at Abu Ghraib he had worked at the Greene County Prison in Pennsylvania, a super-maximum-security prison where an overwhelming majority of the state's death row prisoners live. Graner developed this reputation at Greene County Prison after serving eight years in the marines. His ex-wife took out two restraining orders against him, documenting that he beat her, threatened her with guns, and stalked her. Needless to say, it is troubling, although not surprising, that the Defense Department would send Graner to Iraq, given his history. Cusac points out that "guards at the Greene facility behaved in ways that eerily anticipate the allegations from Abu Ghraib."[15]

Once in Iraq, Graner was one of the few MPs from the 372nd company assigned to work at the prison who had previous experience as a prison guard. Upon their spring 2003 arrival in Iraq, the personnel in this division were assigned to routine traffic and police duties. When they were transferred to Abu Ghraib prison in October, it appears that Graner's work at Greene County Prison in Pennsylvania had simply been a rehearsal for the leadership role he assumed at Abu Ghraib. His shift from US prison work to Abu Ghraib is an example of the rotation of prison, military, and police officials nationally and internationally, apparently depending on who is dodging recent charges of abuse and who is most needed to teach a new cohort of privates how to torture detainees.[16] In this age of globalization, the "interlocking directorate" that C. Wright Mills referred to almost fifty years ago in relation to an elite group of men who control the US domestic economy is currently operating in the US prison system on an international scale.[17]

Graner certainly does not represent the military elite, but his shifting work—first as a marine, then as a notorious US prison guard, and then as a supervising guard at Abu Ghraib—speaks to an interlocking connection between prisons and the military and the shifting of troubled personnel from one location to the next. What he was expected to do in Iraq was not different from what he had been doing in Pennsylvania. Since the early 1990s, US prison officials have become increasingly militaristic in their approach to operating prisons. This influence is evident in boot-camp-style punishment, in prison technology, and at prison and law enforcement conferences. The circulation of personnel between and among locations and the blurring of functions make it easier to elude accountability when abuses are made public. We would expect that dissociation on the part of prisoners and those employed in prisons is a widespread response, given that "sadism, in some locations, is casual and almost routine."[18]

## THE IRAQIS IN THE PHOTOGRAPHS

To date, there is very little information available on the abuse from the perspective of the Iraqi detainees. The lion's share of the political analysis produced by the US-based media consisted of profiles of Graner, England, and other military personnel at Abu Ghraib, while the lives of those who were abused were rendered invisible. This imbalance in reporting reinforces the dominant gaze assumed in the photos themselves.[19]

This focus also harks back to the normative portrayal of the slave on the auction block, which typically centers on the white bidder's assessment of the slave, rather than the slave's assessment of the bidders. Historian David Roediger describes the situation: "Consider a slave on the auction block, awaiting sale. Imagine the slave being seen, indeed examined, by the potential bidders. Imagine what she felt. . . . Such attempts to imagine looking in on the auction block and to empathize with those for sale have found a hard-won place in the mainstream of American culture. But little prepares us to see her as looking out, as studying the bidders. And yet . . . slaves on the block often searched out every clue in sizing up the whites who would own them."[20] By failing to incorporate investigative journalism written from the point of view of the Iraqi detainees, the political analysis ignores their subjectivity—a knowledge that exists even in the most dire of circumstances.

Despite the dearth of attention paid by the US media to Iraqi prisoners, the Red Cross, Amnesty International, and other watch groups have all documented horrendous abuse—people exposed for prolonged periods in the sun while forced to wear hoods; inmates living in outdoor tents where the temperature exceeded 138 degrees; sodomy; prisoners forced to defecate on themselves; rape of women and men; children interrogated and tortured in front of their relatives; and extended solitary confinement.[21] While we do not yet have testimony from those detainees who were actually photographed, we do have information on the psychological damage that Iraqi detainees in general have experienced at the hands of the US military. The Red Cross evaluated people who had been subjected to solitary confinement in Iraq; the prisoners were "presenting signs of concentration difficulties, memory problems, verbal expression difficulties, incoherent speech, acute anxiety reactions, abnormal behavior, and suicidal tendencies." The Red Cross concluded, "These symptoms appeared to have been caused by the methods and duration of interrogation."[22] We do know that between 70 and 90 percent of those held were guilty of no crime. They were simply picked up during widespread sweeps of neighborhoods, which the US military appeared to conduct indiscriminately.[23]

The impact of being abused and then photographed is shaped by culture, religion, and gender. Rape as a form of torture is devastating in any context, but in Iraq there is an additional reality for women: if they speak openly about having been raped, they run the risk of being slain for behaving dishonorably—what is referred to as honor killing.[24] It remains to be seen whether the scapegoating of women who have been raped will be extended to those whose abuse was captured in the photos—if they will be made to carry the shame that should belong to those who abused them. We do know that photographs of torture forever imprison expressions of the desperation of those being abused.

Photographs also expose the abuse to a wide audience, a deeply shaming fact for people whose sexual privacy is a cornerstone of their religion and worldview. The sexual content of the abuse, when captured in a photograph, further complicates the possibility of coming to terms with it. To those who were tortured, the abuse was sexualized and racialized. To some viewers, the photos were just the latest pornography writ large for the world to see. The photographed Iraqis have no control over the second interpretation. Iraqi detainees' responses to the torture are inevitably complicated by the knowledge that there is an audience that they cannot control, see, understand, or get to know, an audience that will continue to have access to the photos, well into the future. Historically, a key characteristic of rape and other sexual abuse has been its privatized nature—the abuse is hidden from public view, is treated as taboo, and is often blamed on the victim if the abuse is revealed. With Abu Ghraib, what has traditionally been hyperprivate became hypervisible. While the documentation may help to counter the denial, amnesia, and blocking typically associated with privatized domination, its hypervisibility carries its own horrendous liabilities.

### THE AUDIENCE

While the military personnel and the Iraqi detainees at Abu Ghraib are the two most obvious parties involved in the production process of the photographs, there is another party as well—the audience. Blogger the Plaid Adder provided an astute political analysis of the photographs: "One of the first questions I had, after I saw the pictures from Abu Ghraib was 'Who's behind the camera?' CBS says the pictures were taken by American soldiers working as military police at the prison. But the real reason they're so disturbing—even more disturbing than the pictures of the more seriously maimed and mutilated civilian bodies that have been destroyed by the violence we unleashed there—is that those pictures put us all behind the camera."[25]

Dissociative responses of those who viewed the photographs from "behind the camera"—the audience around the world—may be the most difficult to document given that, by definition, most of the audience will remain anonymous. In a media-saturated culture it is virtually impossible to avert one's gaze, to avoid seeing, and, at least to some extent, not to internalize the photos. Such avoidance would essentially require the life of a hermit. The virtual silence about the toll that such viewing exacts is problematic, given the pervasiveness of the imagery. It is as if there is an inverse relationship between the amount of imagery we are exposed to and the amount of attention that is paid to the toll such spectatorship takes on our psyches and humanity.

Accounting for the psychological state of those witnessing abuse has always been complicated, in part because of the concern that attending to the witness's vantage point, particularly his or her psychological distress, may divert attention from those "actually" abused. And yet, as psychoana-

*Children in Sadr City, Iraq, playing in front of a mural depicting the Abu Ghraib atrocity of 2003. "Iraqi Boys Play in Front of a Mural." Photograph by Awad Awad. Collection A F P. Getty Images News, 50901881.*

lyst Dori Laub describes, research on trauma has demonstrated that the witness to trauma "comes to be a participant and a co-owner of the traumatic event: through his very listening [in this instance, seeing] he comes to partially experience trauma in himself."[26]

Many of the political analyses of the audience's role in viewing the photos have focused on those who have seen the images as pornographic. The Plaid Adder observes, "Like many strains of pornography, these pictures display all that dehumanizes flesh not so much for its own sake as to titillate the viewer's lust for power. They're assuming a viewer who will get hard over humiliation, who will be more gratified by the sight of a degraded Iraqi body than he would be by any image you could find of any Playmate of the Year."[27]

On one occasion when soldiers ordered Iraqi detainees to perform sexual acts while the military personnel watched, England pointed to one of the detainees and announced, "He's getting hard."[28] With this pronouncement, England projected onto the subject what we may guess was

the actual sexual experience of some of the soldiers (as well as an anonymous number of those viewing the photos) who saw this as pornography,
using the Iraqis as the basis of their own pornographic gaze. Many commentators identified the photographs as pornographic, racist, and part of a
brutal colonial mentality. As Douglas Kellner commented, "The *Washington Post* noted that the cache of more than 1000 digital pictures that they
had received revealed that the young American troops took pictures of
camels, exotic vistas of Iraq, and scenes of ordinary people, as well as the
copious prisoner abuse and disgusting prison pictures. Many of the quasi-
pornographic images released of the Iraqi male prisoners depicted a femi-
nization of them, naked or in women's garments, and passively humiliated
and emasculated. There is, of course, a long Western colonial tradition of
taking exotic pictures of faraway places and feminizing and sexualizing
exotic cultures, just as there is a tradition of documenting bloody atrocity
scenes in wartime. In a digital age, these genres and impulses merged
together."[29]

By assessing the photos as pornography and evidence of an enduring
colonialist mentality, the analysts are assuming that the audience identifies
with those taking the photos—the troops. The Plaid Adder writes, "When
we look at the pictures from Abu Ghraib, we put ourselves in the position
of the American soldiers who took the photos. We are, like them, forced
to identify not with the faceless pile of flesh on the other side of the camera, but with the American soldier pointing to it. We watch that American
soldier smile at us as we click the shutter. That soldier looks out at us with
a wink and a smile, confident that we're sharing the joke, that we're enjoying this as hugely as he is. Or she. And something in us is afraid that that
soldier may be right."[30]

As a visual audience to images of abuse, the US population has been
behind the camera many times in US history, as Jennifer Wells points out:
"Even without benefit of a photographic image, it is too easy to recall the
picture of a lynching a hundred years ago, a body swaying from a tree
limb. What is not so readily recalled of that horror are images of white folk
smiling for the camera. Lynching as social encounter. Picnic baskets were
packed. Children were included in the outing. Photographs were taken."[31]
Commenting on the connection between lynching photos and those from
Abu Ghraib, literature professor Susan Willis explains, "I see Abu Ghraib
as a re-enactment of lynching and the history of the KKK . . . But instead
of the besieged white woman fearing the lust-driven blacks, she becomes
the dominatrix. Were these women performing for the benefit of the white
male soldiers? Were they, let's say, teasing their white male cohorts? Or

were white male soldiers pleasuring themselves watching white women conduct themselves in aberrant ways? The whole thing is ricocheted. Who's looking at who and who's pleasuring who and who's dominating who?"[32]

While we agree that the photos may serve as pornography and may demonstrate many viewers' attachment to a racist, sexist, and colonialist mentality, we have also noticed that few of the analyses have attended to the possibility of an audience that, having personally experienced similar trauma, most identifies with the Iraqis. From our vantage point, whole categories of people may fall into this group: black people who carry a historical memory of slavery and lynching; those who have been imprisoned; sexual abuse survivors; Holocaust survivors; and other people who have lived through atrocities. From this perspective, it is no coincidence that black activist and political prisoner Mumia Abu-Jamal linked the police's stripping of Black Panther Party members in Philadelphia in the 1970s to the stripping of detainees at Abu Ghraib.[33] Abu-Jamal has been incarcerated for many years at Greene County Prison, perhaps not coincidentally where Graner was a guard before working at Abu Ghraib. Abu-Jamal knew the reality of that connection from frighteningly personal experience, as a victim of police brutality in the 1970s and a victim of torture in prison. Part of the challenge, then, is to understand the psychic cost of such identification for the viewer, particularly given the reality that many subjugated communities see the abusive practices at Abu Ghraib as business as usual.

The fear of retaliation is a key reason why people may not break silence about identifying with those who have been abused. Many poets, writers, and activists who have spoken out about injustice have paid with their lives. Ken Saro-Wiwa was murdered by the Nigerian government for his activism against environmental degradation. Musician Victor Jara was murdered by Pinochet's military junta in Chile. And Anna Mae Aquash was killed in retaliation for her work on behalf of indigenous people in the United States. They are only a few of the many people of conscience who have been killed for speaking about and confronting injustices that have not yet been recognized collectively.

Psychoanalytic theory on witnessing trauma becomes a crucial source for understanding the psychic cost of speaking openly about one's identification with the Iraqi detainees in the photographs. Psychiatrist Dori Laub chronicles her therapeutic work with Holocaust survivors, noting that, for survivors, there are often two holocausts that must be survived— the initial trauma of imprisonment and then a second trauma (a fire, the loss of a loved one, an inexplicable illness) that may be experienced as profoundly as the first. Laub explains, "Through its uncanny reoccurrence, the trauma of the second holocaust bears witness not just to a history that has not ended but, specifically, to the historical occurrence of an event that, in effect, *does not end*. The fear that fate will strike again is crucial to the memory of trauma, and to the inability to talk about it."[34]

Clearly, we are not trying to equate surviving the Holocaust with the experience of witnessing the abuses at Abu Ghraib. However, we do believe that the psychoanalytic dynamic identified among those working with Holocaust survivors—the indelible vulnerability of trauma survivors—may help explain why so little attention has been granted to the psychic experience of subjugated communities who witnessed the photos. Laub continues, "The act of telling might itself become severely traumatizing, if the price of speaking is *re-living*; not relief but further retraumatization."[35] For people who have been incarcerated and abused, the price of acknowledging an identification with the Iraqi detainees includes the risk of further retraumatization, particularly if the devastation caused by the original trauma has not been recognized or honored as real and life-altering.

The supersaturation of the images may also have hindered people from speaking openly about their identification with the Iraqis who were being tortured. The photos were splashed all over our public consciousness, deluging the media market through multiple venues. Paradoxically, such exposure may actually normalize the torture, working against the ability of people who have faced injustice to take seriously their own identification with the victims. The superexposure can trivialize injustice, making it more difficult for survivors to consciously name their identification. Consequently, the association runs the risk of remaining submerged in the unconscious, gnawing at a person's steadiness while unable to name itself as real. Mass marketing, by placing the images in a public space, may also make it hard for those who have been victimized to consciously associate their experiences if their abuse was enacted in privatized spaces.

While there are many viewers of the photographs who may identify with those being tortured, there may also be many who identify with both the victims and the soldiers—the dominant photographic gaze and the one that typically goes unmentioned. Our discussions with each other provided a useful example of this dual association. For Becky, a woman who was abused early in childhood, to whom being restrained or closed in remains a fear, even a brief look at the photographs made her feel sick. After discovering a website on the Internet that features photographs of Lynndie England, Diane began studying them for their detail, thinking that such information was crucial to writing this chapter. When Becky realized that

Diane was really scrutinizing the photos, she pleaded with Diane to close the site immediately, a request that, even at the time, we both thought was unreasonable. To Becky, looking at the photos seemed to be a way of condoning them, of supporting those who saw reason to set up a website featuring Lynndie England. It took many weeks for Becky to be able to articulate why simply looking at the photos seemed so threatening.

As we grappled with our different vantage points, we also wrestled with the possible implications of identifying with one or the other—but not both—of the represented groups. In the process we came to agree that because of our location in the world as US citizens, with race and class privilege, to only name an identification with the victims made it seem that we were abdicating our responsibilities. As US citizens, we are clearly implicated in Bush's military actions. As a white woman growing up in the United States, there is no way Becky can avoid recognizing herself in the visages of England, Graner, and the other military guards. As a black woman who also grew up in the United States, Diane could not simply dismiss the photos as another instance of white depravity. Race, class, and citizenship privilege inevitably implicate us in relation to the photos. This dual reality may trigger a schizophrenic relation to the images as both the oppressor and the oppressed—the simultaneous inflicter of the pain and the object of the terror.

To our knowledge, nothing has been written, until now, about how viewers of the images may feel conflicting identifications with the people in them. Perhaps the most helpful means of understanding this dual dynamic exists in feminist writing on people's multiple identities (on the basis of race, class, gender, sexuality, nationality, etc.). In her brilliant article, "Playfulness, 'World' Travelling, and Loving Perception," philosopher María Lugones explains that, as a child growing up in Argentina, she was taught to "perceive arrogantly" as she watched wealthy people in her life "graft the substance of their servants to themselves." She also learned to "graft my mother's substance to my own." Both experiences taught her to see others as in service to her, to perceive them arrogantly (to use them, take them for granted, and require unreasonable service). At the same time, as a female she learned early that she was the object of others' arrogant perceptions, a position that was extended when, upon migrating to the United States, she was perceived by white people as inferior. She writes, "I learned that I could be seen as a being to be used by White/Anglo men and women without the possibility of identification."[36]

According to Lugones, such dual realities—perceiving people arrogantly while being perceived arrogantly—requires one to travel between these two spaces, to have a double image of oneself. The problem in this traversing, however, was that Lugones was taught to "practice enslavement of my mother and to learn to become a slave through this practice." Resisting this pattern required Lugones to identify and break through this "schizophrenia" in order to make sense out of the "ontological confusion." She needed to try to see the world through her mother's eyes, to "witness her own sense of herself from within her world." Breaking the pattern of perceiving her mother and others arrogantly was a necessary prerequisite for resisting the arrogant gaze of others.[37]

Lugone's philosophical reasoning is helpful in understanding the Abu Ghraib prison photos on a number of accounts. First, Lugones asserts that both realities must be recognized—the reality of identifying with the Iraqi detainees as well as with the abusive guards must be understood before "schizophrenia" can be reckoned with. What Lugones names in philosophical terms as schizophrenia, Marx understood as a false, alienated self that is a result of separation from the process of production. Second, Lugones suggests that by drawing upon one's experience of being perceived arrogantly as an object, it is then possible to see one's role in perceiving others arrogantly. Applying this emerging consciousness to the photos of Abu Ghraib suggests that those viewers with dual affiliations are uniquely able to draw upon their understanding of their role as victim in order to rethink their participation in victimizing others. This vantage point is a version of Du Bois's double consciousness.[38] It is both a burden and a gift.

Third, for Lugones, the point of such investigation is to learn how to be "at ease in a world"—to know oneself and others as neither arrogant nor the object of one's arrogance.[39] This emerging consciousness, of course, depends upon intervening against the estrangement experienced by all of the participants in the production and dissemination of the Abu Ghraib photographs. What Lugones describes as being "at ease in a world" resonates deeply with Marx's understanding of species being—the experience of being in touch with and pleased by one's humanity.

### "MAKE-WORK" IN THE BELLY OF THE BEAST

The Abu Ghraib prison photos reveal forms of alienation that occur in a postindustrial capitalist economy. When the market is saturated with commodities, new forms of employment emerge—in this case, the employment of people trained to imprison other human beings. While our focus in this chapter has been on torture at Abu Ghraib, the process of alienation crosses individual prison and national boundaries. With deindustrialization and corporate flight from the United States, the construction of new prisons and the expansion of old ones has become a booming business. The increase in poverty and economic insecurity since the 1970s has left many poor communities more vulnerable to what Angela Davis terms "criminalization"—policies that have been used to justify an explosion in the incarceration of poor people, people of color in particular.[40] Over five million people in the United States are either in prison, on parole, or on probation.[41]

The ideology used to justify this increase has been based on a fierce and steady campaign to convince people that crime has not only skyrocketed but is also what people should most fear. Militarism—most specifically, the US wars against Iraq in 1991, Afghanistan in 2001, and Iraq again in 2003—has also dramatically expanded the prison industry, marketed both by private corporations and the US government. Alienation in a postindustrial, postproduct society helps explain why prison workers who seem to be perfectly normal people could engage in such horrific acts of violence and be willing to be photographed doing so, with smiles on their faces.

Marilyn Buck, a poet, social theorist, and political prisoner incarcerated in the United States for her antiracist activity in the 1960s and 1970s, provides an insider's perspective on the process of degradation involved when a tangible product is missing in the labor process—when there is nothing in people's work that is regenerative: "The officer's work is not productive labor, its only product being her [the prisoner's] submission or humiliation. It is negative productivity—to 'unmake' or deconstruct her efficacy as a human being in her own right."[42] In prisons all over the country, inmates are required to perform work that makes no pretense of having productive value. The work is typically humiliating and has no usefulness—"make-work," as Buck refers to it. This make-work takes the form of requiring prisoners to dig up recently planted flowers identified as inappropriate for a prison complex, rewashing already immaculate floors, and being awakened in the middle of the night to buff already shiny hallways. Most prisoners work, for fear of reprisals or because keeping busy, even if it is degrading, is easier to take than idle hours. At the same time, Buck explains that refusing to work can be an act of rebellion, an assertion of one's human dignity and worth.[43] In prisons, both the guards and the prisoners are alienated. The prisoners are forced to do work that has little social meaning, earning nothing or very little in wages. The guards are required to uphold make-work policies and are often allowed, if not encouraged, to perform actions that are debilitating and humiliating to the prisoners.

At various times when Becky has visited friends who are in prison, she has been outraged at the behavior of some of the correctional officers—the pretend convivial tone in conversations while they degrade prisoners in small and large ways; the unnecessary scrutiny of women visitors' and inmates' bodies; the officers' strutting body language and extra-loud voices; the condescension toward and manipulation of inmates by requiring them to ask permission to use the bathroom; and the use of brute force in response to the slightest infraction. Becky's anger has been tempered, however, by political prisoners she knows—David Gilbert in particular— who remind her that many correctional officers have families to support and believe that following procedures will ultimately decrease strife in the prison.[44] David reminds Becky that, in terms of socioeconomic class, the guards' position is not so different from that of many prisoners. Both groups have been squeezed out of heavy industry, which provided relatively high-paying, often unionized jobs, as the economy has shifted to service-based, less lucrative, lower-status occupations. Michael Moore's film *Roger and Me,* which traces the decline of the auto industry in Detroit, makes a link between the dramatic rise in the prison population and the whittling down of General Motors' production there. Many of those who became correctional officers ended up guarding men with whom they used to work on the assembly line, the line between them now institutionalized through prison procedures. Prisons do not inflict equal damage on guards and inmates. Guards walk out freely at the end of their shifts; some have the choice to seek work in other occupations. Prisoners are trapped and have almost no control over the work they do. But the whole environment is mad at the level of the psyche and the spirit, oftentimes leaving people completely isolated as they try to resist either being abused or abusing others.

## "A PERSON IS A PERSON THROUGH OTHER PERSONS"

In *Black Skin, White Masks,* Frantz Fanon, a psychiatrist and social theorist from Martinique who worked in Algeria, asserts that people must not only free themselves physically from domination but also decolonize their minds. Colonization involves control of the body as well as manipulation of the mind. Psychological decolonization requires people to recognize that they have internalized the colonial master's ideology.[45] This psychological purging allows them to reclaim their history and, therefore, themselves. Fanon also asserts that in a situation of domination there is always resistance. Domination, by definition, creates resistance because people never lose their desire to be fully human. Fanon's hopeful assertion encourages us to identify resistance—even, and perhaps most especially, in situations of torture and terror. Such resistance reminds us that not all minds have been colonized, that at least one person, and hopefully more, knows that torture is not right.

At Abu Ghraib, that one person, by the name of Specialist Joseph M. Darby, acquired a CD of the photos and slipped an anonymous letter under the door of the Criminal Investigation Division of the US Army.[46] Following his brave act, Darby was castigated by many other military personnel and, upon returning to the United States, was made so unwelcome in his hometown that he and his wife were forced to relocate far from their roots. But his actions did lead to an investigation. When he refused to participate in the degradation of the Iraqi prisoners, he was asserting his own human dignity and worth, as well as that of the prisoners he did not torture.

So, are we left to rely upon individual initiative and conscience as the basis of resisting oppression? Is that what this horrible story implies? Are individual whistle-blowers the crux of social activism in this new millennium? There have been many times in history when individual acts of conscience have provided the essential starting point for a more collective social response. But we can't rely on individual initiative to take the place of group organizing. Resistance is a sociological concept that refers not only to individuals but also to group formation and solidarity.

For signs of this collective work we look to international struggles against alienation in its most extreme form—when the process of production centers on degrading fellow human beings. For the most celebrated and perhaps most far-reaching example in recent world history, we look to the Truth and Reconciliation Commission in South Africa. Under the direction of theologian Desmond Tutu, the commission orchestrated a means for South Africa to move from apartheid to a multiracial democracy by emphasizing principles of peace and reconciliation rather than retaliation and imprisonment. Established in 1995, this commission was composed of seventeen members representing diverse racial, religious, and political backgrounds. The commission was charged with hearing testimony that would fully disclose political crimes committed between the Sharpeville Massacre in 1960 and the first democratic elections in 1994.

At the root of Tutu's theology and the commission's work was the proverb: "A person is a person through other persons."[47] This ethical stance resonates deeply with Marx's concept of species being. The logic of the commission was that more healing could occur by honestly naming and taking responsibility for the violence done by human hands than could be achieved by punishing those responsible for the violence. Given the history of apartheid in South Africa, punishing only those who could be found guilty of violence through a trial would fuel a "few bad apples" ideology that would do little to address the widespread violence at all levels of society. In his autobiography, Tutu explains that a democratic South Africa could not begin with "retribution or punishment." He continues, "In the spirit of *ubuntu,* the central concern is the healing of breaches, the redressing of imbalances, the restoration of broken relationships, a seeking to rehabilitate both the victim and the perpetrator."[48] Although difficult to translate into a Western language, *ubuntu* connotes an understanding that people are "born to belonging."[49] Tutu explains that the concept "speaks of the very essence of being human."[50] It goes to the heart of the commission's work.

In its three years of painstaking labor, the Truth and Reconciliation Commission provided an unprecedented example of an alternative to imprisonment for those who had violated the social contract of civil society. We can imagine that the Iraqi detainees who were tortured and then photographed might have experienced some initial relief if they learned that Graner was sentenced to ten years in prison and that several others have been held legally accountable for abuse. However, these punitive measures do little if anything to ensure that the US government will take responsibility for its export of a punishment industry to Iraq, Guantánamo Bay, and multiple locations internationally. And these measures have done little, perhaps nothing, to stop further abuse. In fact, Amnesty International's report that Guantánamo Bay is this century's version of a Russian gulag was met with the announcement by the Bush administration that the prison at Guantánamo Bay would remain open indefinitely and that the prisons in Iraq would be expanded.

The Truth and Reconciliation Commission ultimately held the South African government responsible for a system that poisoned human relations. The commission could serve as a model for the United States to be held accountable for crimes committed in times of war, as well as state crimes still unaccounted for on domestic soil—beginning with the genocide of Native Americans, centuries of slavery, and current abuses done in the name of war.

For examples of collective struggles against alienation in its most sharpened form we also look to Critical Resistance, a US-based, multiracial organization, cofounded in 1997 by Angela Davis, Ruth Wilson Gilmore, Julia Sudbury, and others.[51] This group is charged with investigating abuses within the prison system and creating alternatives to prison time for those incarcerated. The organization recognizes that something is powerfully wrong when the prison population has doubled since 1990 and when the fastest-growing industry in California and many other states is the prison system, not the educational system.[52] Critical Resistance believes that securing people's rights to basic needs—including food, health care, education, and housing—will be far more successful in creating safe communities than building more prisons will.

This agenda inevitably links the organization's work to global struggles for equity and justice. Taking the abolition of the prison industrial complex as its ultimate goal, Critical Resistance exposes the institutionalized racism, violence, and inequality that characterizes prisons; supports alternative models of justice that nurture communities and individuals; and protests the unbridled expansion of prisons and the criminalization of poverty. Critical Resistance also attempts to foster political alliances across a multitude of movements, seeing links, for example, between ending police brutality and ending torture in prisons.[53] By acknowledging the horrific consequences that such systems as state-sponsored surveillance and the penal system have on poor communities and especially communities of color, the organization confronts the belief that these institutions make our lives safer.

We also look to the Grandmothers of the Plaza de Mayo in Argentina, who for more than thirty years have kept pressure on the government to account for the disappearance of their children and grandchildren at the hands of the US-backed military regime. In defiance of the prohibition against public assembly, fourteen mothers gathered in the Plaza de Mayo in April 1977 to demand accountability for and information on the disappearance of their loved ones who were kidnapped and/or killed by the military junta.[54] Tens of thousands of Argentines—labor organizers, intellectuals, leftists, students, and others labeled "subversives"—vanished during what has become known as the "dirty war." Since 1977, the Grandmothers of the Plaza de Mayo have gathered each Thursday afternoon, wearing white handkerchiefs stitched with the names of their missing relatives, to circle the monument at the center of the plaza in silence. Initially dismissed by the junta as "madwomen," the activists were able to establish a political bulletin, connect with other mothers and grandmothers of the disappeared, and garner international support for their movement. Since the fall of the military regime in 1983, the activists have fought for a broad vision of social justice and continued to pressure the government for accountability and redress.

These and many other grassroots organizations are the lighthouses that keep Marx's concept of species being alive. Ultimately, the three organizations mentioned here are taking stands against militarism in many forms, including the buildup of prisons. The Truth and Reconciliation Commission's work avoided the imprisonment of thousands of people and provided a forum to begin healing the wounds of apartheid. Critical Resistance asks us to view imprisonment as a way of avoiding problems of inequality—racism, classism, and violence. It envisions a society where resources are redirected from prison construction to the building of schools, universities, houses, and community centers. The Grandmothers of the Plaza de Mayo imagine a world where the military has been dismantled, where people do not have to worry about being "disappeared" at the hands of military dictatorships.

The worlds these organizations envision require us to consider the ways in which nationalism has been used to fuel military economies that, as we have argued, eventually distort all human relationships. Historian Howard Zinn contends that whereas nationalism is useful for those in power, it is deadly for those out of power: "National spirit can be benign in a country that is small and lacking both in military power and a hunger for expansion (Switzerland, Norway, Costa Rica, and many more). But in a nation like ours—huge, possessing thousands of weapons of mass destruction—what might have been harmless pride becomes an arrogant nationalism dangerous to others and to ourselves."[55] Although the success of many anticolonial struggles depended on nationalist rhetoric, this method of binding people to each other cannot sustain itself in a life-affirming way over the long run. Ultimately, nationalism relies on coercion and fear, an ideology that there is always someone out there coming to get you—Germans, Russians, Islamic fundamentalists, and the list goes on.

Nationalism assumes that the government speaks for the people when, in fact, the government typically reflects the opinions of a minority of the population. Germany was not the enemy during World War II. The German people included Nazis, Christians who were not Nazis, and Jews. Coercion by the Nazis silenced the other Germans. What was done in the name of national identity was actually much more specific. Similarly, the ideology that the Russians were coming to get us—an ideology that fueled the Cold War and led to a permanent war economy in the United States—depended upon constructing the people of the Soviet Union as totally different from all the other people on the planet. Nationalism rendered invisible the tremendous diversity of opinion, religion, and culture in the Soviet Union. It is not surprising that the latest purported threat to US nationalism—Islamic militancy—does not originate in a single country. Islamic militancy is transnational. And yet Bush's response to this threat has been made on national terms, first targeting Afghanistan and then Iraq. Nationalism is outdated, both as an identity and as a tactic for organizing the world. As the world gets smaller and smaller, we can no longer survive with militarized economics, particularly those justified through nationalism.

One reason that Costa Rica is so beautiful—the multiethnic population, the rain forests, the beaches, the coral reefs, the birds of a thousand colors—is that the government has placed a high priority on honoring the country's natural resources. Costa Rica has no standing army. Even though it is a relatively poor country, its government has been able to sustain this beauty in part because there is no need to divert resources to a military. We think it is worth trying to imagine the United States without a military and, further, to imagine the United States in some way other than in nationalist terms. There is something amiss with a society that requires people to disrobe in order to get on an airplane, trusting that doing so will somehow make us all safe. There is something wrong when community development is simply a code word for building a super-maximum-security prison or another police station. There is something terribly wrong when a woman in her early twenties from a small town in West Virginia sees fighting in Iraq as the way out of working in a chicken-processing plant.

Ultimately, by holding Costa Rica up as a model country because it doesn't have an army, we run the risk of romanticizing it, as does our opening account of our idyllic time there. But our palpable relief when we visited the country, the relaxation our bodies registered in our lowered shoulders and softening eyes, speaks to our desire to keep an imaginative space alive. Abu Ghraib asks us to see militarism as a threat to all of us. The nationalism at the core of the US military has run its course. Experiencing dissociation on multiple levels is no way to live.

# PART FOUR

# BODY

## *The Columbine School Shootings*

CANOPY

*in Auschwitz you lived*
*in a tin can on a metal beam*
*seeped into water*
*children drank to soothe throats*
*rough from crying*

*in Rwanda you slipped*
*under the bed with the boy*
*left speechless*
*his parents found him fetal*
*pulled him close, army circling*

*in Colorado*
*you buckled yourself to the breast*
*of a teacher*
*who covered the children's bodies*
*with his own, tent of mercy*

*in California you*
*carried the voices of women*
*finding Marilyn Buck locked*
*in the hole sixty days darkness*
*post towers roundup*

*Elie Wiesel asked*
*did god die in Auschwitz*
*god colors the water*
*whispers in desert breezes*
*does yoga in still darkness*

— BECKY THOMPSON

# SEVEN

# ÉMILE DURKHEIM AND EMBODIMENT
# IN THE AGE OF THE INTERNET

R ecently, we went over to a campus computer center to get a laptop computer repaired after receiving multiple e-mail messages advertising products for penile enlargement. We could neither stop these messages from arriving in the inbox nor delete them. These announcements, in combination with the numerous other e-mail messages asking if we were interested in going out with a bored housewife, had led us to believe that something had gone wrong with the spam filter. Putting "penile" and "housewife" as the key words on the filter had seemed only to invite further inquiries. Fearing that the ads would become even more in-your-face and invasive, we marched to the computer center seeking help.

When we arrived, the work-study student on duty was barely willing to look up from his computer screen, but then relented with a cursory look and order: "You need to send an e-mail to the help desk and explain your problem. Then we will give you an appointment." When we said that we would be happy to make an appointment now, he replied, "Oh, we don't make appointments in person." We stood there silently wondering how our lives had come to this. Here we were, on a late Friday afternoon, being overpowered by a machine while someone half our age told us that a written statement sent via an electronic impulse was somehow more legitimate than our human voices and human presence. We continued to stare at him, hoping that our status as professors might change his mind. Eventually he said, "If I take the request in person, I may lose it." When we asked why he couldn't help us now, he mumbled that he was busy instant-messaging his friend. Upon asking where his friend was—we assumed Australia or Indonesia, or at least in one time zone away from ours—he finally looked up at us, clearly annoyed by our presence and pointed, "He is over there," pointing to the other male student at the end of the room.

At that point we thought it best to leave with our invitations for penile enlargements dates still glued to the e-mail inside the laptop, thinking that this conversation, if you could call it that, was getting us nowhere fast. We had entered a world that privileged mediated communication over human contact and connection. For a moment we wondered if his supervisor did not want the student's friends in the computer center and so they had decided to communicate through computers—two students' subversive acts on a Friday afternoon. We went back to the office, willing to live with this reasoning until, a few days later, other students informed us—with sighs conveying how hopelessly out-of-touch we were with modern life—that they had been instant messaging while in the same room for years. This activity, they let us know, predated ads for Viagra, promises of sex organ augmentation, and housewives' pleas for company.

The students continued to tell us about how people use chat rooms, which ostensibly allow them to leave their gender, race, culture, age, and sexuality behind. In these "rooms" people can assume any and all identities they choose. A white man can become a single mother from Zimbabwe, a thirteen-year-old girl can become a forty-year-old man, a grandmother can become a co-ed beginning her first year of college. The students praised the Internet, explaining that it frees people from expectations that may otherwise exist for them in their everyday lives. While people across race don't often talk with each other in real life, the Internet—because it doesn't demand face-to-face communication—can lessen distance, even if only momentarily. Was this Internet technology a sign of a new way for people to feel a sense of belonging to each other? Was it a sign of alienation that has not yet been theorized? Or was it a combination of both?

Over the next few weeks, we kept returning to the scene in the computer center, trying to parse out the consequences of this information age and the Internet on people's lives. We had to admit that the Internet linked people in new ways—people using it to find long-lost loved ones, pulling up information and sources quickly that might, in previous years, have taken weeks to uncover if they could be found at all; people selling last year's cross-country skis to buy this year's UGGS; people struggling with bipolar disorder finding each other on the Net and having conversations they might avoid otherwise, out of fear of disclosure and face-to-face interaction.

Just when we agreed to think about the Internet in a more complex way—to try not to be so Luddite and reactionary about it—the fifth anniversary of the 1999 murders in Littleton, Colorado, arrived. Talk shows around the country were attempting to review what people did and did not know about why two students, Dylan Klebold and Eric Harris, came to school with guns, wearing overcoats, and shot their classmates and a teacher, killing thirteen and injuring twenty-three more before killing themselves. Dylan and Eric had been close friends since junior high school. They worked together at a pizza parlor, discussed their anger about bullies, and, as it turns out, shared an interest in buying guns, building bombs, and plotting the destruction of their high school, much of which they planned online. Eric and Dylan spent multiple hours each day both individually and together on the Internet, playing warrior games that featured bombs and firepower. They found information about how to build bombs from the Internet. They created their plans for blowing up their classmates and the school on Internet sites. Isolated from other friends and adults, they spent substantial time doing research on Hitler's life, Nazi philosophy, and other violent movements. On a website that Eric Harris designed, he threatened to kill one of his classmates. The bulk of their time was spent in cyberspace, developing their own site and checking out other sites that revolved around violence.

Of course, computer use did not cause their violence. Long hours at the terminal were neither the primary nor the only sign of trouble. But signs that might have warned of the impending doom were missed.[1] Though seen as quirky and scary in some instances, Dylan and Eric did not fit a profile that people in their neighborhoods or schools saw as dangerous. While psychologists from all over the United States were called in to explain the issues that may have led to these young men's violence, we knew that had they been African American, no such analysis would have been deemed necessary. Explanations for the violence would have harked back to how the media handled the 1989 Central Park jogger beatings, when the alleged black perpetrators were described as "wilding"—acting like wild animals out of a biological tendency toward violence. The boys at Columbine High School were never considered capable of such violence. As a consequence, the warning signs that preceded this tragedy did not reach the radar screen until the two marched into their school on the anniversary of Hitler's birthday, just weeks before their graduation, planted a bomb in the cafeteria, and began murdering people before killing themselves. The result was the Columbine murders, which at the time became the deadliest school shooting in US history.

The indiscriminate quality of the murders raises startling questions about the erosion of social ties that keep people from harming each other. The seeming logic was this: let's kill someone because we have guns and we can; then we'll kill ourselves; they, you, me, no one really matters. Had these boys become so ensconced in virtual identities that seeking connections to fellow students no longer mattered? How had they missed the lesson that there is a social reality that constrains people from killing their classmates? How had they come to believe that freedom meant killing themselves and others rather than caring for themselves and those around them? Is this a Middle America version of a suicide bomber? What was causing these young people—with race, class, and gender privilege—to plot their own and so many others' destruction?

We are left asking if, in this information age of seemingly endless possibilities, people are losing the ability to understand the difference between fantasy and reality. While there certainly is no dearth of examples of violence in the United States throughout history, mass murders coupled with suicide committed by young people are new. The media have long documented black-on-black male violence in urban areas, but all of the school killings (with the exception of two)—including Columbine—have been committed by young white men. This is why sociologist Orlando Patterson urges us to ask "why mass murders seem exclusively the doing of young white men who come from the middle class."[2] What are these young people alerting us to understand? What social forces are we now missing that in previous eras reinforced a sense of moral responsibility? These were, in fact, questions that Émile Durkheim (1858–1917), the late nineteenth-century French sociological theorist, spent his life reckoning with. His work, from his first to his last book, pivoted on the question of the norms and constraints necessary in order for societies to avoid violence and give people a sense of collective belonging.

### ÉMILE DURKHEIM: REVISITING THE FRENCHMAN

As is true of many people trained in sociology, we had been force-fed Durkheim as undergraduates and graduate students. We had been taught about how hard he struggled, how diligent he was, to have sociology recognized as its own, necessary discipline in France. He established the first French journal of sociology, *L'Année Sociologique,* wrote three major studies while mentoring the first generation of sociology scholars in France, and eventually was named a professor of education at the Sorbonne, France's most prestigious university.[3] While our professors in college and graduate school waxed eloquent about a man who seemingly single-handedly put sociology on the map in France, we worried about whether becoming a sociologist was worth it, given Durkheim's driven, almost religious dedication to his work. As is true of many innovators, Durkheim's devotion enabled enormous productivity as well as exacting work standards.[4] Sociology legend has it that Durkheim's nephew and colleague, Marcel Mauss, once tried to hide from Durkheim as he was drinking coffee at a café by the Sorbonne in Paris, for fear that Durkheim would scold him for not working. For us, as budding sociologists, his total focus was both intimidating—out of our reach—and intriguing, since his drive seemed to give so much meaning to his life.

As undergraduates, we suffered through the voluminous accounts of suicide rates in Western Europe that Durkheim used as the basis for the first empirical study on the subject. And we wondered at the time how a subject that was so emotional and fascinating could be reduced to such dry, passionless language. We learned to say Marx-Weber-Durkheim almost as if it were one word, to acknowledge the triumvirate of scholars typically named as the fathers of sociology.

Despite our complaining and running critique, we were convinced early on of the value of teaching Durkheim's concept of "social facts."[5] Arguably Durkheim's most famous concept, social facts are cultural beliefs and actions that extend beyond individual control—forces that are external to and coercive of people. Social facts, although created by people, take on a life of their own, in the process restraining people both materially and morally. Myths, suicide, patriarchy, languages, the division of labor, and racism are all examples of social facts. The concept "social fact" had, over the years, come in handy for us when we taught about how patriarchy seeps into the veins of all people—not even feminists are immune; that racism is a force that, like smog, infects all of us, regardless of who is breathing the air. Like electricity, a social fact may seem invisible, but its consequences are as real as electricity's power.[6] The underlying moral values of a society, and the mechanisms used to enforce these morals, have real consequences. Attempts to resist these social facts are a sure sign of their power.

When teaching social theory, we also credited Durkheim for his exploration of the dangers of individualism and for his interest in moral and spiritual qualities of life that keep societies from spinning out of control. We appreciated his passionate concern about the world and his fierce intellectual hunger. And we admired his principled protest in the 1890s of the anti-Semitism at the root of the French military's imprisonment and deportation of a Jewish army colonel, Alfred Dreyfus, who was falsely accused of spying for Germany.[7]

While we were willing to acknowledge Durkheim's contributions, the truth is that, in our own work and in the classroom, we ultimately portrayed his scholarship as deeply flawed. And we had plenty of reasons to do so. Like other calls for objectivity, his commitment to objectivity—though a method he considered crucial in order for sociology to be granted academic and moral authority—obscured the impact of his own social location (as a Jew in a Catholic country, as a European man) on his vision. Despite the value he placed on the ideals of the French Revolution and the republic, what was often celebrated as his blueprint for a well-ordered society also served as a grand apology and justification for maintaining social inequalities and legitimizing repressive authority. Although he was not a political conservative (in fact he was a socialist all of his life), the primacy he placed on social order rendered his work, and the ways it has often been interpreted, as hopelessly conservative. Durkheim viewed women as less developed human beings than men. He believed that women did not need the degree of intellectual and social stimulation that men needed. "With a few devotional practices and some animals to care for," Durkheim states, "the old unmarried woman's life is full," whereas a man needs others because he is a "more complex social being."[8] From Durkheim's perspective, if what we now name as patriarchy is necessary to keep families working, then so be it.

Durkheim also used terms such as "savage" and "primitive" in reference to people not of European background, revealing his unquestioned hierarchical sense of modern and "primitive" societies. While Durkheim was certainly not alone among white European men of his era in terms of his ethnocentrism, this limit is particularly significant in Durkheim's case, since his early and late work extended beyond Europe in its gaze. (His books *The Division of Labor in Society* and *The Elementary Forms of the Religious Life* theorized about the structures of societies in industrialized and colonized countries.) It is almost impossible to read much of Durkheim without arguing with his basic assumptions. One of the most-cited excerpts from *The Division of Labor in Society* reads: "Likewise, although the savage does not know the pleasures that a very active life procures for us, his compensation is that he is not prey to boredom, that torment of the cultured mind."[9] If only we were guilty of taking his words out of context. Our feelings about his sexism, European elitism, and other problematic assumptions in his work are not benign.[10]

Given our many qualms, you can imagine our surprise when we found ourselves returning to Durkheim's work, flaws and all. But we did. The Columbine murders and suicides seemed to demand it. We painstakingly reread his scholarship, begrudgingly acknowledging that his focus on the necessary ingredients for social order—for the moral and spiritual quality of life in modern society—was exactly the question we were still struggling with.[11] This time, we were asking it in relation to devastating violence that had taken place in the "heartland of America." We realized there were many reasons why we could not give up on Durkheim. Just two paragraphs after the passage on savages and the torments of a cultured mind, Durkheim poses important questions about enjoyment, joy, suffering, and pleasure—concepts few sociologists of his time or since have considered.[12] His lifelong hunger for understanding religious systems globally continues to raise crucial questions about religion as both a necessary social glue and an institution that rationalizes profound social divisions. His encyclopedic knowledge of history, philosophy, and religion makes any easy dismissal of his work anti-intellectual. So we returned to the Frenchman whom we had righteously rejected in previous times.

An academic concerned about the rapid social change from rural agricultural life to urban industrial life, Durkheim argued that modern society must control people's antisocial urges (what he thought of as limitless desires and an overemphasis on individualism) in order to ensure the social bonds that are necessary for social cohesion. Durkheim reasoned that prior to industrialization people were held together by religion, which gave them a shared collective conscience—a consciousness, set of ideals, or shared values that go beyond individual belief or morality.[13] As society became increasingly industrialized, more people moved to the cities, concentrating the population into smaller areas. Industrialism also ushered in a complex division of labor, requiring more complicated and specialized rules. These dramatic changes were taking place during a period when religion was losing its hold over people, replaced by reliance on science as the basis of moral and political power.

Durkheim worried that secularized society would not be enough to provide people with a sense of order and belonging. He asserted that this belonging is particularly fragile during times of rapid economic and political change when people are often bereft of old traditions. As a Jew in an overwhelmingly Catholic country with a history of anti-Semitism, Durkheim knew early in his life what it meant not to belong. At the same time, as a Jew, he knew the necessity of a moral code for holding communities together. He knew about both integration and regulation from his own subject position.

When he went to Paris as a young man, away from his family for the first time, he felt his outsider status even more profoundly. Some have hypothesized that this experience was the seed for his lifelong interest in collective belonging and meaning.[14] Durkheim believed that sociology could provide a science of humanity, addressing many of the issues previously taken up by religion. By the time he began his work on the now classic text *Suicide,* he had come to believe that understanding society required careful and rigorous sociological research methods that he found missing in the philosophical, literary, and historical approaches in which he had been trained. He believed that sociology could, unlike any other discipline, address the most pressing moral issues facing people in contemporary society.

In one of the truly ironic moves in the history of sociology, Durkheim reasoned that the best way to understand social cohesion in society was to study its opposite. Those who commit suicide are assuming the ultimate protest against cohesion, shattering connection by deliberately and permanently removing themselves from their community. In *Suicide,* Durkheim gathered statistics on suicide rates from Protestant, Catholic, and religiously mixed countries and found that the average suicide rate per million was over twice as high in Protestant nations.[15] He argued that "the proclivity of Protestantism for suicide must relate to the spirit of free inquiry that animates this religion."[16] He posited that the free inquiry that was characteristic of the Protestant faith opened a space for individualism while it deemphasized collective goals and a hierarchy of authority that were more characteristic of Catholicism. Durkheim saw that the chain of command in the Catholic Church made possible a clear understanding of who was in charge and how decisions were made. Catholicism provided more moral cohesion than that offered to Protestants, whose faith emphasized individual accomplishment and a direct connection between people and God. In effect, Catholic doctrine provided a moral and social collective fabric unavailable to Protestants. Durkheim also collected statistics that led him to conclude that married people with children were less likely to commit suicide than unmarried individuals.[17] Those with fewer social ties, with fewer obligations to a community, were more susceptible to suicide than those with substantial social responsibilities.

Durkheim used a statistical method to explain one of the most enduring sociological questions: What would lead a person to do the most taboo of acts, the taking of one's own life? At the same time, he offered compelling evidence for a crucial distinction to be made between psychological processes and social facts. While suicide clearly had implications for individuals, its causes could not be reduced to individual psychology. This was important to us as we found article after article attributing the Columbine murders to psychological processes within Dylan and Eric that had no relationship to the social world. Most of the media seemed fixated on one question: How could these acts of violence be explained, given that the two had come from such "normal" families? When one explanation gained national currency—that these young men had become antisocial as a result of living in a computer-generated fantasy world—this account quickly devolved to a simplistic solution: keep young people away from excessive computer use.

Durkheim believed that suicide could not be understood solely as a psychological act, an individual decision. Rather, suicide has social causes; it is rooted in social forces that are beyond individual control. War, economic change, divorce, an erosion of religious life, social dislocation, industrialization, and technological changes were among the social forces that Durkheim identified as having power beyond an individual and affecting suicide rates.

## LONELINESS IN THE HEARTLAND

Durkheim believed that rapid change was responsible for new forms of antisocial behavior. Dramatic economic, political, and social change can make social rules unclear or nonexistent. One of the symptoms and consequences of this rapid change is suicide.[18] Although the specific social upheavals and unrest Durkheim lived through and theorized about are not the same as those in contemporary US society, a shift in moral values that Durkheim linked to social change certainly applies to the United States now. Since World War II, the United States has witnessed the most rapid social change in its history.[19] Among the elements of this change has been the rise of the information age, a postindustrial era in which a sense of community is as likely to be sought from virtual relationships developed on the Internet as it is from familial relationships maintained through frequent-flyer miles and limitless-minute phone plans.

Durkheim helps us see that spending much of one's life in virtual reality is a symptom of an increasingly atomized and individualized society that undermines social solidarity. He linked this dynamic to an increase in suicide. Durkheim's study of suicide revealed four types—anomic, altruistic, egoistic, and fatalistic. Anomic suicide reflects an individual's moral confusion and lack of social direction, which Durkheim believed was linked to dramatic social and economic upheaval. Both Dylan and Eric were facing uncertain futures economically at a time in US history when younger generations are less, rather than more, likely to do as well as their parents financially, when outsourcing and a postindustrial economy make economic security an unknown quantity for an increasing number of people. Chances are that both of them knew that living in the style they had become accustomed to was no longer their birthright. In his interpretation of Durkheim's concept, Ken Thompson writes, "In anomic suicide, insufficient regulation had left individual passions and wants unchecked, leading to irritation, disgust, anger, disappointment, or recrimination."[20]

It is hard to think of an example of a suicide that more fits Durkheim's description of anomic suicide than that of these two teenagers. They were making up the rules as they went along in a world that must have seemed both strangely boring and confusing. Brooks Brown, a former Columbine student and friend of both Eric and Dylan, elaborates: "In real life, things didn't make sense. We saw our classmates being beaten by their parents, who were supposed to love them and nurture them. We heard our friends talking about how much their mommies hated their daddies—kids turned into bargaining chips in custody battles they couldn't even begin to comprehend. We saw racism, sexism, and cultural oppression—not just on TV or on the Internet, but in our own daily lives. These came from the adults we looked up to."[21]

The absence of social rules that made sense—that could be counted on in daily life—left Eric and Dylan looking for reliable and predictable rules elsewhere. Brown explains, "When Eric and Dylan got into the world of video games, they loved it, because it was a world with definite rules. Those rules were preset, and they could not be broken. For a young man in a world like ours, it was a godsend. In the real world, the rules change constantly—and you could be in trouble at a moment's notice. But video games are different. In a video game you only get what you know; nothing changes. So video games are a sort of haven, an escape to a logical, exciting world where two things are certain; justice is done, and you get what is due you based on your actions. Everything happens through your own doing, your own mistakes and your own achievements."[22] As Brown concludes, "Eric and Dylan got sucked into this appealing fantasy because it was an escape from the troubles of everyday life. When you have a place to go—whether it be home, school, a bar, a drug den, or a video game—where things seem perfect, you go to that place as much as you can. It's a type of drug—a fantasy—where happiness exists because things make sense."[23]

Eric and Dylan grew up being taught that they were entitled to a future. Yet they couldn't seem to find a place for themselves in their school or community. When Eric—whose older brother was an accomplished athlete and whose father had a successful career in the Air Force—could not qualify for the Marine Corps because he did not reveal his prescription drug use for depression during the application process, he saw no other real option for himself and his future, even though he had been a strong student.[24] He seemed to find a community on the Internet that gave him an outlet for his anger and fantasies of power. Dylan and Eric kept written diaries of their violent plans that they also placed on websites. There appears to have been little regulation to interrupt their actions. In their case, rage was the passion that went unchecked, rage that few people recognized until Dylan and Eric named it themselves on videotapes they made before the murders, to be played once the deed was done.[25]

Dylan's and Eric's suicides also exemplify another type that Durkheim identified—egoistic suicide. This form of suicide reflects a prolonged sense of not belonging, of not being integrated into a community, an experience of not having a tether, an absence that can give rise to "meaninglessness . . . apathy, melancholy, and depression."[26] Again, Dylan and Eric manifested those states, both expressing a lack of connection or sense of belonging at school and at home. At school, neither fit in with the jocks or the other students considered popular. Both boys were ostracized repeatedly by the popular students. The powerful students in the class (the jocks and others recognized as "popular") repeatedly hurled obscenities at them, shoved them up against lockers, and threw bottles at them through open cars windows.[27] Eric was especially singled out because he had a slight chest deformity, which he could not hide in gym class. He was also short at a time in life when height is a sign of real status, particularly among adolescent boys. As Brown observes, "Mocking a guy for a physical problem he can't control is one of the most humiliating ways to bring him down."[28] In addition, Eric was not originally from Littleton. In fact, his family had moved several times, forcing him to adjust over and over again to new school environments. He never did find a place among the popular students at Columbine High School.

Instead, he and Dylan were members of the "Trench Coat Mafia," a loose affiliation of students that Brown describes as "a pretty diverse lot that made for some interesting conversations. Some were Wiccans, some were Satanists, some didn't proclaim any faith whatsoever. . . . Jocks would call the girls who hung out with the Trench Coat Mafia 'sluts' or 'Nazi lesbians.'"[29] Administrators and teachers saw that the "unpopular students" were ostracized but either encouraged the bullying or ignored it.[30] Brown cited many examples of fights that the jock students initiated that school administrators refused to stop or blamed the Trench Coat Mafia students for, each time allowing the bullying to continue.[31] Amid this bullying, Dylan and Eric stayed close to each other, finding violent games on the Internet to be their common companion. While Durkheim obviously did not account for Internet culture in his assessment of egoistic suicide, his recognition of suicide as a response to a long-term sense of not belonging certainly rings true for both Dylan and Eric. It is frightening that it was only in death that Dylan and Eric became full members of their communities, illustrated in the photo of a row of wooden crosses and altars, one right along side the next, memorializing those who died at Columbine. The first time they belonged was in death. Killing was a way to find their group.

A less evident but nevertheless applicable suicide type that Durkheim described is altruistic suicide, characterized by a sense of being overwhelmed by a group's goals and beliefs. Altruistic suicide is not as common as the other suicide types, due to the emphasis on individualism in modern society. However, examples of this suicide are sometimes seen in the military—a highly regimented and hierarchical institution based on groupthink and acceptance of authority. Eric and Dylan were living in a military town. Eric's family was in the military, and Eric himself had tried to join the Marines, only to be rejected.

Nothing suggests that Eric and Dylan killed themselves for the good of the community, for the good of some stated higher ideal. The centrality of militarism in the ethic of the town, however, suggests little way out for Eric—who wanted to be part of it but could not—and perhaps for Dylan as well, who grew up with a missile plant as an everyday fixture in his community. The two young men were enacting what the military teaches by carefully and methodically planning mass destruction. The mayhem and misery their destruction caused looked little different from a military operation waged against "the enemy." Only this time they were their own enemies as well.

The military was so much a part of their lives—central to the town's economy, a key family profession, at the center of sites they frequented on the Internet, a symbol of manhood—that perhaps there was no space outside of that institution. We know from the testimony of people who have left cults, broken away from domestic abuse, and escaped slavery that release from what sociologist Erving Goffman identified as a "total institution" does not mean the end of the trauma.[32] Being outside of a force that is all-encompassing can be experienced as still being in it—and experienced for a long time after.

What might it mean that these three types describe the Columbine suicides simultaneously? Durkheim frequently suggested that egoistic suicide and anomic suicide were two sides of the same coin.[33] Both types reveal confusion, deep loneliness, and a sense of separation from oneself and one's community. The third type, altruistic, asks us to consider to what

*Dylan Klebold's cross with those of his other classmates on Rebel Hill near Columbine High School following the 1999 massacre. "Eric Harris [misc]; Dylan Klebold [misc]." Photograph by Steve Liss. Time & Life Pictures Collection. Getty Images News, 50661133.*

extent a militarized economy, with the masculinist assumptions embedded in it, offers young men options beyond its script.

The fourth type of suicide that Durkheim identified, fatalistic suicide, describes yet another set of stresses that Eric and Dylan lived with. Durkheim explains, "There is a type of suicide, the opposite of anomic suicide, just as egoistic and altruistic suicides are opposites. It is the suicide deriving from excessive regulation, that of persons with futures pitilessly blocked and passions violently choked by oppressive discipline.... Do not the suicides of slaves, said to be frequent under certain conditions, belong to this type, or all suicides attributable to excessive physical or moral despotism? To bring out the ineluctable and inflexible nature of a rule against which there is no appeal, and in contrast with the expression 'anomie' which has just been used, we might call it *fatalistic suicide*."[34] Might each of these types of suicide—anomic, egoistic, altruistic, and fatalistic—and the stresses that relate to them (alienation, normlessness, ultraconformity, and stultifying regulation) be synergistic in their effect? Might the combination of stresses when experienced together help explain the enormity of the boys' rage, the extent of their violence?

167

Durkheim believed that schools were a source of social cohesion in the nineteenth and early twentieth centuries, public locations that would reflect and pass on the moral values of a culture. To realize that school was the very place where one of the most antisocial acts in recent history occurred is indeed troubling. That the boys who orchestrated these murders were young—individuals who are supposed to be the most protected by family, schools, community programs, and other institutions—tells us, in yet another way, that we are in trouble.

While we can identify an uncertain economic future, vicious bullying, and the town's militarism as key factors leading to the double suicide and the massacre, it is the synergism of these factors that ultimately set the course for that fateful day. In report after report following the massacre, what we were most struck by is how closed the environment of Littleton, Colorado, seemed to be. The town's homogeneity in terms of race, class, and social values doomed those who deviated, even in slight ways, as hopeless outsiders. This exclusion is what social theorist and poet Audre Lorde referred to as "the institutionalized rejection of difference." At Columbine High School, there was no space for Eric's and Dylan's differences. According to Lorde, "In a society where good is defined in terms of profit rather than in terms of human need, there must always be a group of people who, through systematized oppression, can be made to feel surplus, to occupy the place of the dehumanized inferior." Under capitalism and white supremacy, physical, occupational, and sexual differences are ranked, with one group valued and the other devalued. In the process, people are programmed to respond to differences with fear and loathing. We are taught to ignore, copy, or destroy difference. Lorde asserts that "institutionalized rejection of difference is an absolute necessity in a profit economy which needs outsiders as surplus people."[35]

Were Lorde still alive today, she may well have had much to say about how a fear of difference related to the murders in Columbine.[36] Social convention would lead us to believe that Littleton, Colorado, is America's heartland—the center of the American dream of two-car garages, white picket fences, stable heterosexual families, and quality public schools—but the film *Bowling for Columbine,* by Michael Moore, shows us that such a dream has costs. The children in Littleton have scant opportunity to meet and learn from those who are different from them in terms of race, class, and religion. The children grew up in an overwhelmingly white environment; Littleton is 98 percent white.[37] In the United States, we have been taught to equate difference with fear. Lorde tells us that "difference must be not merely tolerated, but seen as a fund of necessary polarities between which our creativity can spark like a dialectic."[38] If difference is the dialectic that sparks the imagination, then boredom and sameness contributed to the lockstep mentality the boys were rebelling against. The mass media's and the academy's continued focus on cultural deficits in black and Latino communities diverts attention from the ways in which white, middle-class locations are missing life-affirming imaginative spaces.

Given the emptiness that can be a product of a homogeneous environment, it is no surprise that white suburban kids are among the biggest consumers of hip-hop music. It is no surprise that all of the school shootings (with one exception) have taken place in white schools. It is also no surprise that these school shootings have been used as justification to further militarize urban black schools—the students still being seen as the source of youth violence even as statistics prove otherwise.[39] There is a reason why white people have historically run to Harlem to go to the clubs, churches, and dances. There is a reason that former President Clinton chose Harlem as the place for his office following his years in the White House. These reaches beyond white homogeneity tell us much about how all-white environments can end up feeling quite stultifying. That certainly appears to have been true for Dylan and Eric.

As it turned out, the rejection of difference at Columbine High School had enormous ramifications. While some of the mainstream media picked up on the cliques within the school, the ways in which white supremacy and patriarchy defined the school's culture were largely unseen. In an article on whiteness and the Columbine murders, critical race geographers Audrey Kobayashi and Linda Peake write, "This was not an urban inner-city school; this was a white school; this was a wealthy school; this was a *normal* school. And so, the perpetrators of this act had to be depicted as abnormal *individuals* who have deviated from the established norm as individuals, not as products of a particular social context."[40] Studied attention to the Columbine murders reveals that it makes little sense to consider Eric and Dylan, or Columbine High School, or Littleton, Colorado, as individual specimens that are unlike other white students, white schools, and white towns. The institutionalized fear of difference at the base of these murders—white supremacy, dominant masculinity—goes to the heart of US culture. "Littleton reminds us that the *entire* US landscape is deeply racialized . . . Processes of racialization are present throughout landscapes that are seemingly free from racial tension or diversity."[41]

While the media focused on Dylan and Eric as individuals, little attention was granted to how the culture of the school created devastating divisions despite its essential racial and class homogeneity. That sameness made other distinctions particularly salient. In an environment where race and class were not used as ways to divide people, strict hierarchies existed between the jocks and preps (the cool kids) and the geeks and losers (the uncool kids).[42] Once Dylan and Eric were labeled uncool—part of the dorks, loners, and geeks—they "struggled under the symbolic weight of the designation." When they gave up on being cool, they embraced their subordinate status fully, dressing in trench coats and maintaining "surly and irreverent antisocial dispositions."[43]

As white, middle-class boys, Dylan and Eric were raised to believe that their masculinity and their race would afford them multiple privileges. Their day-to-day reality, however, was one of being scapegoated, teased, and marginalized. In an analysis of the media representation of the murders, Mia Consalvo explains how the culture of Columbine High School revealed two masculinities—dominant and subordinate. She notes that "although as white males they were supposed to be in a privileged position . . . they were instead shown to be at the bottom."[44] At Columbine High (and many other high schools) there did not need to be any evidence that a boy was gay for him to be gay-baited. Simply refusing to be a jock was enough to be rendered as gay. In a study showing links between adolescent masculinity, homophobia, and violence in a range of school shootings, Michael Kimmel and Matthew Mahler found a "striking pattern from the stories about the boys who committed the violence. . . . Nearly all had stories of being mercilessly and constantly teased, picked on, and threatened. And most strikingly, it was *not* because they were gay (at least there is no evidence to suggest that any of them were gay) but because they were *different* from the other boys—shy, bookish, honor students, artistic, musical, theatrical, nonathletic, 'geekish,' or weird. Theirs are stories of 'cultural marginalization' based on criteria for adequate gender performance, specifically the enactment of codes of masculinity."[45] When the media sought to portray Dylan and Eric as so outside of society that their actions could not, in effect, be understood as anything other than the work of inhuman monsters, the culture that is threatened by difference could not be implicated in the violence.

For Lorde, fear of difference in its multiple forms is one of the fundamental impediments to social cohesion in US society. She identifies this fear as linked with the suppression of what she calls the erotic. In one of her most foundational essays, "The Uses of the Erotic," Lorde explains that the erotic is an expansive concept. It is the power that enables us to share deeply with other people, to experience joy, and to "scrutinize all aspects of our existence." It is a capacity we can experience whether we are "dancing, building a bookcase, writing a poem, examining an idea."[46] Lorde defines the erotic as an essential power within and among us that, like Karl Marx's species being, helps to make us fully human. She conceptualizes the erotic as "an internal requirement toward excellence" and the capacity to feel fully present in one's life, work, and relationships: "The erotic is a measure between the beginnings of our sense of self and the chaos of our strongest feelings. It is an internal sense of satisfaction to which, once we have experienced it, we know we can aspire. For having experienced the fullness of this feeling and recognizing its power, in honor and self-respect we can require no less of ourselves."[47]

Lorde believes that, under capitalism, the erotic is restricted, contained, and confined: "The erotic has often been misnamed by men and used against women. It has been made into the confused, the trivial, the psychotic, the plasticized sensation. For this reason, we have often turned away from the exploration and consideration of the erotic as a source of power and information, confusing it with its opposite, the pornographic. But pornography is a direct denial of the power of the erotic, for it represents the suppression of true feeling."[48] Lorde asserts that the erotic gives people psychic, emotional, and physical joy that is the basis of understanding between one another.

In this way, Lorde's work resonates with the writing of sociologist Herbert Marcuse.[49] He, like Lorde, asserts that capitalism diverts people from joy by teaching them to reach for and then become addicted to false needs — for consumer products that, like candy, bring momentary delight but cannot sustain us for the long term in any deep way. Also like Lorde, Marcuse believes that capitalism teaches us to see sexuality in reductionist terms — as contained solely within particular erogenous zones that are often defined through the pornographic gaze. In a society not built on consumption and profit, sexuality could be experienced as a much larger concept than genital or oral gratification. A fully embodied sexuality certainly includes the ecstasy of two people making love, but it can be manifested in many other ways as well.

Lorde believes that the erotic can serve as a powerful bridge across difference, holding people together who, without this often subterranean and unconscious power, might otherwise be foreign to each other. Lorde did not believe that differences between people necessarily fuel the isolation and individualism that are so characteristic of US society. In fact, Lorde asserts that differences — whether they be racial, ethnic, sexual, class, or religious differences — are what enable creativity, innovation, and advancement. She writes that "recognizing the power of the erotic within our lives can give us the energy to pursue genuine change within our world, rather than merely settling for a shift of characters in the same weary drama."[50]

While celebrating the erotic as a possibility, as a power, and as a principle for social cohesion, Lorde also cautions against the many social forces undermining it. Her words offer powerful warnings about the systems bent on destroying humanity, including those at the foundation of the Columbine murders. Littleton is a leading producer of missiles in the United States. Lorde's work suggests that people raised in an environment based on a system of profit fueled by militarism are not only bereft of the possibilities that difference brings. They are also denied a chance to experience the power of the erotic within themselves. Surrounded by symbols of death and destruction, it is no wonder that young people have trouble gaining access to their deepest life force — the want, the courage, the desire to live life to its fullest. Militarism's emphasis on external directives, hierarchy, discipline, and conformity leaves little or no room for individual human needs. Lorde writes, "When we live outside ourselves, and by that I mean on external directives only rather than from our internal knowledge and needs, when we live away from those erotic guides from within ourselves, then our lives are limited by external and alien forms, and we conform to the needs of a structure that is not based on human need, let alone an individual's."[51] Here, Lorde is linking the destruction of the erotic with a lost sense of an internal guide that leads us toward life and joy rather than toward death and loneliness.

Lorde's attention to the potential destructiveness of being controlled by external forces reinforces Durkheim's description of altruistic suicide — an act of desperation in response to being overwhelmed by a group's goals and beliefs. The psychological conditioning that Dylan and Eric experienced as students, being treated cruelly at school, and their socialization to see violence as a means for restoring their honor — all fueled a sense of desperation.[52] Kimmel and Mahler state, "In our view, these boys are not psychopathological deviants but rather overconformists to a particular normative construction of masculinity, a construction that defines violence as a legitimate response to a perceived humiliation."[53] Both Durkheim and Lorde warn us about the potential damage that all-encompassing institutions can do to our most essential life forces. For Lorde, even if an individual is not physically dead from these social forces, the destruction of the erotic can leave him or her spiritually dead — among the walking wounded.

## EMBODIMENT IN THE AGE OF THE INTERNET

Our attention to militarism, bullying, race segregation, and the suppression of the erotic is our attempt to offset explanations for the Columbine murders that reduce Dylan and Eric to individual crazy people. We also focus on these factors to offset superficial explanations of the murders as primarily signs of Internet overuse. At the same time, we would be remiss to end the chapter without a return to where we began—feeling lost at a campus computer center where our bodies were considered less real than a message we could send electronically. The truth is we still believe that the age of the Internet is also a factor in the Columbine murders.

Technology, it appears, links us together now in a way that religion linked people in the nineteenth century. On the surface, the Internet appears to be a source of freedom; it allows anybody to be anybody for a moment, an hour, a day, or a year. It frees us from the meaning attached to the corporeal body—one's sex, age, or race—and enables us to assume any reality we choose. In this way the Internet gives us freedom to enter into a world that satisfies our individual desires—whomever we choose to be. It takes us out of society and into a virtual reality that is supposedly unfettered by the everyday rules of behavior that bind us to others. The Internet is virtual fantasy and virtual freedom, a space with virtually no rules. After the Columbine murders, however, we found ourselves asking, might this be a new form of anomie—a lack of social control and a condition of normlessness where there is little or no sense of authority or moral guidance?

While it would be absurd to suggest a unidimensional explanation for why Dylan and Eric did not feel a sense of belonging to a larger community, we wonder about the ways in which technology and the information age may contribute to the anomie Durkheim identified. The increased use of computers for human transactions—at the supermarket, at the ticket counter, at the bank—decreases human contact in often imperceptible, daily ways. Spending long hours on the Internet makes the body superfluous. People's physical connections to one another are put on hold because the communication is not physical. People don't see each other's eyes, smell each other, hear each other's voices, or touch each other when they are online. Although the Internet may titillate the mind, it cannot, as a virtual reality, provide a vital life force. This connection lies outside communication on the Internet.

It is no coincidence that Dylan and Eric spent most of their time on the Internet playing a video game in which the main character has "practically unlimited firepower, can run and jump with inhuman stamina and skill," as Consalvo notes. For the two boys, "playing the game might have meant trying on a new and improved masculinity—one that was dominant rather than dominated, picking the fights rather than fleeing them, laughing at, rather than being the object of laughter." Consalvo adds, "The vastness of the Internet worked to [their] advantage, allowing [them] to simultaneously stand out and hide in the multitude of pages."[54]

This standing out and hiding at the same time is a key feature of the virtual reality of the Internet, a virtual reality that has consequences for embodiment. Consalvo observes, "For both boys, computers possibly served as technological 'add-ons' to their bodies. By adding technological prostheses, they could upgrade themselves temporarily—they could become 'Terminators' in a particular time and space. Unfortunately, this virtual cyborgization was not enough, and they progressed to the more deadly real prostheses of automatic weapons and bombs strapped to their chests. In so doing, they transformed their bodies into agents of destruction, terminator cyborgs, and their prostheses not simply extending them but destroying them as well."[55]

The Columbine murders and suicides—and other acts of self-destruction and collective destruction—ask us to consider the particular ways that body consciousness is compromised among young people in this century. For Dylan and Eric, the Internet seemed to be an escape from assaults on their bodies that ended up encasing them in an unreal world. It makes sense that Eric's "imperfect" body has been cited as a key reason why he was ostracized by his peers.[56] Body consciousness goes beyond the idea of body image, a concept that reduces one's embodiment to appearance. The etymology of "consciousness," rather than the more often used term "body image," links an awareness of one's embodiment to social conditions.[57] Consciousness, as Marx and others have used the term, links individual people's social realities, opportunities, and perspectives to social structures. One's race, sexuality, culture, gender, and nationality influence body consciousness, the development of which extends across the life span. Body consciousness is concrete in that breathing, eating, sleeping, and simply being require awareness of one's body. But body consciousness occurs at the imaginative, symbolic, and spiritual level as well. It includes the ability to see oneself as part of one's body and to draw upon that power to expect excellence of oneself and others. The social process of being embodied lies at the root of a person's capacity to know himself or herself as simultaneously unique and connected to the world. Our sense of connection to each other begins in infancy through a bodily connection. Our need to live in, experience, and be guided by our bodies does not lessen as we grow—in fact, it may increase, as multiple factors impinge upon this fundamental capacity.

In a postindustrial society it is no surprise that many people—particularly people living in suburban and urban areas with little access to the rhythms of nature, the seasons, and the earth—live outside of their bodies, having little sense of being connected to their own or other's bodies. One of the most profound characteristics of contemporary society is disconnection from nature—a force that has the power to remind us of our dependence on and home within our bodies. This disconnection takes many forms—being removed from the process of growing, harvesting, and, increasingly, cooking our own food; having little interaction with the seasons, except to be inconvenienced by weather; and having little chance to touch the earth, see plants grow, or watch the natural cycle of birds, insects, trees, the moon. The pace of our lives—working two jobs, juggling paid work and family responsibilities, needing to drive long distances to and from work; barely having time to breathe, have intimate conversations, see the color purple—undermines a sense of living within our bodies.

To us, it is no coincidence that in tapes Dylan and Eric made before the massacre, they explained their actions in terms of not being able to handle the rage they felt in their bodies. In tapes Harris left, he quoted Shakespeare: "Good wombs hath borne bad sons."[58] By this point, he couldn't seem to see himself outside of his badness, outside of his rage, the most constant emotion that both boys made reference to and manifested in their diaries, on their website, and in their videotapes. According to Mai and Alpert, "Both boys masked their inner rage, which they felt was unacceptable to their families."[59] In the videotapes, Dylan also "showed remorse, in advance, about how their actions were going to affect their parents." He told his mother and father that they had been "great parents" who taught him "self-awareness, self-reliance." He added, "I always appreciated that" and "I'm sorry I have so much rage." Eric apologized to his parents for the "hell" his actions were going to put them through and talked about his necessary withdrawal from them for their own good, before his violent act.[60]

Eric and Dylan carried around tremendous pain for years. They were physically assaulted, called sissies and faggots, and spat on. Their eventual response to this cruelty was to be as different as they possibly could, in looks and actions, from those who were taunting them. Over time, they also created strategies of retaliation. Kimmel explains, "Violence is often the single most evident marker of manhood."[61] According to the psychodynamic theory on gender socialization, weakness is shameful for boys, while violence is honorable.[62] Over time, the popular students' cruelty trumped Eric's and Dylan's own sense of self. They became focused on retaliation, not on their own survival. Their life force was distorted into destructive anger, which they understood but seemed to have no way to escape except by destroying their own and others' bodies.

Columbine ask us to grapple with how developing a life-affirming body consciousness on a collective level could heighten and sensitize our capacity to love each other.[63] Marx saw class consciousness as the primary definer of people's status and location in the world. Durkheim considered professional and social affiliations as the primary influences on an individual's consciousness. What might it take to put body consciousness on a par with class and gender and race consciousness as vital aspects of social change? Might body consciousness—a concept that has been given life by the emphasis on the body within the feminist and gay and lesbian movements, a concept made possible by liberation struggles since Marx and Durkheim—help us attend to issues the massacre raises? What changes might we have made so that Eric and Dylan could have felt so grounded and connected to their bodies and communities that the idea of blowing themselves and others up might never have occurred to them?

Ultimately, addressing these questions requires us not to separate the rage that Eric and Dylan expressed from our own, not to see them as alien or inferior to ourselves. We can't afford to chalk up their behavior to two horrifically screwed-up kids, although they were; it is much more involved than that. What might it mean that virtually all of the media coverage and academic analysis of the violence focused entirely on the murders, not on the double suicide? In fact, some of the accounts do not even include the two suicides in the number of people who died that day. Portraying Eric and Dylan as "monsters" and not fully human—their deaths not even countable—stops us from seeing their humanity and from seeing them in ourselves. An unwillingness to count their deaths is not so different from the US government's unwillingness to count Iraqi and Afghan deaths—to try to cordon off those who are considered human from those who are not, based on national affiliation. Durkheim offers us the concept of collective conscience, a holistic worldview that gives people a sense of their interconnectedness.[64] Durkheim believed that the collective conscience was strained beyond recognition in industrial society. The massacre in Littleton asks us to find ways to develop a collective conscience again. Certainly the coach and teacher Dave Sanders—who ran from room to room at the high school to guide students out of the building and who canopied students with his body, saving their lives while losing his own—can give us a start in that direction.

Durkheim instructs us in *The Division of Labor in Society* that rapid social change can outstep the development of morality—that there can be a lag time between social change and the moral forces necessary to maintain harmony and order under new social conditions. The morality "corresponding to this type of society has lost influence, but without its successor developing quickly enough to occupy the space left vacant in our consciousness."[65] As a consequence, he writes, "Our beliefs have been disturbed. Tradition has lost its sway. Individual judgment has thrown off the yoke of the collective judgment."[66] People's faith in each other has been troubled. Individual judgment has, seemingly, been freed from collective judgment. One hundred years later, Durkheim's words still apply.

# CONCLUSION

## *Regeneration*

S ince this book opens with our walking through the streets of San Francisco, we wanted to end it in an embodied way as well, making our voices central to this task. To do so, we decided to present our conclusions in the form of a dialogue, mirroring the conversations we have had while writing this book, as we have reasoned out every point together. While the preceding chapters reflect our training — sustaining complex arguments and organizing our thoughts in a linear form — our first and last chapters are our chance to keep it real, relying less on footnotes and more on lived experience.

We hope this dialogue will kick-start further exchanges. In the end, we think that the best of social theory often comes from writing that is self-reflective, shows some personality, and makes a link between history and biography. The popularity of reality TV and instant messaging tells us of people's hunger for unstaged, unrehearsed, and spontaneous conversation. Here's as close as we might get to reality TV.

BECKY: When we began this book in 2005, we had just returned from Costa Rica. Two years later, we are back in the United States, where, three weeks ago, police killed Sean Bell in his car with a hail of fifty bullets, wounding two other passengers.[1]

DIANE: People have been so afraid since 9/11 that they are willing to shoot anything that moves, especially if the person is dark skinned. Remember when we were watching TV together when Bush announced that the United States was going to bomb Afghanistan? He said they were looking for Osama bin Laden and that the military would find him within a few months. Now the United States is still in Iraq, and over 600,000 Iraqis have died.[2]

BECKY: And Bush is threatening to send more troops to the Persian Gulf, which may mean that the military is getting ready to strike Iran. Times seem to be even more troubled than when we started this project. The United States has become too mean, too harsh, too reactionary, even for its own self.

At the same time, the momentum of vets who are mobilizing against the war is building. The documentary *Sir! No Sir!* that I recently got to see made me try to find out more about what the vets from Iraq are saying now. Before seeing that film, I was still under the impression that there was a huge schism between the vets and the antiwar protesters during the Vietnam War. This film shows that so many vets *were* antiwar protesters. The mobilization against the war, by vets, is building earlier now than during Vietnam. People are fed up with the continued militarization of US society. I am sure that is one reason they turned the Republicans out of office last November.

DIANE: People are starting to fight back. Many people who haven't marched in years took to the streets in New York City to protest the Sean Bell killing. After James Brown, the "godfather of soul" died at seventy-three years old, thousands of people stood in the cold for hours, waiting to get into the Apollo Theater to pay their respects to him and his legacy. He told us to be black and proud. The sixties aren't dead, and people remember that there is still work to do.

My students, who can be so apathetic, have gotten some life back in the last couple of years. I don't have to work so hard to get them upset. They are upset on their own. In my Introduction to Sociology class this semester, for the first time in many years, students were angry that the history they had been taught was skewed. They were angry, not defensive, after realizing that they had only heard about the dreaming Martin Luther King, not the one who was against the war in Vietnam. And Malcolm X, well, they had just heard he was a crazy man. Once they saw a clip of him at a rally in Harlem, they were just as mesmerized by his charm and intelligence as I had been as a young woman. Many of the upper-class white students said they could understand him.

In that class, we also studied the sociologist and activist Jane Addams, including her notion of social ethics.[3] She believed that you can only be an ethical person in the world if you walk with people who are different from you. If you stay in your house, bound up with your family, you will continue to repeat your own set of ideas and will not learn anything else. Addams's ideas made sense to my students. They felt how limited and isolated their experience had been, in their Columbine-like environments. Even though the benefits of society are in front of them, they are serious and sad. They are overtrained, overprivileged, and high-achieving. In the past, not talking was a way they made sure they were safe. Now they know that staying silent is no longer working. They want to find ways to connect with each other that override their differences. They understand Marx's concept of alienation from species being, because that is what they have been feeling.

BECKY: I went to high school in an all-white environment where I felt like I was suffocating. I could not wait to get out of there.

DIANE: Even in all-white environments, they make someone the "other." If you are odd in any way—a dyke, or raised by a Communist-voting, single mother, in your case—you'll need to leave to save yourself. There is only a certain kind of whiteness that is acceptable. That is the whole point about Columbine.

In recent years so much of the space in the United States has been privatized, separating people from each other. People don't talk with each other outside of their immediate circles. Since the sixties, we have been so anxious to make sure that everybody has an identity. People have learned to think of each other in broad categories—Asian American, Hispanic American, African American, Italian American, et cetera. In the process we have been careful not to really see each other, not to talk with each other. A student came to me a few years ago who said he knew me because he had been watching Bill Cosby reruns. He was trying to be nice, saying he knew about middle-class black people.

BECKY: As bell hooks says, people eat each other (eat Chinese food, soul food) and simulate knowledge of each other through the television, but they do not necessarily see each other.[4] Like the color blindness ideology, this is another way not to really see difference. The unsaid logic: I see myself as appropriate and cosmopolitan because I eat Chinese food, but I don't really know Chinese people.

DIANE: One of the characteristics of a dysfunctional family is that people don't really talk with each other. People are afraid that if they talk, the house might blow up. US society operates like a dysfunctional family. There is so much information available, so much media chatter, that people think they are communicating. But face-to-face conversation is largely missing. This is why body consciousness is important. If you are in your own body and conscious of other people's bodies, it may be harder to abstract others, to think of them as different, as dangerous. I want people to be good neighbors. People are hungry for a sensuous relationship with the world that allows them to feel safe and free.

BECKY: Your good-neighbor policy sounds like you are whitewashing power inequalities. It is hard to be a good neighbor if you are homeless. Most of us who have houses don't seem to have a clue about how to be good neighbors to homeless people.

DIANE: If we really listen to each other, we can see who really has the power. What Mayor Bloomberg did after the police killed Sean Bell that was different from what former mayor Giuliani did when the police shot Amadou Diallo forty-one times is that Bloomberg called people in and talked with them.[5] When Giuliani remained silent, he assured people that fear and distance would be maintained. When people came to talk with Bloomberg, they did not come there thinking that they had as much power as the police or the mayor. But smelling each other's breath, looking into each other's eyes, seemed to be a way to communicate with each other so the city could move forward.

BECKY: You are making it sound like we should all just hold hands.

DIANE: No. We need to talk with each other because we are upset about the world we are living in. The pain is too great; enough is enough. People are feeling like they are going to choke on how stultifying their lives are, the mindlessness of TV, the violence that is all around them. We don't need to talk about global warming now since we know we are out of sync. It is sixty degrees, and it is Christmas in the Northeast.

BECKY: We are also living in a time when people are more paranoid than ever, particularly white people.

DIANE: Yet, they still have all the guns.

BECKY: Yes, but on some level people know that guns don't really protect them. All the military in the world could not protect against the 9/11 attacks. When people of color (in this instance, al-Qaeda) can strike at the heart of whiteness, embodied by Wall Street, the fantasy that being from the United States or being white or having money can protect people dissolves. When people can use computers and planes to crash into the World Trade Center, white supremacy has been, at least momentarily, shaken.

DIANE: The attack on the World Trade Center could be interpreted as a "Fanonian" moment—when violence has the effect of decolonizing people's minds.[6] It seems to me that the logic of al-Qaeda was that violence was the only way to get Western attention. We know that Fanon believed that a crucial element of domination is obedience. Fanon argued that people who have been colonized never escape this oppression until they are willing to fight back. When al-Qaeda did violence against the symbols of whiteness, this strategy furthered the creation of a pan-national identity that is distinctly not white. Taking up arms negates the training toward subservience. It opens up the possibility for a new group identity.

BECKY: Historically, armed resistance has often signaled a fundamental change within an organization's identity. When I went to South Africa in 1994, I learned that when the African National Congress decided that nonviolence could no longer be their only strategy for eliminating apartheid, they were forever changed as an organization. In 1961 Mandela asserted that the government's relentless violence against nonviolent protesters had forced them to rethink their fifty-year endorsement of nonviolence.[7] They formed a militant organization that supported armed struggle, which gave new energy and resolve to the antiapartheid movement. Clearly, the ANC's shift in policy was compelling.

DIANE: You're not equating ANC with al-Qaeda are you?

BECKY: You know I am not saying that. There are *many* crucial differences between al-Qaeda and the ANC. Al-Qaeda's only real strategy is violence. Violence is both the means and the end for that network. The ANC saw violence as a means of self-defense but treated this strategy as one of many, including negotiating, changing laws, building community, practicing civil disobedience, and creating peaceful alliances.

DIANE: I see that they are different, but I wonder whether, when we call upon Fanon, people will think we are in some way justifying al-Qaeda's violence.

BECKY: Fanon's theory for decolonizing the mind is seductive, but both of us know it eventually backfires. Fanon was wrong to assert that violence against oppression is the only way that oppressed groups can find an identity. That strategy mimics the oppressors' tactics.

DIANE: With his support of violence as a necessary response to oppression, Fanon advocated the use of the "master's tools," which Audre Lorde taught us come back to haunt us.[8]

BECKY: While the United States has bombed people all over the world and we both understand why people of color all over the world are angry at white supremacy, there is still no justification for the 9/11 attacks.

DIANE: This was the point of the Truth and Reconciliation Commission—to give people a means to deal with violations without causing more violence. Some people don't want to reconcile. They just want to keep dropping bombs. I have always hated bullies. In one of my classes we recently discussed how only one-eighth of the world is white and that when you travel outside of the United States, Europe, Australia, and New Zealand, white people are in the minority. In the past, when white people went places that were primarily composed of people of color, they had to treat them as welcomed guests. Now white people are often ignored or rendered suspect. This means that there are fewer places white people can go. I have traveled all over the world in countries that are populated by people of color. No matter where I go, even China, they decide I am one of them—that I somehow belong. It is starting to dawn on some white people that something is missing for them.

BECKY: On some level, white people know that we will never really belong in the world as long as we are trying to dominate it. The degree of killing done in the name of the United States, killing people we can't see, with automatic weapons—this passionless violence—has a devastating effect on the human psyche. The blackout of the media coverage of the war takes the violence away from our bodies as the images are left unprocessed in our psyches.

DIANE: Perhaps one reason that people were so captivated, seemingly obsessed, with the Abu Ghraib photos is that at least they gave evidence that a real war was being fought. To be honest, I found myself looking at the photos to see what the Iraqis look like. Were they muscular? Tall or short? Did they have kinky or straight hair? They had not felt real to me before. I had heard about them, seen a few Iraqis on television, but all of it was abstract, removed.

BECKY: We are haunted by an invisible presence that is heightened during war. When the United States is at war internationally, state violence domestically seems to escalate too. With the military, with the buildup of prisons and state violence, we are at war on both fronts. The police are very jumpy. Another circling of the wagons.

DIANE: It is not so different from during the nineteenth century, when Marx, Weber, and Durkheim were looking at changes from the rural to the urban, from agriculture to industrialization, from small groups of people to large groups of people, from the religious to the secular. Now the shifts are from the nation-state to a global economy, from white supremacy to another racial formation, from an industrial age to an age of information, from uncontested patriarchy to a patriarchy that is beginning to show cracks.

While the specifics are different, both were times of great change. That is why we revisited the classical theorists. In our minds, it is up to us, as public sociologists, to name these changes and help guide history.

BECKY: Even though I came into this project dreading reading Durkheim, he was right that we need rituals as guides. Durkheim was worried about the end of religious rituals. Through the book, we kept asking if there are rituals that will help fill the void so many people are feeling.

If there is anything that working on this book has taught me, it has been that we are living in the age of the spectacle—which, as we have talked about, is a form of failed ritual. Bin Laden and al-Qaeda were banking on creating a spectacular spectacle that could be played over and over again, eventually taking on a life of its own. The constant replaying of the attack on the towers intensified the experience—it made people feel out of control, like the disaster would never stop—constantly evoking the original fear.

DIANE: A spectacle is something that keeps on giving at the expense of not being able to stop it, to make meaning out of it, to move on.

BECKY: In another context, Dylan Klebold and Eric Harris were creating their own spectacle. They were practicing to make this spectacle right before graduation. They wanted their orchestrated spectacle to give them some kind of immortality, some kind of importance, some way of belonging that they already knew graduation would not provide.

DIANE: Eric and Dylan created a spectacle that succeeded in keeping them in the national memory in a way that nothing else in life might have done for them. I understand their need to be seen.

BECKY: Charles Graner was also trying to create a spectacle with the photos. He sent a birthday notice to his family—one of the photos of his and England's abuse of the Iraqi detainees—that would beat all birthday notices. The photographs became his spectacle, his claim to fame, his evidence that he was in charge, retaliating after the 9/11 attack.

DIANE: On some level, Graner knew that he was from the lowest rung, doing the lowest work, unable to catapult himself out of the business of degrading other people.

BECKY: Katrina, like the other catastrophes we visited, created its own spectacle as women held babies above their heads, as the water rose, calling for help that never came. They became the spectacle that brought no relief. More than a year later, the government is still refusing to see them.

For many years, I have admired the Vietnam Veterans Memorial because it resists becoming a spectacle. Maya Lin created a visual presence to honor those who were killed through the listing of names, one right after the next, etched into marble. This memorial cannot move. The marble has a sensual, living, breathing quality to it—it stays steady, in place for everyone to see. It is a democratic monument, one that anyone can touch, anyone can visit without a fee. Anyone can see her or his reflection in it. The memorial refuses to entertain. It refuses projections. It refuses to be anything other than what it is: a cold, hard naming of thousands of people destroyed by war.

DIANE: The problem with a spectacle is that it titillates but it doesn't go any deeper. It is addictive, but it leaves people feeling empty, not nourished. A spectacle doesn't link us together. There are many examples of failed rituals that people have tried to compensate for by creating a spectacle in their place. So many of the rituals we have now no longer serve the purposes for which they were first created.

BECKY: Thanksgiving used to be a ritual, but it has turned into spectacle. The nostalgic story needs to be replaced by a more complicated and nuanced version of colonial history, a version that shows a chink in white supremacy—that white people never could have survived without Native people, whose generosity they met with genocide. The reliance upon spectacle is one reason why George Bush had no advice for people after 9/11 except that we should go shopping. He had no rituals to offer. We are in need of rituals that can draw communities together in thanks and celebration that are not based on an enduring colonial mentality and consumerism. This is what I like about the Day of Mourning overlooking Plymouth Rock.[9] There is great music, drumming, and real food.

DIANE: Well, you know, I am the first one to eat the turkey. I love the food on Thanksgiving, but it has been reduced to shopping and stuffing ourselves, while looking at Mickey Mouse in the Macy's Thanksgiving Day Parade and football games with over-the-top halftime shows. I'll be convinced about Thanksgiving when they get rid of the racist mascots.

BECKY: I am looking for rituals that aren't spectacle. That's why I wanted to focus on the people in Union Square lighting candles after 9/11, building makeshift altars, reading people's "portraits" in open spaces, working round the clock—all were rituals that helped people mourn. That was much better than shopping.

DIANE: Millions of people made a ritual of reading the portraits every day that were printed in the *New York Times*. This gave me something to talk about with people I had hardly ever spoken to previously. We talked about the people who had died as if we knew them. The portraits were not written as typical, formulaic obits. They gave us lively, unique, intimate pictures of people's families, habits, and inspirations. The portraits were a created ritual—they were, on a mass scale, like what my uncle did by talking about my mother for hours on the day of her funeral. The portraits were a collective witnessing, an honoring of lives lost.

BECKY: Part of the power of that ritual was that it came from the trauma itself. It was not superimposed. It was original and spontaneous. It was not a ritual borrowed from, recycled from, another disaster. It was particular to, and therefore honoring of, 9/11.

DIANE: My friend Ismail is right: the state continues to try to impose rituals that have nothing to do with what we need.[10] Each year, there is a state-sponsored 9/11 event that is so stiff and staged that it has virtually no resemblance to a memorial. Often the state offers up the spectacle of war in place of rituals of mourning and reckoning. Rituals come from the people, but then the state or the market intervenes, supervising rituals that are empty of meaning. Kwanzaa has been so penetrated by the market that it runs the risk of simply becoming a black Christmas, with no spiritual content.[11]

BECKY: We need to create rituals that are regenerative, not destructive. That is why I wanted to call this chapter "Regeneration." With the Abu Ghraib prison abuses, profoundly alienated workers were trying to call attention to themselves, to let the world be a witness to the destruction they were causing. The abuse at Abu Ghraib teaches us that emotional labor in the service of violence requires that workers be angry. In order to do their work, they must violate others and therefore themselves.

DIANE: The problem with portraying Graner and England as "the bad apples" is that the military requires work that is the opposite of re-generative. If guards are taught that all of the prisoners are potential terrorists, it makes sense that they will treat them in a hostile manner. That becomes part of their job.

BECKY: While the military and prisons may be the most obvious ex-amples of institutions that require angry workers, these two institutions aren't exceptions. The idea is that everyone should be angry, or at least mistrustful. No wonder people looked angry to us when we came back from Costa Rica. They are.

The challenge is to rearrange work that can move us from a con-suming to a regenerative society. People deserve to have work that is life-affirming, well-paying, and respected. If people who take care of children, keep company with old people, and feed hungry people are paid well, that is a big step toward regeneration. Marx teaches us that people realize themselves through their work. People create themselves through their work.

DIANE: Part of the reason that Habitat for Humanity and alternative spring breaks, where students travel to do work in communities, are both popular enterprises is that students come back with a sense of being useful and empowered. They return feeling less alone and confused, as having stretched themselves, without the attitude of having helped those "pitiful" people somewhere else. Habitat for Humanity has managed to cut out the missionary approach to service work. Students also get excited about sustainable development, growing vegetables, and learning how to farm. Many of the vegetables that we eat in the cafeteria at school are grown by students working on local farms.

BECKY: It seems like you think it was worth going back to read the three dead white men and Du Bois, to immerse ourselves again. At the beginning of the book we said we had fallen in love with sociology, then became disillusioned and ran to other places. Was it worth coming back?

DIANE: Reading their work again made me understand Western culture better. After having spent so many years in women's studies, where we critique the mind/body split, I had forgotten that the classical theorists were struggling with the mind/body split too. Weber thought that this dualism would never be overcome. When Durkheim could get away from his conservative and overarching categories, when he could give an individual more space to breathe, he and Marx understood the need to heal the mind/body dualism. Marx didn't really leave any space for the irrational as Durkheim did.

BECKY: Even though Durkheim didn't treat "the body" as its own concept, his work on the irrational left some space for the body.

DIANE: Where he ended up (assuming that individual freedom must be subservient to collective moral authority) is not where I would reach, but at least he was grappling with the consequences of a dualistic society. Marx became too dependent upon science, even as he talked about alienation. Du Bois, better than any of them, was trying to heal the mind/body dualism by grappling with the paradoxes of double consciousness.

I remember being blown away as an undergraduate when I first learned about yin and yang, the notion in Chinese philosophy of complementarity. The image of yin and yang curled around each other is so much different from the dichotomies at the base of Western thought: heaven and earth, black and white, male and female, civilized and uncivilized. These dichotomies cut people off from each other, forcing them to get on one side or the other. Religion, whether it be Islam, Christianity, or Judaism, tells people what they need to do to get on the "right side"—whether you are going to inherit the earth or live forever, whether you are going to burn in hell or go to heaven. That is why religion is comforting—the narratives give people road maps. The problem is that those in power can use these narratives to divide and manipulate people.

While doing this project, something finally clicked for me: Western culture makes it so that there is always someone up and another down, someone with power and someone without it. People are never side by side. People become means, not ends. You either get something from the person above you or take something from the person below you.

BECKY: This time around, I still found reading the classical work in the original intimidating. Although in college I had a terrific social theory professor, Michael Kimmel, going to graduate school ate away at my confidence. The grad professor was so obtuse and I could not figure out how the theory had any relation to activism or the real world. I dreaded going to class. The only idea I remember from the whole course is when my professor would take a quarter out of his pocket and ask us how that quarter got its meaning. He would hold that quarter in his hand and, for what seemed like hours, ask us about that quarter. At that point, I never would have thought I would devote two years of my life to explaining why the theorists still matter—that we need to think about that ridiculous quarter. I really feel for students who try to make sense out of the nuances of Marx's alienation or Durkheim's four types of suicide or Weber's minefield of explanations on rationality and irrationality without having teachers who are in love with the material and really know how to make it come alive. That's why I enjoy sitting in on your classes.

I got a kick out of learning more about the individual theorists' biographies—that Marx had terrible boils; that Weber had a long-standing love affair that enabled him to write a spectacular essay on the erotic; that Du Bois loved beautiful clothes, smoked one cigarette after each meal, and went to bed at ten o'clock no matter what; that he persevered even when the academy had little clue about how to support his big, big mind.

DIANE: I teach about these theorists as flawed human beings who were passionately concerned about the world. If I teach these theorists as authoritative voices from afar, students cannot relate to them as human beings. Reading about the theorists as people who struggled *and* who wanted to understand and change the world gives students some hope.

At the same time, they didn't struggle enough, because they didn't have a clue about gender. After doing this book, I understand even better why multicultural feminist theory has been absolutely necessary, that none of the classical theorists should be read without also reading some of the founding women sociologists, as well as contemporary theorists including Patricia Hill Collins, Patricia Williams, Gloria Anzaldúa, María Lugones, and Angela Davis, among others.

BECKY: I think that Anzaldúa is starting to get some of the recognition she deserves. I wish that could have happened more when she was still alive.

DIANE: My women students love Anzaldúa because she gives them a rest from Western dualism. Her concept of the borderlands is a place many of my students want to live or already live. At a coed school, many of the women students are really trying to be men—high-achieving, Hillary Clinton–type career women. But they are finding it hard to compete with the men on men's terms, and women are hesitant to give up the irrational. They are still more concerned about how their classmates feel during a discussion than in making a linear argument. They still have the courage to talk about their personal lives (to not split themselves off into professional/personal compartments). Similarly the black and Latino students typically come to college with a deep respect for the world, which their mothers helped create for them (a respect for the unknown as much as the known, where everything does not have to be proven to be believed, where dance, music, and good food are crucial parts of everyday life).

Once they're in college, these students are taught that, to be successful, they must give up that world for a colder, more rational space. They come to college living in what Anzaldúa referred to as a borderland—a "liminal space"—between a rational and irrational world. Anzaldúa knows there is a world that goes way beyond the rational world that people can inhabit. This possibility affirms the women students and students of color. Reading Anzaldúa puts them in another space that is softer and rounder than the spaces they have to occupy in most of what they read. While the white male students often begin by feeling impatient with Anzaldúa, if they can start listening, her work can help them name why they feel uneasy, less certain, than when they started the course.

BECKY: I think that this book has given us a chance to move beyond Western dualism, including moving beyond the mind/body split.

DIANE: Right. Getting on one side of the line or another is an attempt to feel safe, to find the rationality. That is how we have been trained to think, and we have been rewarded for that. That skill is essential for getting a PhD. That rational way of thinking has a method, a hierarchy, a supposed objectivity that professes to give us a certain piece of mind. At the same time, we chafe against it. Both of us spend as much time as we can in the world of the irrational—music, poetry, film, dance, and play—where the body reigns. And we know that I play more often than you do. But the irrational is something we have been taught to give up, to cordon off, to do when we are not working. We have been taught to squeeze the irrational in and then go back to work. This project made me so anxious because we were trying to create with a mind-body dialectic, where one feeds the other. I couldn't say that what we did was play or work. It was both. I wouldn't say it was fantasy or a purely intellectual event. I know we felt compelled to do it.

We need to be able to incorporate the mind-body dialectic into what we do in the world, so maybe we don't have to "play" or "work" so hard. We can just live. Watching the football games on Christmas Day, people seemed desperate to have a good time—to be seen, to show that they are enjoying themselves, to show that they can feel young and carefree. People are angry through their workday and then spend their evenings trying to "have a good time" in an extreme way. We are so afraid, in part, because we are so split off, so fragmented. Technology moves us toward guns that are supposed to keep us safe from the irrational that we are afraid to let in.

BECKY: We tried to makes space for the irrational in our writing. This is one reason we wrote the book without a contract. I knew a contract would make me feel pressured, and you were afraid it might make us censor ourselves. We gave the irrational free reign early on—by not thinking about the long-term consequences, not thinking if there was a product at the end of the process, not considering whether the scope of the project would overwhelm us. We made a leap of faith to do it.

DIANE: Because I hadn't written a scholarly book before, it was a bit of magical thinking to decide I was going to write on topics that required such detailed and methodical research.

BECKY: Wasn't the magic of the project being able to translate your lightbulb ideas and insights onto the written page?

DIANE: Well, there was some of that, but what I am trying to get to here is the nervousness and anxiety I had about this project. We kept finding that the dialectic between the mind and body, between rational and irrational thought, was the source of a certain intellectual creativity. If something is only irrational, then I need to decide only whether or not it pleases me. If something is only rational, then I have an outside evaluation—does it have all of the footnotes? does it meet scholarly standards? et cetera. With a writing project that puts the rational and irrational together, I found myself anxious because I didn't know how to measure this intellectual creativity.

When I step back from that anxiety, I realize that our approach speaks to the need to put play and work together—to have a new way to reimagine our world. Instead of being split off, we need to be able to join these parts of ourselves. One can feed the other.

BECKY: The anxiety I felt—and I am assuming we are not talking about anxiety as a psychological pathology but rather a socially induced state that Anzaldúa refers to as "psychic restlessness"—related to the type of research that we needed to do given the upheavals we focused on.[12] All of them were recent events and required us to get to alternative news sources, often found in esoteric and out-of-the-way websites. You did all of that research online, as the one of us with those skills. I think particularly back to the work we needed to do for the chapters on Katrina, knowing New Orleans's profoundly mixed-race and multiracial background. We knew we needed to learn about how the Hondurans and the Jamaicans, the Hmong, and the Native Americans were coping, because they were nowhere to be seen in the media spectacle during and after the hurricane. What that meant, however, is that you would send me articles from many sources that I had not heard of. They would come to me in a strange electronic format, separate from the other articles that might have appeared with them in printed text, in a uniform font that made them all look the same.

I had never written a book that relied heavily on Internet sources. I have always craved reading whole books. For me, reading a chapter of a book from an anthology without seeing the other chapters made me feel like I was looking at a few puzzle pieces with no sense of the whole puzzle. I am someone who has rarely used Xeroxed copies of articles in my classes. I assign whole books because I don't want to cut up the author's creation, to fragment the work of creativity and scholarship. That, to me, is a form of Marx's alienation, to cut the production of a book into its parts, to decontextualize it, to remove it from its community.

DIANE: They call it cherry picking.

BECKY: The anxiety for me has been needing to rely upon often decontextualized Internet sources, which then caused more troubles for us when we came to the necessary job of checking and double-checking sources. I want people who are reading books to be able to follow the intellectual trail that footnotes provide. I want people to still be able to hold books in their hands. I did not want to use citations for websites that might disappear by the time this book is out. Our reliance upon the Internet made me feel like we were living in a virtual reality, even as one of the central pleas of the book is for people to have sensual relationships with what they read, feel, and think about. I felt like we were caught up in a process of alienation that is a result of the "advances" of technology.

On the one hand, it was a luxury to get FedEx packages from you with so many Xeroxed copies of articles you had quickly found on the Internet. On the other hand, these packages felt like little bits of information, coming from nowhere to anywhere. This was disorienting for someone who grew up intellectually by sitting on the floor of libraries, between the stacks, pulling books down from the shelves, seeing how whole bodies of scholarship sat next to each other, sidled up to each other. In the past, doing research in a library helped me see conceptual links that I needed to also feel by holding the books. In this project, I felt like technology was being dumped on me. When I did research the old-fashioned way, there was something about reading and writing and thinking that felt sexy to me, that was erotic. With all this technology I lost that connection.

DIANE: The Internet is not what I would call sensual, but I enjoyed going online because that task drew upon my critical skills of being able to decode which of the hundred articles available on a given topic were the three we needed to study closely. The Internet kept me on the rational side of the divide. That is the easy part for me. It was comforting and rational for me to type in three keywords and then narrow down the list of articles that would come up. While these searches overwhelmed you, made you feel impatient and depressed, I felt competent and efficient. I sent you articles that you often thought had no intellectual tether, while I felt quite accomplished about having found ones I knew you needed to read. When you would question a source or the relevance of an article, or want to know about the author, including the author's political background, I would take umbrage because I felt like all of my training was about finding the most relevant existing sources.

BECKY: I feel like I yelled a lot—demanding context, demanding more information about the authors, asking you to find as many sources as possible in printed books. I never overcame my anxiety about writing in the age of the Internet. I also vowed not to write another scholarly book for a long time. The poet in me that I am trying to nurture was fed up with footnotes. I know that footnotes are a political act, a way to show an argument's relationship to a larger political and intellectual community; they are the connective tissue. But the poet in me craves living in a more resonant register, a more unconscious, more irrational place that goes deeper than proof and logic. That is one reason we decided to include poems and photographs and make the writing accessible.

DIANE: Even though trying to fuse the rational and irrational, the conscious and unconscious self, creates anxiety, I don't think we should give up on that fusion. I don't think that this is solely a scholarly book or solely a creative project. It is an attempt to be part of a new intellectual consciousness. As it turns out, we both had a similar anxiety about trying to find that fusion, although it manifested itself in different ways.

The scholarly approach might seem too narrow for you now, but to think of it as merely linear does not reflect the process we used to write—the trances we found ourselves in as we wrote, how we drew upon our own experience, the urgency we felt about doing it, the joy of writing, and the leaps of faith. I don't think this type of writing is more superficial than poetry. In fact, I think it can be deeper and broader than poetry because more people have access to it. It is like lifting weights and walking on the treadmill at the same time.

BECKY: I guess I am looking for writing that is more like yoga and salsa than weight training.

DIANE: *The Souls of Black Folk* is so marvelous because Du Bois is lifting weights, running on the treadmill, doing yoga, and dancing at the same time. It is a creative intellectual piece. His novels, on the other hand, are unremarkable. And some of his later polemical writing is just that. *The Souls of Black Folk* is the fusion we are seeking. It remains a model for us.

I used to think that people couldn't really do sociology until they were older, because when they are young, they really don't know anything yet. I know things now I couldn't have known twenty years ago. I didn't understand the power of the unconscious twenty years ago. I didn't understand the seductive power of consumption. I didn't understand how frightened people are, how fearful most people are every day. It took me the years I am now to appreciate anything about Durkheim. Having come from such a conservative background myself, for a long time I could not tolerate reading his work. I also would have dismissed Condoleezza Rice as simply a Tom twenty-five years ago.

BECKY: This may seem a little harsh, but I think I spent my twenties and thirties projecting onto others what I was most afraid of in myself. I think twenty years ago I would have been so horrified and disturbed by the cast of characters we deal with in this book that I could not have tried to get inside their heads. Twenty years ago I wouldn't have known how to work so intimately with someone whose ways of working and thinking are so different from mine. I would not have been able to trust that the magical process of creating new thought would come to us as long as we kept talking. At this stage of my life I don't have as much to prove in terms of my scholarship, so I could relax a little bit.

DIANE: I often get the big points first, and then you push us to flesh out the nuances. You are a stickler for detail but easily lose your patience if we don't get time to talk about the creative ideas too. Your desk is always in order. If I write anything down, it's on little pieces of paper I tuck in sometimes unfound pockets. From the beginning of this project, we had to deal with my feeling that giving order to the ideas would make me feel trapped and exposed. I was afraid that once I wrote my ideas down for publication, I wouldn't have a chance to change my mind. Those ideas are what I would become to people. When people say to writers, "I know you—you wrote that book," I cringe. I felt like writing would rob me of my privacy, that people would decide who I was and limit me to that. I thought writing would freeze my identity. As we both know, as the project grew, I got more and more chaotic, which made it hard for both of us.

BECKY: I don't think you are alone in terms of feeling trapped and exposed. I think many very bright people don't want to get pinned down by words on the page. Their minds go too fast, their imaginations are too fierce for such a pinning. What you have talked about has also reminded me of Darlene Clark Hine's culture of dissemblance.[13]

DIANE: Hine is right that, as a black woman, the only way I feel whole is to have a private space that no one else can go to, that no one else can see or have access to. I don't want people to get ahold of me and twist me out of shape, or try to hold me down. The culture of dissemblance still lives for me and many other black women. Because I am in touch with the ancestors, I am trying to make sure that I am not violated the way they were.

BECKY: We also ended up disagreeing with each other about accountability and forgiveness, about right and wrong. We could not go into the chapter on Columbine thinking of Dylan Klebold and Eric Harris as individual monsters. We could not approach the Abu Ghraib prison abuses without trying to see them from the point of view of Lynndie England. We definitely needed to understand the critiques underlying al-Qaeda's attack.

DIANE: Unlike you, I haven't gotten over believing that some people are bad and others are good. I am less postmodern than that. I can be sympathetic to anybody's point of view, but I am not without judgment. So many people have been let off the hook for atrocious acts. We have circled back to my student who asked me if we would be talking about the slave master's point of view. I can think about the slave master as someone caught in a society he didn't make, caught up in rules he didn't create, and being a flawed human being. But at the end of the day, I don't have time to worry about him. At the end of the day, someone has to be accountable.

BECKY: Of course I agree with that. But I think we tried to push ourselves to hold people individually accountable and look to the systemic reasons for their behavior. There are social forces and institutions that influence us in ways we often cannot even see. The Durkheimian move in our logic was to recognize the power of social facts in each catastrophe. And that meant staring down, and in some instances undoing rigid ideas about right and wrong, good and bad, et cetera. The rage that Graner and England manifest is widespread. Harris and Klebold's hopelessness lives inside many of us. Rice's opportunism does not stop with her. Osama bin Laden's logic and tactics come out of material realities. Dismissing him as a crazy religious fanatic will not move us forward.

DIANE: One of the themes that weaves through all of the chapters is the taken-for-granted presence of violence in US society. People will be shot. People will have guns. Movies will be violent. Our national pastimes (sports, television shows) will be violent. We can solve all problems with violence. One way that the twenty-first century is different from the nineteenth century is that even though people were at war with each other then, they did not have weapons of mass destruction and the threat of nuclear war.

BECKY: In this age of no innocence, 90 percent of those who die in war are civilians; 75 percent are women and children. A century ago, 90 percent of those who died were men in uniform. This shift changes the nature of living itself.

DIANE: Violence continues to fuel fear. They both heighten suspicion, making it hard to have a cohesive society. Violence diverts vital resources away from life-affirming programs. When I was in China for the UN World Conference on Women in 1995, this tragedy became clear to me when women from several countries in Africa talked about how the money used in warfare was making it impossible for their daughters to go to school and for them to keep themselves and their families healthy. Governments, including the United States, that spend most of their money on the military rob people of basic resources.

BECKY: So we need to imagine a society that is nonviolent.

DIANE: I fear that we will sound like "pie in the sky" again. Another touchy-feely moment.

BECKY: But there are some examples of societies that have made inroads into creating more peaceful places. When we were recently in Tunisia, we were both struck by how much more peaceful it seemed there than in the United States. Some of that is because there is little drug addiction, partly because drug and alcohol use is against Muslim law. There are few guns, and extended families are still intact, which provide a sense of continuity and belonging for Tunisians. Tunisia is not suffering from the overwrought individualism that seems to be endemic to Western society.

DIANE: The collective conscience that Durkheim talks about still exists in Tunisia, partly because of the five-times-a-day call to prayer and reverence for the sacred that are still practiced by many there. Also, the relaxed quality in the air and the county's beauty seemed to make room for imagination.

BECKY: In his book *Freedom Dreams,* Robin Kelley says we need to tap into imagination to change the world.[14] He writes that struggling for change unleashes the mind's most creative capacities. This creativity is what Marx recognizes in his concept of species being. It is the heart of Anzaldúa's mestiza consciousness. It is what Weber considers as the foundation of the mystical.

At the Black Nations/Queer Nations? Conference in New York City in 1995,[15] the social critic and performance artist Coco Fusco showed an extraordinary video clip of South African black women. Faced with bulldozers threatening to mow down their homes and police preparing to arrest them, the women took off their clothes and began dancing and singing in front of the machines. As women who have had to protect their bodies from the white male gaze and violations for so long, their acts of defiance so overwhelmed the police and bulldozer operators that both groups of white men backed off. As the women sang and danced, their naked bodies proudly bearing their full figures—completely in their bodies as they refused to step away from the menace of the tractors—the men and their machines retreated.

At that moment in South African history (the early 1990s), all that the black women had as an immediate resource was their bodies, and that is what they used, collectively and spontaneously. They showed us the power of imagination to stop violence. In the moment when the women were about to watch their entire community be destroyed, they imagined that they could indeed save it. They had no guns, no legal authority, and no money. All they had were their bodies and their imagination. The decades-long antiapartheid struggles for freedom—including the Freedom Charter of the African National Congress; the 1976 Soweto uprising; and Nelson and Winnie Mandela's leadership—allowed the women to dream their freedom. In the crucial moment when the women danced in front of the bulldozers, what they were for—saving their community—took precedence over what they were against. They had to catapult themselves into a consciousness of possibilities, despite the powers against them. Their creativity, innovation, and embodiment are what saved them, and their children, from homelessness.

DIANE: What the women did is another vivid example of body consciousness, of using one's body in the service of liberation. Looking back on it now, I understand that people willingly putting their bodies on the line is one of the reasons that the civil rights movement was so powerful. The South African women's way of stopping destruction also reminds me of Thich Nhat Hanh and his understanding of mindfulness.[16] Both of us have drawn on his writing for years.

BECKY: Of course, I am hesitant to even use the term "mindfulness" because of the way it has been so commercialized, so taken out of context and made into some kind of Hallmark mission.

DIANE: It has been so commodified—"Do these three things and you will find mindfulness." It is true that first white people went native, and now they have gone East, in search of a spiritual salve. At the same time, the whole process of writing this book has been a practice in mindfulness, hasn't it?

The best moments for us were when we were doing it, when we weren't worrying, is this going to be understood, will people read it, are we making sense, will we get a contract? The most productive moments, the most creative moments, were when we lost ourselves in the process, listening to each other deeply. During these times, we would be surprised to find that what seemed like twenty minutes was two hours. We were what athletes have referred to as being "in the zone," when nothing mattered except what we were creating together. Thich Nhat Hanh believes that mindfulness can relieve suffering, can enable people to find creative and positive strategies for bringing peace to the world.[17]

BECKY: Our attention to mindfulness, to being willing to stay in one's body during pain, and refusing to retaliate, can sound like pie in the sky again except that there are multiple examples of people using mindfulness to overcome hardship and discrimination. In *Finding Freedom*, Jarvis Jay Masters, a man on death row in California, chronicles the transformation in his life from being a furious man caught up in a system that encourages men to attack each other to becoming someone able to come up with creative and courageous actions to save other people's lives. He deliberately walked in front of a gay inmate to stop the man from being killed. He convinced three people on death row to flood the floor to stop others from retaliating against two guards who were mistreating them.

Masters never lost his awareness and sense of outrage about the cruelty of prison officials. Nor did he ever lose sight of the multiple hardships that so many prisoners faced as children (child abuse, poverty, neglect, impoverished schools, et cetera) that set so many of the prisoners up for initial incarceration. He understood from personal experience, and from all he saw around him, how the rage and hurt that boys experience can get translated into shame and humiliation. He writes that shame and memories of abuse are locked up in the scars so many men have all over their bodies.[18] He also never lost sight of the injuries caused by those in prison—the crimes they committed that often threatened, if not took, human life. But mindfulness helped him know he did not have a monopoly on suffering. The hardest part of suffering is feeling isolated and alone.

By understanding that suffering is part of the human condition and can be survived, Masters was able to reach across all kinds of differences in the prison to help relieve his own and others' suffering.[19] Meditation gave Masters a way to see he belonged to the world. He asks us to look for signs of belonging.

DIANE: What you are saying about Masters's development of an embodied spirituality reminds me of when we got to hear Armando Hart, the former minister of culture in Cuba, speak when we traveled there together in 2001.[20] He spoke on a range of interrelated topics, beginning with the role of young people in Cuba as older people pass on their batons. Hart explained many of the economic and cultural changes in Cuban society since the Soviet Union collapsed. He talked about José Martí, a leading poet and writer who was one of Castro's cultural heroes.[21] Martí had spent time in the United States and had fallen in love with Walt Whitman, Ralph Waldo Emerson, and other transcendentalists who believed that a human-centered government must glorify spiritual life. Castro, as Martí's philosophical heir, had expected the United States to be more supportive of the Cuban revolution. When the United States rebuked Cuba, Castro was forced to seek Russian support.

Hart said that the primary problem with the Russian view of socialism is that it made no room for spirituality. Socialism had taken into account many moral and ethical principles not accounted for under capitalism. But Hart told us that socialism collapsed in many contexts precisely because it did not account for the spirit. Hart said that spirituality was *the* missing piece in the socialist project in Cuba and that socialism cannot exist over time without attending to matters of the heart and spirit.

BECKY: Since the fall of the Soviet Union, Cuban leadership has been moving more toward Martí's view of society, by validating the presence of spirituality in everyday life. We witnessed this in Cuban art that blended African, Spanish, and Mexican images of divinity. We felt it in African ceremonies held on New Year's Day where African dancing, sculptures, and altars graced the roadways and alleys of entire neighborhoods.

DIANE: They were singing and dancing, but they didn't have much to eat. Meanwhile, the government now depends upon tourism so much that they were willing to arrest a young Afro-Cuban teenager in a tourist-marked section of Havana for simply spending the day with us. It was then that we were so relieved that you had not brought your son, La Mar, with you.

BECKY: Yes. We might not have been able to convince the police that I am his mother.

DIANE: They might just have seen him as another Afro-Cuban boy in the wrong part of town. There was such frisson between how wonderful it was to be there and how terrible that scene was.

BECKY: Yes. I felt so sad that candid talk about bisexual and lesbian life in Cuba was relegated to whispered conversations in bars after the officials had gone off the bed. Many of the artists we met also complained bitterly about difficulties in getting visas to travel outside the country—hardly a sign of imagination and art given free reign. A revolution that makes space for the spirit and imagination is a work in progress in Cuba. An economic-based revolution began in 1959. A revolution that includes the spirit has just begun.

Armando Hart humbly reveals the cost for a society that runs away from spirituality. Jarvis Jay Masters gives us a real example of how meditation and mindfulness expand consciousness. Audre Lorde's work on the erotic shows us that spiritual consciousness is grounded in the body. Kelley's work shows us liberatory locations in the world, where the erotic is manifest in music, art, social change, and the imagination. Thich Nhat Hanh offers mindfulness as a method to feel joy. Put together, the erotic, the imagination, and mindfulness become three crucial elements for healing.

DIANE: We need those theorists now. Classical sociologists electrified people because they offered grand narratives to explain the world. Looking at these writings from the twenty-first century, we know they were not inclusive which is why, in the twentieth century, many people left them behind. But we don't want to ignore their work. It has helped us understand many gut-wrenching catastrophes. We know that activists need social theory.

When I teach my classes, students talk about feeling trapped in a world they didn't make and one they do not know how to change. They become exhausted by all of the analysis if they don't also hear about solutions. I tell them that solutions are all around them. Just today I read an article in the *New York Times* that this is the four-hundredth anniversary of the founding of Jamestown, Virginia. The Virginia legislature issued a statement condemning slavery and the treatment of Native Americans in Virginia. It is not an apology, because there are no reparations attached. If people really apologize, then they need to take steps to repair the damage. That legislature has not done that yet, but it is a beginning.

BECKY: Despite its limits, the Virginia example *is* a sign of hope. Histori-cally in this country, we have been behind ourselves in terms of deal-ing with socially induced upheavals. As a culture, the United States has not stopped long enough to talk about social dis-eases. In Weberian terms, the Protestant ethic about keeping a stiff upper lip and being stoic keeps the United States in forward motion, even when stopping and reflecting might, in the long run, enable us to deal with the up-heavals in more humane and creative ways.

It wasn't until after the 9/11 attacks that Congress offered a formal apology for lynching. When the United States could have been grap-pling with the deep concerns implicit in anti-US sentiment, instead it was dealing with lynching, an injustice that needed to have been con-fronted more than a century ago.

Because the United States has not come to terms with its history of genocide, slavery, and imperialism, it is in a state of arrested develop-ment, stuck in adolescence, destined to repeat the same mistakes over and over again.[22] When the country might have focused on why, in fact, so much of the world is angry at it, why the 9/11 attacks are simply the tip of the iceberg in terms of world rage about US domination, instead we are just beginning to come to terms with slavery.

This book is our attempt to say, "Time out. Stop. Let's slow down a bit, take stock, look at ourselves, and try to make sense out of the deep meaning of these recent catastrophes. Let's not let them pile up, un-accounted for, left for a future that promises to bury them with other destruction."

DIANE: As long as we are one or two or three traumas behind, we aren't in real time. The need to be in real time relates to the need for the irrational that Weber wrote about. The imagination comes from the irrational. Being in the present is what enables people to use their imaginations fully, because they are not stunted by trauma.

BECKY: If we could really take seriously the first traumas—the slave trade and Native genocide—we might then be able to go forward in creative ways. Until reparations are made, we will still be reenacting the old slave-master drama by using violence to control our fears. We all know that slavery would never have been possible without coercion and violence, traumatizing both blacks and whites. Since we never got over that trauma, it is no surprise that police are afraid of an unarmed Sean Bell.

DIANE: It may seem too simple to say that the police saw Sean Bell as an escaped slave but their actions suggest that association still exists. The reason that England, Graner, and others could move right into terror-izing the "Arab colored other" is that slavery remains in white people's historical memory. One solution is to have a truth and reconciliation commission about slavery and then get serious about reparations. We can't get serious about reparations until we have a real conversation. The violence will continue until we are willing to do that.

BECKY: Healing and repairing can take place simultaneously, but they both need to happen. We saw healing in Cuba, but the government does not have enough economic wealth for repair.

DIANE: What is hopeful about the United States is that we have the wealth needed to repair. But we have not yet found the will. If we deal with the traumas in the past, we will then be able to take care of the traumas we focus on in this book.

BECKY: In a recent talk, Cornel West spoke of Mamie Till's eloquence at the memorial for her fourteen-year-old son in 1955 after she had insisted that there be an open casket. Fifty thousand people came to witness his body. At the time, she said "I don't have a minute to hate. I will pursue justice for the rest of my life." West juxtaposed this ethic against Bush's reference to the military's mission to kill all of the cockroaches in response to 9/11.[23] West's reference to Till's composure teaches us again that solutions are all around us when we are listening. West has long said that the struggle for justice always relies upon cour-age. Ultimately we envision a world where humanity is sacred, where all people know they belong.

# NOTES

## INTRODUCTION

1. For a helpful summary of the limits and uses of postmodernism in an activist-based sociology, see Joe R. Feagin and Hernán Vera, *Liberation Sociology* (Boulder, CO: Westview, 2001), 219–223.

2. The sociologist Herbert Gans used the term "public sociology" in 1988 to describe sociologists who write accessibly and with imagination, publish in both scholarly and popular publications, engage in a wide range of subjects and social concerns, and use rigorous methods to explicate deep social concerns. While the term itself is recent, the existence of public sociology goes back to the beginning of sociological inquiry. See Herbert Gans, "Sociology in America: The Discipline and the Public; American Sociological Association 1988 Presidential Address," *American Sociological Review* 54 (February 1989), 1–16.

3. Patricia Hill Collins, "W. E. B. Du Bois: Preeminent Public Sociologist," panel presentation, Presidential Plenary, "W. E. B. Du Bois: Lessons for the 21st Century," ninety-ninth annual American Sociological Association, San Francisco, August 13, 2004.

4. Gloria T. Hull, Patricia Bell Scott, and Barbara Smith, eds., *All the Women Are White, All the Blacks Are Men, but Some of Us Are Brave: Black Women's Studies* (New York: Feminist Press, 1982).

5. Karl Marx, "Manifesto of the Communist Party," in *The Marx-Engels Reader,* ed. Robert C. Tucker (New York: Norton, 1972), 331–362.

6. Max Weber, *The Protestant Ethic and the Spirit of Capitalism* (New York: Charles Scribner's Sons, 1958), 181.

7. W. E. B. Du Bois, *The Souls of Black Folk* (New York: Vintage, 1990); C. W. Mills, *The Sociological Imagination* (New York: Oxford, 1959).

8. Johnnetta B. Cole, *Anthropology for the 1990s* (New York: Free Press, 1988); Gerrit Huizer and Bruce Mannheim, eds., *The Politics of Anthropology: From Colonialism and Sexism toward a View from Below* (Paris: Mouton Publishers, 1979).

9. Mills, *Sociological Imagination,* 15.

10. Hans Gerth and Saul Landau, "The Relevance of History to the Sociological

Ethos," in *Sociology on Trial,* ed. Maurice Stein and Arthur Vidich (Englewood Cliffs, NJ: Prentice-Hall, 1963), 31.

11. Steven Seidman, *Contested Knowledge: Social Theory in the Postmodern Era* (Cambridge, MA: Blackwell, 1994), 3–4.

12. Alvin W. Gouldner, "Anti-Minotaur: The Myth of a Value-Free Sociology," in *Sociology on Trial,* ed. Maurice Stein and Arthur Vidich (Englewood Cliffs, NJ: Prentice-Hall, 1963), 35.

13. Patricia J. Williams, *The Alchemy of Race and Rights: Diary of a Law Professor* (Cambridge, MA: Harvard University Press), 73.

14. Patricia Hill Collins, *Black Feminist Thought: Knowledge, Consciousness, and the Politics of Empowerment* (Boston: Unwin Hyman, 1990), 26; Adrienne Rich, *Blood, Bread, and Poetry: Selected Prose, 1979–1985* (New York: Norton, 1986), 210–231; Williams, *Alchemy of Race and Rights,* 3.

15. Du Bois, *Souls of Black Folk,* 8.

16. Karl Marx, *The Economic and Philosophic Manuscripts of 1844,* ed. Dirk J. Struik (New York: International Publishers, 1964).

17. Frantz Fanon, *Black Skin, White Masks* (New York: Grove Press, 1967); Frantz Fanon, *The Wretched of the Earth* (New York: Grove Press, 1963).

18. Audre Lorde, *Sister Outsider* (New York: Crossing Press, 1984), 53–59.

19. Ralph Ellison, *Invisible Man* (New York: Random House, 1947).

20. There are many psychic and spiritual connections between blacks and Mormons as well as Mormons and native people of the US West and Southwest. For example, many Las Vegas businesses are owned by Mormons who, according to their theology, forbid alcohol use, premarital sex, and other "sins of the flesh." In a parallel way, many American Indians are now financing their schools and communities through the profits from casinos all over the country. Both Mormons and Native people are creating "good hells"—pleasure palaces from which many people, once they go, never want to return home. The making of money wrapped up with pleasure is a quintessential American concept.

21. For an analysis of the complications of such an identification in terms of anti-racism, see Becky Thompson, "Time Traveling and Border Crossing: Notes on White Identity," in *Names We Call Home: Autobiography on Racial Identity,* ed. Becky Thompson and Sangeeta Tyagi (New York: Routledge, 1996), 92–109.

22. Akasha Gloria Hull, *Soul Talk: The New Spirituality of African American Women* (Rochester, VT: Inner Traditions, 2001).

### CHAPTER ONE

1. Paul Frymer, Dara Z. Strolovitch, and Dorian T. Warren, "New Orleans Is Not the Exception: Re-politicizing the Study of Racial Inequality," *Du Bois Review: Social Science Research on Race* 3, no. 1 (2006): 37–57.

2. Anthony Paul Farley, "The Station," in *After the Storm: Black Intellectuals Ex-*

*plore the Meaning of Hurricane Katrina,* ed. David Dante Troutt (New York: New Press, 2006), 148.

3. Michael Eric Dyson, *Come Hell or High Water: Hurricane Katrina and the Color of Disaster* (New York: Basic Books, 2006).

4. Angela Y. Davis, "Race and Criminalization: Black Americans and the Punishment Industry," in *The House That Race Built: Black Americans, U.S. Terrain,* ed. Wahneema Lubiano (New York: Pantheon, 1997), 267.

5. Highly visible conservative Latinos include Linda Chavez, former secretary of labor, author, and pundit; Manny Diaz, the mayor of Miami; Alberto Gonzales, US attorney general in the second Bush administration; Abel Maldonado, a California state senator; and others.

6. Jean Hardisty, *Mobilizing Resentment: Conservative Resurgence from the John Birch Society to the Promise Keepers* (Boston: Beacon, 1999); Cornel West, *Race Matters* (Boston: Beacon, 1993).

7. Du Bois, *Souls of Black Folk.*

8. For a dynamic and beautifully written anthology of essays on Du Bois's relevance today, see Gerald Early, ed., *Lure and Loathing: Essays on Race, Identity, and the Ambivalence of Assimilation* (New York: Penguin Press, 1993).

9. High-profile black conservatives include, among others, Clarence Thomas, a strict constructionist interpreter of the Constitution and the second black Supreme Court justice in the history of the Court; Thomas Sowell, an economist and senior fellow at the Hoover Institution on War, Revolution and Peace at Stanford University; Glenn Loury, a former professor at Harvard University's Kennedy School of Government; Tony Brown, a journalist who has a widely watched syndicated talk show; and Alan Keyes, a Harvard-trained political scientist and a former Republican presidential contender.

10. Combahee River Collective, "The Combahee River Collective Statement," in *Home Girls: A Black Feminist Anthology,* ed. Barbara Smith (New Brunswick, NJ: Rutgers University Press, 1983, 2000), 264. Citations are to the 2000 edition.

11. Robin Givhan, "Condoleezza Rice's Commanding Clothes," *Washington Post,* February 25, 2005, CI.

12. Martin Luther King Jr., "I Have a Dream," in *I Have a Dream: Writings and Speeches That Changed the World,* ed. James M. Washington (New York: HarperCollins, 1992), 105.

13. Michael K. Brown, Martin Carnoy, Elliott Currie, Troy Duster, David B. Oppenheimer, Marjorie M. Shultz, and David Wellman, *Whitewashing Race: The Myth of a Color-Blind Society* (Berkeley: University of California, 2005), 3.

14. Eduardo Bonilla-Silva, *Racism without Racists: Color-Blind Racism and the Persistence of Racial Inequality in the United States,* 2nd ed. (Lanham, MD: Rowman and Littlefield, 2006).

15. Nicholas Lemann, "Without a Doubt," *New Yorker,* October 14 and 21, 2002, 171.

16. Ibid., 172.

17. *W. E. B. Du Bois Speaks: Speeches and Addresses, 1890–1919,* ed. Philip Foner (New York: Pathfinder, 1970), 27.

18. Du Bois's autobiographical work, and other work as well, underscores his yearning to do sociology, even when his appointments were in other departments and his activism took him in other directions. In Berlin, he actively sought out sociologists, including Max Weber and Gustav Schmoller, who encouraged his career as a sociologist. At Wilberforce College, Du Bois offered to teach a sociology course, unpaid, but the administration turned him down. During his first years at Atlanta, Du Bois taught many courses with sociological content, although his official appointment was in history and economics. In fact, it was not until 1934, when he returned to Atlanta University for the second time, that he officially taught sociology, now as chair of the sociology department at the university. Du Bois also organized an association of sociologists in 1897, almost a decade before the American Sociological Association was founded, and he trained many scholars who went on to careers in sociology. We emphasize Du Bois's devotion and contribution to sociology, since what some have called the sociological fraternity (white sociologists in positions of authority) has often written Du Bois out of the sociological canon. See *W. E. B. Du Bois on Sociology and the Black Community,* ed. Dan S. Green and Edwin D. Driver (Chicago: University of Chicago, 1978), 39.

19. *Du Bois Speaks,* 32.

20. W. E. B. Du Bois, *The Philadelphia Negro: A Social Study* (Millwood, NY: Kraus-Thomson, 1973).

21. *Du Bois on Sociology,* 37.

22. *Du Bois Speaks,* 37.

23. *Du Bois on Sociology,* 12–13.

24. Herbert Aptheker and Fay Aptheker, "Personal Reflections on W. E. B. Du Bois: The Person, Scholar, and Activist," in *Against the Odds: Scholars Who Challenged Racism in the Twentieth Century,* ed. Benjamin P. Bowser and Louis Kushnick (Amherst: University of Massachusetts, 2002), 165.

25. *Du Bois Speaks,* 39.

26. Aptheker and Aptheker, "Personal Reflections," 166.

27. *Du Bois Speaks,* 50.

28. W. E. B. Du Bois, *Black Reconstruction in America, 1860–1880* (New York: Free Press, 1998).

29. Aptheker and Aptheker, "Personal Reflections," 166.

30. *W. E. B. Du Bois: Writings* (New York: Library of America, 1986), 551.

31. David Levering Lewis, *W. E. B. Du Bois: Biography of a Race, 1868–1919* (New York: Henry Holt, 1993), 1–10.

32. *The Oxford W. E. B. Du Bois Reader,* ed. Eric J. Sundquist (New York: Oxford, 1996), 624.

33. Aptheker and Aptheker, "Personal Reflections," 187.

34. Ibid., 189.

35. Ibid.

36. Gerald Horne, *Race Woman: The Lives of Shirley Graham Du Bois* (New York: New York University Press, 2000).

37. *Du Bois: Writings*, 792.

38. Martin Luther King Jr., "Honoring Dr. Du Bois," in *Du Bois Speaks*, 16.

39. Aptheker and Aptheker, "Personal Reflections," 185. Sundquist writes, "In finding the voice of his own leadership, Du Bois had to balance his northern birth against his desire to speak also for the black South; his elite intellectual tastes against his commitment to the equal importance of folk art; his immersion in a political tradition of liberal individualism against his evolving belief that socialism promised a more just world; his hope to link African America's liberation to anticolonial movements in Africa against the view of some Africans that he had little to offer them; and his own mixed race heritage against the suspicions of those American blacks who considered him, by reason of his birth and his privileged education, inherently a traitor to the racial cause" (*Oxford Du Bois Reader*, 7–8).

40. *The Souls of Black Folk* was reprinted twenty-four times by 1940 and then reissued again in the 1960s, with substantial attention since. Historian William Ferris identified *Souls* as "the political Bible of the Negro race" (*Oxford Du Bois Reader*, 8). John Edgar Wideman has called it "a beacon, a rallying cry." He professes, "If I could put one and only one book into the hands of students to whom I was teaching post–Civil War American history, I would choose without hesitation *The Souls of Black Folk*" (introduction to *Souls of Black Folk*, xi, xii).

41. *Oxford Du Bois Reader*, 15.

42. For a new introduction to *The Souls of Black Folk* that pays special attention to Du Bois's love for and writing about black music, see Farah Jasmine Griffin, introduction to *The Souls of Black Folk*, by W. E. B. Du Bois (New York: Barnes and Noble Classics, 2003), xv–xxviii.

43. Du Bois, *Souls of Black Folk*, 8–9.

44. Ibid., 226.

45. Ibid., 150–155.

46. Antonia Felix, *Condi: The Condoleezza Rice Story* (New York: New Market Press, 2005), 47.

47. Richard Cullen Rath, "Echo and Narcissus: The Afrocentric Pragmatism of W. E. B. Du Bois," *Journal of American History* 84, no. 2 (September 1997): 484.

48. *Oxford Du Bois Reader*, 305.

49. Ibid.

50. Ibid.

51. Du Bois, *Souls of Black Folk*, 68–82.

52. Donald B. Gibson, introduction to *The Souls of Black Folk* (New York Penguin, 1989), xii.

53. Felix, *Condi*, 43.

54. In 1989, while Rice was a tenured professor in political science at Stanford University, Brent Scowcroft, the national security adviser for former president George H. W.

Bush, appointed Rice to the National Security Council in Washington D.C.; during this time she met and became friends with the president and Mrs. Bush. While a provost at Stanford University, Rice became a protégée of former secretary of state George Shultz, who facilitated Rice's increasing contact with George W. Bush; in 1999, Rice became Bush's top foreign-policy adviser (Lemann, "Without a Doubt," 164, 166). As a girl whose relationship with her father was both close and directive, Rice learned early how to negotiate relationships with powerful men — facilitating the role she played with many influential men later.

55. Felix, *Condi*, 12–13.

56. Our interpretation of double consciousness reflects that of scholars who have traced the formative influence of African philosophy, particularly Du Bois's understanding of animism, collective souls, and ancestor communication, on *The Souls of Black Folk*. This scholarship interprets double consciousness as multiple and collective, as both benefit and liability. Other scholars have interpreted double consciousness as a division and fragmentation within the individual psyche that requires eventual unification. For a nuanced and detailed discussion of the merits of the first interpretation of double consciousness, see Rath, "Echo and Narcissus," 477–484.

57. Ibid., 478.

58. Karen Fields, "Individuality and the Intellectuals: An Imaginary Conversation between W. E. B. Du Bois and Emile Durkheim," *Theory and Society* 31 (2002): 445.

59. Ibid.

60. The belief in having access to one's ancestors can be seen in numerous African American death rituals. For example, after Diane's mother's death, Diane's uncle spoke about his sister, telling stories about her for six hours and never repeating himself. On this occasion, Diane realized what it meant to have a griot in the community, and the import of such a figure. Her uncle was helping her mother journey into the land of the ancestors, bringing people together as a community, and celebrating her life, all while telling stories that embodied her spirit. The people who gathered ate the cake she had baked right before she died. The material embodiment of her spirit was taken into their bodies through the food.

61. Rath, "Echo and Narcissus," 484.

62. Stanley Crouch and Playthell Benjamin, *Reconsidering the Souls of Black Folk: Thoughts on the Groundbreaking Classic Work of W. E. B. Du Bois* (Philadelphia: Running Press, 2002), 6.

63. Rath, "Echo and Narcissus," 482–483.

64. Felix, *Condi*, 70.

65. Lemann, "Without a Doubt," 169.

66. Felix, *Condi*.

67. Lemann, "Without a Doubt," 168.

68. Patricia Hill Collins, *Fighting Words: Black Women and the Search for Justice* (Minneapolis: University of Minnesota Press, 1998), 14.

69. P. H. Collins, *Black Feminist Thought*, 11–13.

70. Ibid.; Judith Rollins, *Between Women: Domestics and Their Employers* (Phila-

delphia: Temple University Press, 1985); Margaret Walker, *Jubilee* (New York: Bantam Books, 1966).

71. Lemann, "Without a Doubt," 167.

72. Ibid., 171.

73. P. H. Collins, *Fighting Words,* 20.

74. Ibid., 35.

75. Patricia Williams, "From Birmingham to Baghdad," *Nation,* December 13, 2004, 12.

76. Thank you to Ethelbert Miller and Cornell Coley for helping us conjure up the name for the twenty-first-century neo-Mammy.

## CHAPTER TWO

1. John M. Broder, "Amid Criticism of Federal Efforts, Charges of Racism Are Lodged," *New York Times,* September 5, 2005, A9.

2. Ibid.

3. Allen Ginsberg, *Howl and Other Poems* (San Francisco: City Lights Books, 1959); Toni Morrison, *Beloved* (New York: Plume, 1987); Toni Morrison, *The Bluest Eye* (New York: Washington Square Press, 1972).

4. David E. Stannard, *American Holocaust: Columbus and the Conquest of the New World* (New York: Oxford University Press, 1992), 151.

5. John Edgar Wideman, "In Praise of Silence," in *The Writing Life: Writers on How They Think and Work,* ed. Marie Arana (New York: Public Affairs, 2003), 114.

6. James Dao and N. R. Kelinfield, "More Troops and Aid Reach New Orleans," *New York Times,* September 3, 2005, A1.

7. Ralph Ranalli, "Evacuees Say They Were Told Little Before Arrival," *Boston Globe,* September 10, 2005, B7.

8. Patricia Williams, "The View from Lott's Porch," *Nation,* September 26, 2005, 10.

9. Brian MacQuarrie and Tatsha Robertson, "For Many, Frustrated Attempts to Reunite," *Boston Globe,* September 7, 2005, 3rd edition, A12.

10. Lee Jenkins, "After the Deluge, A Football Foothold in Houston," *New York Times,* September 10, 2005, B15.

11. Sarah Schweitzer, "Elite Colleges' Welcome Brings Unexpected Boon," *Boston Globe,* September 10, 2005, A1, 13.

12. Storm and Crisis: Government Responses. Photo with caption, "After Two Weeks, a Rescue," *New York Times,* September 14, 2005, A23, national edition.

13. Peter Kihss, "Benign Neglect," *New York Times,* March 1, 1970, A1, 69.

14. Manning Marable, *How Capitalism Underdeveloped Black America* (Boston: South End Press, 1983), 118.

15. Ralph Blumenthal. "'Prison City' Shows a Hospitable Face to Refugees from New Orleans," *New York Times,* September 6, 2005, A22.

16. Philip D. Curtin, *The Atlantic Slave Trade: A Census* (Madison: University of Wisconsin Press, 1969).

17. Gil Scott-Heron and Brian Jackson, "Peace Go with You, Brother," on *Winter in America* (TVT Records, 1998).

18. Du Bois, *Souls of Black Folk,* 16.

19. Hazel V. Carby, *Race Men* (Cambridge, MA: Harvard University Press, 1998).

20. Darlene Clark Hine, "'In the Kingdom of Culture': Black Women and the Intersection of Race, Gender, and Class," in *Lure and Loathing: Essays on Race, Identity, and the Ambivalence of Assimilation,* ed. Gerald Early (New York: Penguin, 1993), 338. See also Patricia Hill Collins, *Black Sexual Politics: African Americans, Gender, and the New Racism* (New York: Routledge, 2005).

21. Zillah Eisenstein, "Katrina and Her Gendering of Class and Race," *National Women's Studies Association Action* 17, no. 1 (Fall 2005): 8.

22. Darlene Clark Hine, "Rape and the Inner Lives of Black Women in the Middle West: Preliminary Thoughts on the Culture of Dissemblance," in *Words of Fire: An Anthology of African-American Feminist Thought,* ed. Beverly Guy-Sheftall (New York: New Press, 1995), 380.

23. Ann duCille, "The Occult of True Black Womanhood: Critical Demeanor and Black Feminist Studies," *Signs: Journal of Women in Culture and Society* 19, no. 3 (Spring 1994): 605.

24. Quoted in Hine, "Rape and the Inner Lives of Black Women," 380.

25. Cornel West, "Exiles from a City and from a Nation," *Observer,* September 11, 2005, 19.

26. Sharon Malinowski and Anna Sheets, eds., *The Gale Encyclopedia of Native American Tribes* (Detroit: Thomson Gale, 1998), vol. 1, 395–399, 444–448.

27. Before the Louisiana Purchase in 1803, Louisiana was settled by the French, under Spanish rule. The French ceded Louisiana to Spain in 1762, regained it in 1800, and then sold it to Thomas Jefferson in 1803.

28. Amy Goodman, "Honduran Immigrants in New Orleans: Fleeing Hurricanes Mitch, Katrina and Now the U.S. Government," *Democracy Now!* September 13, 2005, http://www.democracynow.org/article.pl?sid=05/09/13/1354211.

29. Ibid.

30. Brenda Norrell, "Tunica-Biloxi Shelter Storm Refugees," *Indian Country Today,* September 7, 2005, A1, and "Louisiana Tribes Receive No Federal Aid," *Indian Country Today,* October 5, 2005, A4; Daffodil Altan, "After Katrina, Where Have All the Hondurans Gone?" Pacific News Service, September 13, 2005, http://news.pacificnews.org/news/, and "Ethnic Communities Rally to Help Katrina Survivors," Pacific News Service, September 7, 2005, http://news.pacificnews.org/news/; C. Stone Brown, "Katrina's Forgotten Victims: Native American Tribes," Pacific News Service, September 11, 2005, http://news.pacificnews.org/news/.

31. Gloria Anzaldúa, *Borderlands/La Frontera: The New Mestiza* (San Francisco: Aunt Lute Books, 1987).

32. Ibid., 3.

33. Ibid., 77.

34. Ibid., 78. For Anzaldúa, psychic restlessness was part of her lived reality as a mestiza woman. It was reflected, for example, in her realization that she had to leave Texas, where she was finishing her PhD, after learning that the faculty in her department did not believe that Chicana literature existed or was worth studying. She could not be at home in the state where she was raised in order to study the writing of women, like herself, who fashioned words based on their multiple identities. Anzaldúa's and Cherríe Moraga's decision to co-edit *This Bridge Called My Back: Writings by Radical Women of Color* (New York: Kitchen Table Women of Color Press, 1983)—which is widely considered a foundational text of the multiracial feminist movement of the 1970s and 1980s in the United States—was motivated by a psychic restlessness she experienced when, after moving to the San Francisco Bay area, the white feminists she met tended to include her writing as an example of their liberalism rather than for her theoretical contributions. Anzaldúa's psychic restlessness also motivated her to revise the mythology of Mesoamerican earth goddesses, including Coatlicue, whom the conquering Aztecs portrayed as monstrous but whom Anzaldúa envisioned as embodying both male and female, light and dark, upper and lower world—in effect, a multidimensional, powerful goddess. For Anzaldúa, psychic restlessness requires creativity and healing at the level of the body, mind, and spirit.

35. For an analysis of the resonant connections between Anzaldúa's and Du Bois's writing, see Theresa A. Martinez, "The Double-Consciousness of Du Bois and the 'Mestiza Consciousness' of Anzaldúa," *Race, Class, and Gender* 9, no. 4 (2002): 158–176.

36. Edwidge Danticat, "Another Country," *Progressive*, November, 2005, 25, 26.

37. Monica Campbell, "Post Katrina Easing of Labor Laws Stirs Debate," *Christian Science Monitor*, October 4, 2005, 1.

38. Helene Cooper, "Rice's Hurdles on Middle East Begin at Home," *New York Times*, August 10, 2006, A1, A12.

39. A. Leon Higginbotham, "An Open Letter to Justice Clarence Thomas from a Federal Judicial Colleague," in *Race-ing Justice, En-gendering Power: Essays on Anita Hill, Clarence Thomas, and the Construction of Social Reality*, ed. Toni Morrison (New York: Pantheon, 1992), 5.

40. Joetta L. Sack, "Teachers' Jobs in Hurricane-Ravaged Areas in Limbo," *Education Week*, November 16, 2005, 3, 17.

### CHAPTER THREE

1. James Der Derian, "9/11: Before, After, and In Between," in *Understanding September 11*, ed. Craig Calhoun, Paul Price, and Ashley Timmer (New York: New Press, 2002), 182.

2. Max Weber, *From Max Weber: Essays in Sociology*, ed. H. H. Gerth and C. W. Mills (New York: Oxford University Press, 1946), 10.

3. Ibid., 11; Fred Pampel, *Sociological Lives and Ideas: An Introduction to the Clas-

*sical Theorists* (New York: Worth, 2000), 96. Although the bulk of the scholarly attention to Weber's breakdown focuses on his relationship with his father, Weber also left documentation of being tormented by sexual feelings from 1898 until the end of his life. Given his strict Calvinist upbringing (which made little or no room for pleasure) and his extramarital affairs, it makes sense to account for this stress in his life as well. Arthur Mitzman writes that "a major cause of his breakdown and the painful years of recovery was probably the compounding of his guilt over his father's death by a parallel guilt over his inability to control his sexual impulses" (*The Iron Cage: An Historical Interpretation of Max Weber* [New York: Grosset and Dunlap, 1969], 285).

4. *From Max Weber,* 24.

5. Ibid., 25.

6. Max Weber, "Science as a Vocation," in *From Max Weber,* 129–156.

7. *From Max Weber,* 27.

8. Rationality and irrationality may also be among his most complicated concepts. Weber uses the term "rationality" in multiple ways. As Rogers Brubaker notes, "No fewer than sixteen apparent meanings of 'rational' can be culled from this highly schematic summary of Weber's characterization of modern capitalism and ascetic Protestantism: deliberate, systematic, calculable, impersonal, instrumental, exact, quantitative, rule-governed, predictable, methodical, purposeful, sober, scrupulous, efficacious, intelligible and consistent" (*The Limits of Rationality: Essays on the Social and Moral Thought of Max Weber* [London: Allen and Unwin, 1984], 2). Weber wrote about the terms across his life span and in relation to many different regions, religions, and historical time periods (from rationality in China to its sources in the United States, from formal rationality characteristic of juries and bureaucracies to substantive rationality characteristic of slave owners and monarchies).

Weber uses the term "irrationality" in equally expansive and ambiguous ways, from irrationality evident in romantic love and the irrationality of a charismatic leader's authority to the irrationality (illogic, destructiveness) that arises as a protest against the stranglehold of rationalization. To further complicate the situation, while the English translation for "rational" and "irrational" suggest that these two terms are antonyms, the German words Weber uses do not imply that the terms are opposites. Weber's work on rationality and irrationality can also be confusing since his writing has been interpreted in various, often contradictory ways since the 1930s, interpretations that speak both to the versatility of his work and to its ambiguity.

9. Max Weber, *Protestant Ethic.*

10. Pampel, *Sociological Lives and Ideas,* 98.

11. Some scholars have argued that the relationship between Protestantism and capitalism may be more dialectical than Weber assumed and that he was wrong to assert that capitalism did not exist in Asian and Middle Eastern countries. The point we are interested in, however, is how religious ethics and economics may interface. R. H. Tawney, *Religion and the Rise of Capitalism* (New York: Transaction Publishers, 1998).

12. Frank Parkin, *Max Weber* (London: Routledge, 1982), 44.

13. Lawrence A. Scaff, "Remnants of Romanticism: Max Weber in Oklahoma and

Indian Territory," in *The Protestant Ethic Turns 100: Essays on the Centenary of the Weber Thesis*, ed. William H. Swatos and Lutz Kaelber (Boulder, CO: Paradigm Books, 2005), 81.

14. While Weber's belief in a connection between the Protestant ethic and the growth of capitalism is accurate, his focus on that connection obscured the centrality of white theft of native land and slavery in the rapid industrialization of the United States. What Weber saw as an astonishing accumulation of wealth (which he attributed to the Protestant ethic) was a direct result of the work of slaves, whose labor was the cornerstone of industrialization, and the white takeover of billions of acres of land formerly cared for by Native people. Slavery and internal colonialism ensured that this wealth was overwhelmingly in white hands.

15. Max Weber, *Protestant Ethic*, 71.

16. Ibid., 53.

17. Ibid., 181.

18. "Disenchantment of the world" is a phrase originally coined by Fredrich Schiller that Weber then developed in his own work. See *From Max Weber*, 51, 155, 350.

19. Anthony Giddens, *Capitalism and Modern Social Theory: An Analysis of the Writings of Marx, Durkheim, and Max Weber* (New York: Cambridge University Press, 1971), 183.

20. Max Weber, *Protestant Ethic*, 182.

21. Julien Freund, *The Sociology of Max Weber* (New York: Vintage, 1968), 25.

22. Ernest Becker, *The Denial of Death* (New York: Free Press, 1973), ix.

23. Weber's nuanced understanding of rituals in premodern societies is one of many indicators that he did not see history as necessarily progressing over time—i.e., he did not regard rationally based, modern society as better or more advanced than earlier social organizations. In fact, in many places in his work he emphasized the costs of change, including how societies that are rooted in scientific knowledge and calculation give people theoretical access to knowing but little lived experience to make knowing real. See, for example, Max Weber, "Science as a Vocation," in *From Max Weber*, 139. See also Freund, *Sociology of Max Weber*, 20–21.

24. *From Max Weber*, 347.

25. Ibid.

26. Marianne Weber wrote eight books of social analysis and was widely recognized as a social theorist, a sociologist of law, and an activist. She also wrote *Max Weber: A Biography* (New Brunswick, NJ: Transaction Books, 1988) and was responsible for the posthumous publication of many volumes of Weber's work. Patricia Madoo Lengermann and Gillian Niebrugge, *The Women Founders: Sociology and Social Theory, 1830–1930* (New York: Waveland, 2007), 193.

27. Mitzman, *Iron Cage*, 148–157.

28. Ibid., 253–254, 271, 274, 296.

29. Max Weber, *Protestant Ethic*, 105.

30. Freund, *Sociology of Max Weber*, 25.

31. *From Max Weber*, 52.

CHAPTER FOUR

1. The temporary creation of new communities as a response to trauma has been documented by other sociologists as well, in particular by researchers who study disaster. See Kai T. Erikson's important work including *Everything in Its Path: Destruction of Community in the Buffalo Creek Flood* (New York: Simon and Schuster, 1976) and *A New Species of Trouble: The Human Experience of Modern Disasters* (New York: Norton, 1995).

2. Janet Abu-Lughod, "After the WTC Disaster: The Sacred, the Profane, and Social Solidarity," Social Science Research Council, After September 11: Terrorism and Democratic Virtues, October 19, 2001, http://www.ssrc.org/sept11/essays/abu-lughod.htm.

3. Moustafa Bayoumi, "How Does It Feel to Be a Problem?" in *Asian Americans on War and Peace,* ed. Russell C. Leong and Don T. Nakanishi (Los Angeles: UCLA Asian American Studies Center Press, 2002), 83.

4. Judith Greenberg, "Wounded New York," in *Trauma at Home: After 9/11,* ed. Judith Greenberg (Lincoln: University of Nebraska, 2003), 23.

5. Allen Cohen and Clive Matson, eds., *An Eye for An Eye Makes the Whole World Blind: Poets on 9/11* (Oakland, CA: Regent Press, 2002); William Heyen, ed., *September 11, 2001: American Writers Respond* (Silver Spring, MD: Etruscan Press, 2002).

6. *From Max Weber,* 354.

7. Ibid., 51, 155, 350.

8. David R. Loy, "The Means/Ends Problem in Modern Culture," *International Studies in Philosophy* 26, no. 4 (2002): 50.

9. Toni Morrison, "The Dead of September 11," in Greenberg, *Trauma at Home,* 1.

10. Ibid.

11. Here we are drawing on Cathy Caruth's *Unclaimed Experience: Trauma, Narrative, and History* (Baltimore and London: Johns Hopkins University Press, 1996), which is quoted in Greenberg, "Wounded New York," 23.

12. Max Weber, *Protestant Ethic,* 181.

13. Tram Nguyen, *We Are All Suspects Now: Untold Stories from Immigrant Communities after 9/11* (Boston: Beacon, 2005).

14. In New York City's taxi industry, which is 60 percent South Asian and 85 percent Muslim, drivers experienced verbal and physical abuse and damage to their taxis long after the 9/11 attacks. This abuse was rarely reported as a hate crime, because of the difficulty in "proving" the motivation (racism and religious discrimination) underlying the violent acts. Monisha Das Gupta, "Hate Crimes," in *Keywords of Contemporary America/Gendai Amerika No Kiiwaado,* ed. Mari Yoshihara and Yurin Yaguchi (Tokyo: Chuo Koron Shinsha, 2006), 130–134.

15. Monisha Das Gupta, "Bewildered? Women's Studies and the War on Terror," in *Interrogating Imperialism: Conversations on Gender, Race, and War,* ed. Robin Riley and Naeem Inayatullah (New York: Palgrave, 2006), 129–130.

16. Ibid., 130. See also Monisha Das Gupta, *Unruly Immigrants: Rights, Activism, and Transnational South Asian Politics in the United States* (Durham, NC: Duke University Press, 2006).

17. Anne Cvetkovich, "Trauma Ongoing," in Greenberg, *Trauma at Home,* 64.

18. Amardeep Singh, "'We Are Not the Enemy': Hate Crimes against Arabs, Muslims, and Those Perceived to Be Arab or Muslim after September 11," *Human Rights Watch,* November 2002.

19. Suheir Hammad, "first writing since," in Greenberg, *Trauma at Home,* 141.

20. Nguyen, *We Are All Suspects Now,* xvii–xviii.

21. Carol D. Leonnig, "More Join Guantánamo Hunger Strike: Detainees Demand Hearings, Allege Beatings by Guards," *Washington Post,* September 13, 2005, A3.

22. Nguyen, *We Are All Suspects Now.*

23. Peter Brooks, "If You Have Tears," in Greenberg, *Trauma at Home,* 49.

24. Jyoti Puri, *Encountering Nationalism* (Malden, MA: Blackwell, 2004), 2.

25. Ibid., 3–11.

26. Michael Watts, "Revolutionary Islam: A Geography of Modern Terror," in *Violent Geographies: Fear, Terror, and Political Violence,* ed. Derek Gregory and Allan Pred (New York: Routledge, 2007), 175–203.

27. This agreement set the stage for Britain and France to put kings, sheikhs, and dictators in power who would answer to the priorities of Western governments, including their demands for control over oil supplies.

28. Political analyst Robert Fisk writes poignantly about US rhetoric to spread democracy in the Middle East. In relation to US claims about democratizing Iraq, Fisk states, "It isn't the first time that the US has threatened the Arabs with democracy, but it's a dodgy project for both parties: first, because the Arabs don't have much democracy; second, because quite a lot of Arabs would like a bit of it; and third, because the countries where they would like this precious commodity include Saudi Arabia, Egypt and other regimes that the Americans would like to protect rather than destroy with democratic experiments. The Palestinians, President Bush has told us, must have a democracy. The Iraqis must have a democracy. Iran must have a democracy. But not, it seems, Saudi Arabia, Jordan, Egypt, Syria, and the rest. Naturally, all these ambitious projects have set off a good deal of discussion in the Arab world" ("September 11—Reflections: A View from the Middle East—Worlds of Difference," *Independent,* September 11, 2002, 16–17).

29. Shibley Telhami, Fiona Hill, Abdullatif A. Al-Othman, and Cyrus H. Tahmassebi, "Does Saudi Arabia Still Matter? Differing Perspectives on the Kingdom and Its Oil," *Foreign Affairs* 81, no. 6 (November/December 2002): 167.

30. John Foran, "Confronting an Empire: Sociology and the U.S.-Made World Crisis," *Political Power and Social Theory* 16 (2004): 224–225.

31. David Ross and Michael Parenti, "Exposing the Terrorist Trap: David Ross Interviews Michael Parenti," *International Socialist Review,* no. 24 (July 20, 2002): 20–23.

32. Watts, "Revolutionary Islam," 185.

33. Foran, "Confronting an Empire," 219.

34. Arundhati Roy, *An Ordinary Person's Guide to Empire* (Boston: South End Press, 2004).

35. Abu-Lughod, "After the WTC Disaster."

36. Puri, *Encountering Nationalism,* 8.

37. Joel Beinin, "The New McCarthyism: Policing Thought about the Middle East," in *Academic Freedom after September 11,* ed. Beshara Doumani (New York: Zone Books, 2006), 237–266.

38. Foran, "Confronting an Empire," 228.

39. Ibid. The United States had also used the position of women in Afghanistan as justification for its 2001 invasion, a particularly disingenuous rationale, given the earlier US support of Afghanistan (with little concern for women's rights in that country then). Monisha Das Gupta urges us to "rethink the simplistic opposition between women's rights and Islamic fundamentalism, an opposition that has been mobilized again and again in the case of women in Afghanistan as justification for invading the country" ("Bewildered?" 132). For nuanced discussions of patriarchy and Muslim women, see Homa Hoodfar, "The Veil in Their Minds and on Our Heads: Veiling Practices and Muslim Women," in *The Politics of Culture in the Shadow of Capital,* ed. Lisa Lowe and David Lloyd (Durham, NC: Duke University Press, 1997), 248–279; and Nayereh Tohidi, "Gender and Islamic Fundamentalism: Feminist Politics in Iran," in *Third World Women and the Politics of Feminism,* ed. Chandra Talpade Mohanty, Ann Russo, and Lourdes Torres (Bloomington: University of Indiana Press, 1991), 251–270.

40. Freund, *Sociology of Max Weber,* 25.

41. BBC News, "Bush God Comments 'Not Literal,'" October 7, 2005, http://news.bbc.co.uk/1/hi/americas/4320586.stm.

42. After 9/11, Bush told the people of the United States to go shopping—a truly ironic and confused response from a man who claims a deep religious belief. He did not encourage people to report to their nearest temple, church, synagogue, mosque, rock formation, or forest to honor their grief. Instead, he asked people to draw upon consumer therapy as their source of comfort.

43. Bruce Lawrence, introduction to *Messages to the World: The Statements of Osama bin Laden,* by Osama bin Laden, ed. Bruce Lawrence (New York: Verso, 2005), xx.

44. Ibid.

45. Osama bin Laden, *Messages to the World,* 160–172.

46. Karen Armstrong, "Fundamentalism," in *Nothing Sacred: Women Respond to Religious Fundamentalism and Terror,* ed. Betsy Reed (New York: Thunder's Mouth Press, 2002), 11–13.

47. Weber was misguided in treating Islam and Puritanism as polar opposites. His focus on seventh-century Islam should not have led him, or others, to generalize about Islam across history or region. Weber was also shortsighted in his assumption that capitalism developed only in the West. In fact, characteristics of capitalism can be seen historically in China, India, and elsewhere.

48. Bassam Tibi, *Islam between Culture and Politics,* 2nd ed. (New York: Palgrave, 2005), 247.

49. Mitzman, *Iron Cage,* 207.

50. Thanks to Becky's mother, Sally Abood, for helping us understand this crucial point about the embodiment of the sacred in public spaces throughout many regions in the Middle East. Her thirty-two-year marriage to Eddie Abood, a Lebanese American, included many trips to the Middle East. Becky's connection to his life (and his dying) is the feeling behind her poem "Questions."

51. There are Middle Eastern–based airlines that take out the backseats in their airplanes to create room to pray during flight. Even in a city as cosmopolitan as Alexandria, one can see people praying along the shore of the Mediterranean Sea and in parks.

52. Rosemary Radford Ruether, "The War on Women," in Reed, *Nothing Sacred,* 3.

53. Quoted in Mitzman, *Iron Cage,* 211–212.

54. Ibid., 212.

55. Lawrence, introduction to bin Laden, *Messages to the World,* xvii.

56. Mitzman explains that, for Weber, "the tension and hostility between the warrior and the saint stem from the saint's rejection of the brutality of the struggle waged by the warrior community and the warrior's rejection of the saint's pacifism. The ascetic position to which Weber also attributes a 'cheerful stupidity' about questions of ultimate meaning, has no qualms, in his view, about accepting worldly violence as part of the divine scheme" (*Iron Cage,* 213).

## CHAPTER FIVE

1. In this chapter, we focus on Charles Graner and Lynndie England, whose abuses garnered the most media attention when the photos were first released. Our focus, however, should not be interpreted as a condemnation of Graner and England as somehow guiltier than the many others who also perpetrated the torture, either directly or as supervisors of those involved. A lengthy report written by Major General Antonio M. Taguba showed "collective wrongdoing and the failure of Army leadership at the highest levels" (Seymour Hersh, "Torture at Abu Ghraib," *New Yorker,* May 10, 2004, 47). Philip Zimbardo, an expert adviser for one of the court martial trials, viewed hundreds of images that he said were "worse than those originally leaked to CBS' 60 Minutes II program on its April 2004 exposé." In an op-ed essay, Zimbardo identified many reasons why the Bush administration and the Pentagon were so eager to gain control over and stop the dissemination of the photos. He concluded, "These photos are testimony to the total breakdown of military discipline and failure of Command accountability." Philip G. Zimbardo, "The 'Trophy Photos': Abu Ghraib's Horrors and Worse," October 25, 2005, http://www.zimbardo.com/downloads/Trophy%20Photos%20OP%20ED%20.pdf.

2. Douglas Kellner, "Baudrillard, Globalization and Terrorism: Some Comments on Recent Adventures of the Image and Spectacle on the Occasion of Baudrillard's 75th Birthday," *International Journal of Baudrillard Studies* 2, no. 1 (January 2005), http://www.ubishops.ca/BaudrillardStudies/vol2_1/kellner.htm.

3. Susan Sontag, "Regarding the Torture of Others," *New York Times*, May 23, 2004, 2.

4. Bruce Brown, *Marx, Freud, and the Critique of Everyday Life: Toward a Permanent Cultural Revolution* (New York: Monthly Review Press, 1973), 15.

5. Pampel, *Sociological Lives and Ideas*, 3.

6. Karl Marx, "The German Ideology: Part I," in *The Marx-Engels Reader*, ed. Robert C. Tucker (New York: Norton, 1978), 160.

7. Ibid.

8. Once a product is exchanged on the market, it has moved beyond what Marx referred to as having "use value" to having "exchange value." With that shift the product becomes a "commodity." For more on this distinction, see especially Chapter One in Marx, *Capital: Volume I*.

9. Karl Marx, *The Economic and Philosophic Manuscripts of 1844*, ed. Dirk J. Struik (New York: International Publishers, 1964), 106–119.

10. Ibid., 78–91; Marx, *Capital: Volume I*, 125–163, 283–339.

11. Marx, *Economic and Philosophic Manuscripts*, 108.

12. Ibid., 110.

13. George Ritzer, *Sociological Theory*, 4th ed. (New York: McGraw-Hill, 1996), 58.

14. Arlie Russell Hochschild, *The Managed Heart: Commercialization of Human Feeling*, 2nd ed. (Berkeley: University of California Press, 2003), 7.

15. Lisa Lowe, "Work, Immigration, Gender: New Subjects of Cultural Politics," in Lowe and Lloyd, *Politics of Culture*, 354–374.

16. Rollins, *Between Women*; Mary Romero, *Maid in the USA* (New York: Routledge, 1992).

17. Rhacel Salazar Parreñas, "The Care Crisis in the Philippines: Children and Transnational Families in the New Global Economy," in *Global Woman: Nannies, Maids, and Sex Workers in the New Economy*, ed. Barbara Ehrenreich and Arlie Russell Hochschild (New York: Henry Holt, 2002), 39–54; Pierrette Hondagneu-Sotelo, "Blowups and Other Unhappy Endings," in Ehrenreich and Hochschild, *Global Woman*, 55–69.

18. Denise Brennen, "Selling Sex for Visas: Sex Tourism as a Stepping-stone to International Migration," in Ehrenreich and Hochschild, *Global Woman*, 154–168; Frederique Delacoste and Priscilla Alexander, eds., *Sex Work: Writings by Women in the Sex Industry* (Pittsburgh: Cleis Press, 1987).

19. Jennifer Wells, "Leashes, Lynchings, and Lynndie England," *Toronto Star*, February 20, 2005, A13.

20. Marx, *Economic and Philosophic Manuscripts*, 108.

21. Ibid., 109.

22. Ibid., 112.

23. Ibid.

24. Sontag, "Regarding the Torture of Others," 3.

25. Kellner is drawing on Jean Baudrillard's concept of "immanent reversal" in his analysis of Abu Ghraib. Kellner, "Baudrillard, Globalization and Terrorism." See also Douglas Kellner, *Media Spectacle* (New York: Routledge, 2003), and *From September 11 to Terror War: The Dangers of the Bush Legacy* (Lanham, MD: Rowman and Littlefield, 2003); and Jean Baudrillard, *The Spirit of Terrorism and Requiem for the Twin Towers* (New York: Verso, 2002).

26. Hersh, "Torture at Abu Ghraib," 42.

27. Stanley Milgram, *Obedience to Authority* (New York: Harper Perennial, 1983); Craig Haney, W. Curtis Banks, and Philip Zimbardo, "Interpersonal Dynamics in a Simulated Prison," *International Journal of Criminology and Penology* 1 (1973): 69–97. For a more in-depth description of these two experiments and their applicability to Abu Ghraib, see the Plaid Adder, "The Pictures from Abu Ghraib," Democratic Underground, May 5, 2004, http://www.democraticunderground.com/plaidder/04/p/21 .html.

28. The Plaid Adder, "Pictures from Abu Ghraib."

29. In his introduction to *The Economic and Philosophic Manuscripts*, editor Dirk J. Struik offers a useful explanation of the logic behind the translator's eventual decision to use the word "alienation" as the translation for the German word Marx used, *entäussern*. See Marx, *Economic and Philosophic Manuscripts of 1844*, 58.

30. Peter Worsley, *Marx and Marxism* (New York: Routledge, 1982), 25.

31. Marx, *Economic and Philosophic Manuscripts*, 114.

32. Ibid., 111.

33. Ibid., 116.

34. Worsley, *Marx and Marxism*, 26.

### CHAPTER SIX

1. Marx, *Economic and Philosophic Manuscripts*, 128; Marx, *Capital: Volume 1*, 163–177.

2. Ibid., 110.

3. Robert Jay Lifton, "Conditions of Atrocity," *Nation*, May 31, 2004, 4.

4. Kate Zernike, "Behind Failed Abu Ghraib Plea, a Tangle of Bonds and Betrayals," *New York Times*, May 14, 2005, national edition, A13.

5. T. A. Badger, "Guilty Plea on Abu Ghraib," *Boston Globe*, May 3, 2005, A2.

6. Ambuhl was permitted to marry Graner only by proxy since he is now serving a ten-year prison sentence and, as coconspirators, the two could not be in the same room for their marriage ceremony. The levels of estrangement in this debacle abound. Zernike, "Behind Failed Abu Ghraib Plea," A13.

7. Badger, "Guilty Plea on Abu Ghraib," A2.

8. Sheldon Alberts, "Soldier Admits Humiliating Iraqis," *National Post* (Canada), May 3, 2005, A3.

9. Zernike, "Behind Failed Abu Ghraib Plea," A13.

10. Ibid.

11. Anne-Marie Cusac, "Abu Ghraib, USA," *Progressive*, July 2004, 20; David Finkel and Christian Davenport, "Records Paint Dark Portrait of Guard: Before Abu Ghraib, Graner Left a Trail of Alleged Violence," *Washington Post*, June 5, 2004, A1.

12. Written correspondence between Monisha Das Gupta and the authors, June 27, 2006.

13. Aihwa Ong, "The Gender and Labor Politics of Postmodernity," in Lowe and Lloyd, *Politics of Culture*, 73.

14. David S. Cloud, "Private Gets Three Years for Iraq Prison Abuse," *New York Times*, September 28, 2005, A20.

15. Cusac, "Abu Ghraib, USA," 20.

16. Ibid., 22. Major General Geoffrey Miller, the former commander of Guantánamo Bay prison, was named deputy commander for containment operations for the Iraqi detention centers (Neil Mackay, "The Pictures That Lost the War," *Sunday Herald*, May 2, 2004: 12). Lane McCotter, former director of the Utah Department of Corrections, was named in a suit by the family of Michael Valent, an inmate who was tortured to death in a Utah prison; six years later, McCotter was one of the officials sent by the Justice Department to reconstruct Iraq's prisons (Dan Frosch, "Exporting America's Prison Problems," *Nation*, May 12, 2004, http://www.thenation.com/doc/20040524/frosch). Ivan "Chip" Frederick, who was the senior enlisted officer in charge at Abu Ghraib between October and December 2003 and who tortured prisoners there, was a former correctional officer in the Virginia prison system, which is considered one of the worst systems in the country and has a long history of abusing inmates (Laura La-Fay, "Abu Ghraib in Virginia," *Southern Exposure* 32 [Winter 2005]: 12).

17. C. W. Mills, *The Power Elite* (New York: Oxford University Press, 1956 [1970]), 7. Often seen as a maverick and an outspoken critic among the conformist and bland academics of the mid-1950s, Mills gives us a framework for understanding what we see today. With globalization, corporations such as the Corrections Corporation of America own more and more prisons and provide technology and training for corrections officers around the world. While some government officials may feign surprise at revelations of yet another instance of abuse, since 9/11 several secret prisons have begun operation in various parts of the world. For prison personnel, military and prison elite depend on those who cannot find a good job in the current global economy.

18. Cusac, "Abu Ghraib, USA," 20. Cusac writes, "In conversations over the past few weeks, I have heard outrage and anger over the abuse at Abu Ghraib. I have rarely heard such reactions in connection with abuse of prisoners in the United States. When we tolerate abuse in US prisons and jails, it should not surprise us to find US soldiers using similar methods in Iraq" (ibid., 23). She recalls, "When I first saw the photo, taken at the Abu Ghraib prison, of a hooded and robed figure strung with electrical wiring, I thought of the Sacramento, California, city jail. . . . When I learned that the male inmates at Abu Ghraib were forced to wear women's underwear, I thought of the Maricopa County jails in Phoenix, Arizona. And when I saw the photos of the naked

bodies restrained in grotesque and clearly uncomfortable positions, I thought of the Utah prison system" (ibid., 19).

19. An important exception to this bias is Tara McKelvey's investigative journalism on the women held at Abu Ghraib, a story that includes interviews with Iraqi women who had been detained. See Tara McKelvey, "Unusual Suspects: What Happened to the Women Held at Abu Ghraib," *American Prospect,* February 2005, 18–24.

20. David R. Roediger, introduction to *Black on White: Black Writers on What It Means to Be White,* ed. Roediger (New York: Schocken Books, 1998), 3.

21. Cusac, "Abu Ghraib, USA," 20.

22. The Red Cross documentation is quoted in ibid., 22.

23. Sontag, "Regarding the Torture of Others," 4.

24. McKelvey, "Unusual Suspects," 22.

25. The Plaid Adder, "Pictures from Abu Ghraib."

26. Dori Laub, "Bearing Witness *or* the Vicissitudes of Listening," in *Testimony: Crises of Witnessing in Literature, Psychoanalysis, and History,* ed. Shoshana Feldman and Dori Laub (New York: Routledge, 1992), 57.

27. The Plaid Adder, "Pictures from Abu Ghraib."

28. Hersh, "Torture at Abu Ghraib," 44.

29. Kellner, "Baudrillard, Globalization and Terrorism."

30. The Plaid Adder, "Pictures from Abu Ghraib."

31. Wells, "Leashes, Lynchings, and Lynndie England," A13.

32. Quoted in ibid.

33. Mumia Abu-Jamal, "In the Shadow of Abu-Ghraib Prison," Mumia Abu-Jamal's Radio Broadcasts, Prison Radio, recording and transcript, May 3, 2004, http://www.prisonradio.org/maj/maj_5_3_04_shadow.html.

34. Laub, "Bearing Witness," 67.

35. Ibid.

36. María Lugones, "Playfulness, 'World' Travelling, and Loving Perception," in *Making Face, Making Soul/Haciendo Caras: Creative and Critical Perspectives by Women of Color,* ed. Gloria Anzaldúa (San Francisco: Aunt Lute Foundation Books, 1990), 391, 392.

37. Ibid., 392, 394.

38. Du Bois, *Souls of Black Folk,* 8.

39. Lugones, "Playfulness," 397.

40. Davis, "Race and Criminalization."

41. Ibid., 267.

42. Marilyn Buck, "Women in Prison and Work," *Feminist Studies* 30, no. 2 (Summer 2004): 453. For autobiographical information and political analysis from Marilyn Buck, see Becky Thompson, *A Promise and a Way of Life: White Antiracist Activism* (Minneapolis: University of Minnesota Press, 2001).

43. Buck, "Women in Prison and Work," 453–454.

44. David Gilbert, *No Surrender: Writings from an Anti-imperialist Political Prisoner* (Montreal: Abraham Guillen Press, 2004); Thompson, *A Promise.*

45. Fanon, *Wretched of the Earth.*

46. Hersh, "Torture at Abu Ghraib," 44.

47. Desmond Tutu, *No Future without Forgiveness* (New York: Doubleday, 1999), 31.

48. Ibid., 54–55.

49. Mab Segrest, *Born to Belonging: Writings on Spirit and Justice* (New York: Rutgers, 2002), 2.

50. Tutu, *No Future without Forgiveness,* 31.

51. Joy James, ed., *Imprisoned Intellectuals: America's Political Prisoners Write on Life, Liberation, and Rebellion* (New York: Rowman and Littlefield, 2003), 63.

52. For a special journal issue on Critical Resistance as an organization and an international movement, see Craig Gilmore, Donna Hunter, Christian Parenti, Dylan Rodriquez, Cassandra Shaylor, Nancy Stoller, and Julia Sudbury, eds., "Critical Resistance to the Prison-Industrial Complex," special issue, *Social Justice* 27, no. 3 (2000).

53. Steve Martinot and Jared Sexton, "The Avant-Garde of White Supremacy," *Social Identities* 9, no. 2 (2003): 169–181.

54. Rita Arditti, *Searching for Life: The Grandmothers of the Plaza de Mayo and the Disappeared Children of Argentina* (Berkeley: University of California Press, 1999), 35.

55. Howard Zinn, "The Scourge of Nationalism," *Progressive,* June 2005, 12.

### CHAPTER SEVEN

1. Among other incidents, Eric and Dylan had been suspended from school for computer misuse, arrested for vandalizing a van, and required to attend anger management courses. Katherine S. Newman, Cybelle Fox, David J. Harding, Jal Mehta, and Wendy Roth, *Rampage: The Social Roots of School Shootings* (New York: Basic Books, 2004), 257–258.

2. Orlando Patterson, "When 'They' Are 'Us,'" *New York Times,* April 30, 1999, 34.

3. Pampel, *Sociological Lives and Ideas,* 68.

4. Ken Thompson, *Emile Durkheim* (New York: Routledge, 2002), 28.

5. Émile Durkheim, *The Rules of Sociological Method* (New York: Free Press, 1982), 50–84.

6. Pampel, *Sociological Lives and Ideas,* 58.

7. In 1894 Captain Alfred Dreyfus, the first Jewish general staff officer in France's army, was court-martialed for treason, publicly shamed in a military degradation ceremony, and deported to a prison in Guyana. See Fields, "Individuality and the Intellectuals," 439–441.

8. Émile Durkheim, *Suicide: A Study in Sociology,* trans. John A. Spaulding and George Simpson (New York: Free Press, 1951), 215, 216.

9. Alan Sica, ed., *Social Thought: From the Enlightenment to the Present* (New York: Pearson, 2005), 291.

10. It turns out we are not alone in sidelining Durkheim. As Randall Collins explains, "He is regarded as a conservative defender of the status quo by the Left, as an arch-functionalist by the anti-functionalists, as a naïve unilinear evolutionist by the historicists. The subjectivistic sociologies tend to see in Durkheim, if not always a materialist, at least a social reductionist of a disturbingly deterministic sort. For the humanists, Durkheim is the anti-Christ; for the micro-sociologists, Durkheim is the most reified of the macro. It is small wonder that his reputation is at its ebb" ("The Durkheimian Tradition in Conflict Sociology," in *Durkheimian Sociology: Cultural Studies,* ed. Jeffrey Alexander [New York: Cambridge University Press, 1988], 107). On the other hand, Ken Thompson notes that there has been a revival in interest in Durkheim in the last twenty years, as the fall of communism in 1989 renewed interest in theory about civil society. Thompson points out that Durkheim's concept of "collective effervescence" has "proved particularly useful in the study of nationalism, revolutionary politics and theories of social movements" and that there are also striking parallels between Durkheim's and Foucault's focus on self-surveillance in liberal society (*Emile Durkheim,* xi). We agree with Steven Lukes that Durkheim's work offers a wealth of ideas worth grappling with, both to refine and redefine; see Steven Lukes, *Emile Durkheim: His Life and Work* (New York: Harper and Row, 1972).

11. Émile Durkheim, *The Division of Labor in Society,* trans. W. D. Halls (New York: Free Press, 1984); Durkheim, *Suicide;* Durkheim, *The Elementary Forms of the Religious Life: A Study in Religious Sociology,* trans. Carol Cosman (New York: Oxford, 2001).

12. Sica, *Social Thought,* 292.

13. Durkheim, *Suicide,* 297–325.

14. The sociologist Charles Lemert suggests that Durkheim's decision not to become a rabbi, as his father, grandfather, and great-grandfather had been, meant that "he lost the collective conscience of his childhood, for which he sought a new morality in the science of modern life" (*Sociology after the Crisis* [Boulder, CO: Paradigm, 2004], 42).

15. Durkheim, *Suicide,* 152.

16. Ibid., 158.

17. Ibid., 180.

18. Again, from his own social location, Durkheim understood how disruptive unexpected social upheaval can be. German troops invaded his town when he was not yet a teenager. According to sociologist Alan Sica, this memory "seemed to haunt him in that he suddenly was forced to comprehend what it meant to endure a normless, anomic social condition, and to lose the benefits of collective well-being which were fostered through proper social control and commonly held beliefs" (*Social Thought,* 290).

19. Women have entered the workforce in unprecedented numbers, putting enormous new strains on them and shifting family dynamics. The gay, lesbian, bisexual, and transgender movement has offered new understandings of sexuality and gender that have destabilized heteronormative notions of what constitutes a family and simultaneously challenged masculine privilege. White flight from cities to the suburbs has

replaced the vibrant ethnic enclaves previously characteristic of Chicago, New York, and many other urban areas with a sanitized white culture that rewards conformity and promises security. Middle-class white people often live in sterilized and homogeneous communities where entertainment often centers on going to the mall, drinking, and doing drugs, activities that leave emptiness and boredom in their wake. New immigrants are challenging the notion of the United States as a white country. Unemployment has become a long-term state rather than a temporary one for an increasing number of people, in large part a consequence of the movement of jobs from the United States to other countries and the replacement of human labor with what has been promoted as technological "innovation." An unprecedented number of people, most of whom are children, go to sleep at night with no roof over their heads. The buildup of a massive prison industry, an epidemic of alcohol and drug addiction, an escalation of multiple forms of violence against the most vulnerable populations, and a resurgence of white supremacy and right-wing fundamentalist religions are all signs of distress in the face of these rapid social changes.

20. K. Thompson, *Emile Durkheim*, 119.

21. Brooks Brown and Rob Merritt, *No Easy Answers: The Truth behind Death at Columbine* (New York: Lantern Books, 2002), 39–40.

22. Ibid., 39.

23. Ibid.

24. Newman et al., *Rampage*, 359–360; Rebecca Y. Mai and Judith Albert, "Separation and Socialization: A Feminist Analysis of the School Shootings at Columbine," *Journal for the Psychoanalysis of Culture and Society* 5, no. 2 (Fall 2000): 273.

25. Mai and Albert, "Separation and Socialization," 266–267.

26. K. Thompson, *Emile Durkheim*, 119.

27. Mai and Albert, "Separation and Socialization," 276.

28. Brooks Brown and Merritt, *No Easy Answers*, 51.

29. Ibid., 69.

30. Newman et al., *Rampage*, 286.

31. Brooks Brown and Merritt, *No Easy Answers*, 50–51.

32. Erving Goffman, *Asylums: Essays on the Social Situation of Mental Patients and Other Inmates* (New York: Doubleday, 1961), 4.

33. K. Thompson, *Emile Durkheim*, 119–120.

34. Durkheim, *Suicide*, 276.

35. Lorde, *Sister Outsider*, 114, 115.

36. For an outstanding biography of Audre Lorde, see Alexis De Veaux, *Warrior Poet: A Biography of Audre Lorde* (New York: Norton, 2004). See also these works by Audre Lorde: *A Burst of Light* (Ithaca, NY: Firebrand, 1988), *Zami: A New Spelling of My Name* (Boston: Persephone Press, 1982), and *The Cancer Journals*, 2nd ed. (San Francisco: Spinsters Ink, 1980).

37. Mia Consalvo, "The Monsters Next Door: Media Constructions of Boys and Masculinity," in *Feminist Media Studies* 3, no. 1 (2003): 37.

38. Lorde, *Sister Outsider*, 111.

39. William Ayers, Bernardine Dohrn, and Rick Ayers, eds., *Zero Tolerance: Resisting the Drive for Punishment in Our Schools* (New York: New Press, 2001).

40. Audrey Kobayashi and Linda Peake, "Racism Out of Place: Thoughts on Whiteness and an Antiracist Geography in the New Millennium," *Annals of the Association of American Geographers* 90, no. 2 (2000): 395.

41. Ibid., 392.

42. Consalvo, "Monsters Next Door," 34.

43. Murray Forman, "Freaks, Aliens, and the Social Other: Representations of Student Stratification in US Television's First Post-Columbine Season," *Velvet Light Trap*, no. 53 (Spring 2004): 72.

44. Consalvo, "Monsters Next Door," 35.

45. Michael S. Kimmel and Matthew Mahler, "Adolescent Masculinity, Homophobia, and Violence," *American Behavioral Scientist* 46, no. 10 (June 2003): 1445.

46. Lorde, *Sister Outsider*, 57.

47. Ibid., 54.

48. Ibid.

49. Herbert Marcuse, *Eros and Civilization* (New York: Vintage, 1955); Herbert Marcuse, *One-Dimensional Man* (Boston: Beacon, 1964).

50. Lorde, *Sister Outsider*, 59.

51. Ibid., 58.

52. Mai and Albert, "Separation and Socialization," 279.

53. Kimmel and Mahler, "Adolescent Masculinity, Homophobia, and Violence," 1440.

54. Consalvo, "Monsters Next Door," 39.

55. Ibid., 39–40.

56. Brooks Brown and Merritt, *No Easy Answers*, 51.

57. Becky Thompson, *A Hunger So Wide and So Deep: A Multiracial View of Women's Eating Problems* (Minneapolis: University of Minnesota Press, 1994), 16–21.

58. Mai and Albert, "Separation and Socialization," 266.

59. Ibid., 267.

60. Ibid.

61. Michael S. Kimmel, "Masculinity as Homophobia: Fear, Shame, and Silence in the Construction of Gender Identity," in Barbara Balliet and Patricia McDaniel, eds., *Women, Culture, and Society: A Reader* (Dubuque: Kendall/Hunt, 1998), 227–242, quoted in Consalvo, "Monsters Next Door," 31.

62. Mai and Albert, "Separation and Socialization," 279.

63. Lorde, *Sister Outsider*, 57.

64. Durkheim, *Suicide*, 297–325.

65. Durkheim, *Division of Labor*, 339.

66. Ibid.

## CONCLUSION

1. Robert D. McFadden, with contributions by Cara Buckley, Roja Heydarpour, Daryl Kahn, and Angela Macropoulos, "Police Kill Man after a Queens Bachelor Party," *New York Times,* November 26, 2006, A1.

2. Gilbert Burnham, Riyadh Lafta, Shannon Doocy, and Les Roberts, "Mortality after the 2003 Invasion of Iraq: A Cross-Sectional Cluster Sample Survey," *Lancet* 368 (October 21, 2006): 1426.

3. Lengermann and Niebrugge, *Women Founders,* 65–104.

4. bell hooks, "Eating the Other," in *Black Looks: Race and Representation* (Boston: South End Press, 1992), 21–39.

5. Diane Cardwell and Sewell Chan, with contributions by Daryl Khan, Michelle O'Donnell, and William K. Rashbaum, "Bloomberg Calls 50 Shots by the Police 'Unacceptable,'" *New York Times,* November 28, 2006, A1; Delario Lindsey, "To Build a More 'Perfect Discipline': Ideologies of the Normative and the Social Control of the Criminal Innocent in the Policing of New York City," *Critical Sociology* 30, no. 2 (July 2004): 343, 347.

6. Fanon, *Wretched of the Earth,* 29–83; Fanon, *Black Skin, White Masks.*

7. Nelson Mandela asserted, "If the government reaction is to crush by naked force our non-violent struggle, we will have to reconsider our tactics. In my mind we are closing a chapter on this question of non-violent policy" (*Long Walk to Freedom: The Autobiography of Nelson Mandela* [London: Abacus, 1994], 320).

8. See "The Master's Tools Will Never Dismantle the Master's House," in Lorde, *Sister Outsider,* 110–113.

9. The Day of Mourning is organized by the United American Indians of New England at the top of Cole's Hill in Plymouth, Massachusetts, and takes place on Thanksgiving Day every year.

10. Thank you to Ismail Rashid, professor of Africana Studies at Vassar College, for this crucial insight.

11. Kwanzaa, a cultural and community ritual created in 1966, is an attempt on the part of many African Americans to supplement Christmas with a week of days that are linked to spiritual messages, Ujima, Nia, and other spiritual reminders.

12. Anzaldúa, *Borderlands/La Frontera,* 78.

13. Hine, "Rape and the Inner Lives of Black Women," 380.

14. Robin D. G. Kelley, *Freedom Dreams: The Black Radical Imagination* (Boston: Beacon, 2002).

15. Shari Frilot, *Black Nations/Queer Nations?* video (New York: Third World Newsreel, 1995).

16. Thich Nhat Hanh, *The Miracle of Mindfulness: A Manual on Meditation* (Boston: Beacon, 1975); Thich Nhat Hanh, *For a Future to Be Possible: Commentaries on the Five Mindfulness Trainings* (New York: Parallax Press, 1993); Thich Nhat Hanh, *Peace Is Every Step* (New York: Bantam Books, 1992). See also Hilda Gutiérrez Baldoquín, ed.,

*Dharma, Color, and Culture: New Voices in Western Buddhism* (Berkeley, CA: Parallax Press, 2004).

17. Nhat Hanh, *Peace Is Every Step.*

18. Jarvis Jay Masters, *Finding Freedom: Writings from Death Row* (Junction City, CA: Padma, 1997), 67–71.

19. Masters writes, "Through meditation I learned to slow down and take a few deep breaths, to take everything in, not to run from the pain, but to sit with it, confront it, give it the companion it had never had" (*Finding Freedom,* 111).

20. The Committees of Correspondence is a socialist organization founded by people who left the Communist Party USA in 1991 in protest of its exclusionary policies regarding people of color in leadership positions.

21. *José Martí: Selected Writings,* trans. and ed. Esther Allen (New York: Penguin Books, 2002).

22. For example, not having come to terms with Vietnam and other imperialist wars in the twentieth century, the United States seemed destined to repeat a facile politics of retaliation after 9/11. When terrorists attacked American embassies in Kenya and Tanzania in 1998, the first major violence that can be traced to Osama bin Laden, the Clinton administration retaliated with little to no recognition of the critique of Western values at the root of the terrorism. A different initial response by the United States might have anticipated or perhaps even stopped the attacks on 9/11.

23. Cornel West, "Black Music Matters," Berklee College of Music, Boston, February 1, 2007. See also West, *Race Matters;* and *The Cornel West Reader* (New York: Basic Civitas Books, 1999).

# BIBLIOGRAPHY

Abu-Jamal, Mumia. "In the Shadow of Abu-Ghraib Prison." Mumia Abu-Jamal's Radio Broadcasts, Prison Radio, recording and transcript, May 3, 2004. http://www.prisonradio.org/maj/maj_5_3_04_shadow.html.

Abu-Lughod, Janet. "After the WTC Disaster: The Sacred, the Profane, and Social Solidarity." Social Science Research Council, After September 11: Terrorism and Democratic Virtues, October 19, 2001. http://www.ssrc.org/sept11/essays/abu-lughod.htm.

Alberts, Sheldon. "Soldier Admits Humiliating Iraqis." *National Post* (Canada), May 3, 2005, A3.

Altan, Daffodil. "After Katrina, Where Have All the Hondurans Gone?" Pacific News Service, September 13, 2005. http://news.pacificnews.org/news/.

———. "Ethnic Communities Rally to Help Katrina Survivors." Pacific News Service, September 7, 2005. http://news.pacificnews.org/news/.

Anzaldúa, Gloria. *Borderlands/La Frontera: The New Mestiza.* San Francisco: Aunt Lute Books, 1987.

Aptheker, Herbert. Introduction to *The Philadelphia Negro: A Social Study,* by W. E. B. Du Bois. Millwood. New York: Kraus-Thomson, 1973.

Aptheker, Herbert, and Fay Aptheker. "Personal Reflections on W. E. B. Du Bois: The Person, Scholar, and Activist." In *Against the Odds: Scholars Who Challenged Racism in the Twentieth Century,* edited by Benjamin P. Bowser and Louis Kushnick, 158–192. Amherst: University of Massachusetts, 2002.

Arditti, Rita. *Searching for Life: The Grandmothers of the Plaza de Mayo and the Disappeared Children of Argentina.* Berkeley: University of California Press, 1999.

Armstrong, Karen. "Fundamentalism." In *Nothing Sacred: Women Respond to Religious Fundamentalism and Terror,* edited by Betsy Reed, 11–21. New York: Thunder's Mouth Press, 2002.

Ayers, William, Bernadine Dohrn, and Rick Ayers, eds. *Zero Tolerance: Resisting the Drive for Punishment in Our Schools.* New York: New Press, 2001.

Badger, T. A. "Guilty Plea on Abu Ghraib." *Boston Globe,* May 3, 2005, A2.

Baldoquín, Hilda Gutiérrez, ed. *Dharma, Color, and Culture: New Voices in Western Buddhism.* Berkeley, CA: Parallax Press, 2004.

Baudrillard, Jean. *The Spirit of Terrorism and Requiem for the Twin Towers.* New York: Verso, 2003.

Bayoumi, Moustafa. "How Does It Feel to Be a Problem?" In *Asian Americans on War and Peace,* edited by Russell C. Leong and Don T. Nakanishi, 81–88. Los Angeles: UCLA Asian American Studies Center Press, 2002.

BBC News. "Bush God Comments 'Not Literal.'" October 7, 2005, http://news.bbc .co.uk/1/hi/world/americas/4320586.stm.

Becker, Ernest. *The Denial of Death.* New York: Free Press, 1973.

Beinin, Joel. "The New McCarthyism: Policing Thought about the Middle East." In *Academic Freedom after September 11,* edited by Beshara Doumani, 237–266. New York: Zone Books, 2006.

bin Laden, Osama. *Messages to the World: The Statements of Osama bin Laden.* Edited by Bruce Lawrence. New York: Verso, 2005.

Blumenthal, Ralph. "'Prison City' Shows a Hospitable Face to Refugees from New Orleans." *New York Times,* September 6, 2005, A22.

Bonilla-Silva, Eduardo. *Racism without Racists: Color-Blind Racism and the Persistence of Racial Inequality in the United States.* 2nd ed. Lanham, MD: Rowman and Littlefield, 2006.

Bowser, Benjamin P., and Louis Kushnick, eds. *Against the Odds: Scholars Who Challenged Racism in the Twentieth Century.* Amherst: University of Massachusetts, 2002.

Brennen, Denise. "Selling Sex for Visas: Sex Tourism as a Stepping-stone to International Migration." In Ehrenreich and Hochschild, *Global Woman,* 154–168.

Broder, John M. "Amid Criticism of Federal Efforts, Charges of Racism Are Lodged." *New York Times,* September 5, 2005, A9.

Brooks, Peter. "If You Have Tears." In Greenberg, *Trauma at Home,* 48–51.

Brown, Brooks, and Rob Merritt. *No Easy Answers: The Truth behind Death at Columbine.* New York: Lantern Books, 2002.

Brown, Bruce. *Marx, Freud, and the Critique of Everyday Life: Toward a Permanent Cultural Revolution.* New York: Monthly Review Press, 1973.

Brown, C. Stone. "Katrina's Forgotten Victims: Native American Tribes." Pacific News Service, September 11, 2005. http://news.pacificnews.org/news/.

Brown, Michael K., Martin Carnoy, Elliott Currie, Troy Duster, David B. Oppenheimer, Marjorie M. Shultz, and David Wellman. *Whitewashing Race: The Myth of a Color-Blind Society.* Berkeley: University of California, 2005.

Brubaker, Rogers. *The Limits of Rationality: Essays on the Social and Moral Thought of Max Weber.* London: Allen and Unwin, 1984.

Buck, Marilyn. "Women in Prison and Work." *Feminist Studies* 30, no. 2 (Summer 2004): 451–455.

Burnham, Gilbert, Riyadh Lafta, Shannon Doocy, and Les Roberts. "Mortality after the 2003 Invasion of Iraq: A Cross-Sectional Cluster Sample Survey." *Lancet* 368 (October 21, 2006): 1421–1428.

Campbell, Monica. "Post Katrina Easing of Labor Laws Stirs Debate." *Christian Science Monitor,* October 4, 2005, 1.

Carby, Hazel V. *Race Men.* Cambridge, MA: Harvard University Press, 1998.

Cardwell, Diane, and Sewell Chan, with contributions by Daryl Khan, Michelle O'Donnell, and William K. Rashbaum. "Bloomberg Calls 50 Shots by the Police 'Unacceptable.'" *New York Times,* November 28, 2006, A1.

Caruth, Cathy. *Unclaimed Experience: Trauma, Narrative, and History.* Baltimore and London: Johns Hopkins University Press, 1996.

Cloud, David S. "Private Gets Three Years for Iraq Prison Abuse." *New York Times,* September 28, 2005, A20.

Cohen, Allen, and Clive Matson, eds. *An Eye for An Eye Makes the Whole World Blind: Poets on 9/11.* Oakland, CA: Regent Press, 2002.

Cole, Johnnetta B., ed. *Anthropology for the 1990s.* New York: Free Press, 1988.

Collins, Patricia Hill. *Black Feminist Thought: Knowledge, Consciousness, and the Politics of Empowerment.* Boston: Unwin Hyman, 1990.

———. *Black Sexual Politics: African Americans, Gender, and the New Racism.* New York: Routledge, 2005.

———. *Fighting Words: Black Women and the Search for Justice.* Minneapolis: University of Minnesota Press, 1998.

———. "W. E. B. Du Bois: Preeminent Public Sociologist." Panel presentation, Presidential Plenary, "W. E. B. Du Bois: Lessons for the 21st Century," ninety-ninth annual meeting of the American Sociological Association, San Francisco, August 13, 2004.

Collins, Randall. "The Durkheimian Tradition in Conflict Sociology." In *Durkheimian Sociology: Cultural Studies,* edited by Jeffrey Alexander, 107–128. New York: Cambridge University Press, 1988.

Combahee River Collective. "The Combahee River Collective Statement." In *Home Girls: A Black Feminist Anthology,* edited by Barbara Smith, 264–274. New Brunswick, NJ: Rutgers University Press, 1983, 2000.

Consalvo, Mia. "The Monsters Next Door: Media Constructions of Boys and Masculinity." *Feminist Media Studies* 3, no. 1 (2003): 26–43.

Cooper, Helene. "Rice's Hurdles on Middle East Begin at Home." *New York Times,* August 10, 2006, A1, A12.

Crouch, Stanley, and Playthell Benjamin. *Reconsidering the Souls of Black Folk: Thoughts on the Groundbreaking Classic Work of W. E. B. Du Bois.* Philadelphia: Running Press, 2002.

Curtin, Philip D. *The Atlantic Slave Trade: A Census.* Madison: University of Wisconsin Press, 1969.

Cusac, Anne-Marie. "Abu Ghraib, USA." *Progressive,* July 2004, 19–23.

Cvetkovich, Anne. "Trauma Ongoing." In Greenberg, *Trauma at Home,* 60–66.

Danticat, Edwidge. "Another Country." *Progressive,* November 2005, 24–26.

Dao, James, and N. R. Kelinfield. "More Troops and Aid Reach New Orleans." *New York Times,* September 3, 2005, A1.

Das Gupta, Monisha. "Bewildered? Women's Studies and the War on Terror." In *Interrogating Imperialism: Conversations on Gender, Race, and War,* edited by Robin Riley and Naeem Inayatullah, 129–153. New York: Palgrave, 2006.

———. "Hate Crimes." In *Keywords of Contemporary America/Gendai Amerika No Kiiwaado,* edited by Mari Yoshihara and Yurin Yaguchi, 130–134. Tokyo: Chuo Koron Shinsha, 2006.

———. *Unruly Immigrants: Rights, Activism, and Transnational South Asian Politics in the United States.* Durham, NC: Duke University Press, 2006.

Davis, Angela Y. "Race and Criminalization: Black Americans and the Punishment Industry." In *The House That Race Built: Black Americans, U.S. Terrain,* edited by Wahneema Lubiano, 264–279. New York: Pantheon, 1997.

Delacoste, Frederique, and Priscilla Alexander, eds. *Sex Work: Writings by Women in the Sex Industry.* Pittsburgh: Cleis Press, 1987.

Der Derian, James. "9/11: Before, After, and In Between." In *Understanding September 11,* edited by Craig J. Calhoun, Paul Price, and Ashley Timmer, 177–190. New York: New Press, 2002.

De Veaux, Alexis. *Warrior Poet: A Biography of Audre Lorde.* New York: Norton, 2004.

Du Bois, W. E. B. *Black Reconstruction in America, 1860–1880.* New York: Free Press, 1998.

———. *The Oxford W. E. B. Du Bois Reader.* Edited by Eric J. Sundquist. New York: Oxford University Press, 1996.

———. *The Philadelphia Negro: A Social Study.* Millwood, NY: Kraus-Thomson, 1973.

———. *The Souls of Black Folk.* New York: Vintage, 1990.

———. *W. E. B. Du Bois on Sociology and the Black Community.* Edited by Dan S. Green and Edwin D. Driver. Chicago: University of Chicago, 1978.

———. *W. E. B. Du Bois Speaks: Speeches and Addresses, 1890–1919,* edited by Philip Foner. New York: Pathfinder, 1970.

———. *W. E. B. Du Bois: Writings.* New York: Library of America, 1986.

duCille, Ann. "The Occult of True Black Womanhood: Critical Demeanor and Black Feminist Studies." *Signs: Journal of Women in Culture and Society* 19, no. 3 (Spring 1994): 591–629.

Durkheim, Émile. *The Division of Labor in Society.* Translated by W. D. Halls. New York: Free Press, 1984.

———. *The Elementary Forms of the Religious Life: A Study in Religious Sociology.* Translated by Carol Cosman. New York: Oxford, 2001.

———. *The Rules of Sociological Method.* New York: Free Press, 1982.

———. *Suicide: A Study in Sociology.* Translated by John A. Spaulding and George Simpson. New York: Free Press, 1951.

Dyson, Michael Eric. *Come Hell or High Water: Hurricane Katrina and the Color of Disaster.* New York: Basic Books, 2006.

Early, Gerald, ed. *Lure and Loathing: Essays on Race, Identity, and the Ambivalence of Assimilation.* New York: Penguin, 1993.

Ehrenreich, Barbara, and Arlie Russell Hochschild, eds. *Global Woman: Nannies, Maids, and Sex Workers in the New Economy.* New York: Henry Holt, 2002.

Eisenstein, Zillah. "Katrina and Her Gendering of Class and Race." *National Women's Studies Association Action* 17, no. 1 (Fall 2005): 8.

Ellison, Ralph. *Invisible Man.* New York: Random House, 1947.

Erikson, Kai T. *Everything in Its Path: Destruction of Community in the Buffalo Creek Flood.* New York: Simon and Schuster, 1976.

———. *A New Species of Trouble: The Human Experience of Modern Disasters.* New York: Norton, 1995.

Fanon, Frantz. *Black Skin, White Masks.* New York: Grove Press, 1967.

———. *The Wretched of the Earth.* New York: Grove Press, 1963.

Farley, Anthony Paul. "The Station." In *After the Storm: Black Intellectuals Explore the Meaning of Hurricane Katrina,* edited by David Dante Troutt, 147–159. New York: New Press, 2006.

Feagin, Joe R., and Hernán Vera. *Liberation Sociology.* Boulder, CO: Westview, 2001.

Felix, Antonia. *Condi: The Condoleezza Rice Story.* New York: New Market Press, 2005.

Fields, Karen. "Individuality and the Intellectuals: An Imaginary Conversation between W. E. B. Du Bois and Émile Durkheim." *Theory and Society* 31 (2002): 435–462.

Finkel, David, and Christian Davenport. "Records Paint Dark Portrait of Guard: Before Abu Ghraib, Graner Left a Trail of Alleged Violence." *Washington Post,* June 5, 2004, A1.

Fisk, Robert. "September 11—Reflections: A View from the Middle East—Worlds of Difference." *Independent,* September 11, 2002, 16–17.

Foran, John. "Confronting an Empire: Sociology and the U.S.-Made World Crisis." *Political Power and Social Theory* 16 (2004): 215–235.

Forman, Murray. "Freaks, Aliens, and the Social Other: Representations of Student Stratification in US Television's First Post-Columbine Season." *Velvet Light Trap,* no. 53 (Spring 2004): 66–82.

Freund, Julien. *The Sociology of Max Weber.* New York: Vintage, 1968.

Frilot, Shari. *Black Nations/Queer Nations?* Video. New York: Third World Newsreel, 1995.

Frosch, Dan. "Exporting America's Prison Problems." *Nation,* May 12, 2004. http://www.thenation.com/doc/20040524/frosch.

Frymer, Paul, Dara Z. Strolovitch, and Dorian T. Warren. "New Orleans Is Not the Exception: Re-politicizing the Study of Racial Inequality." *Du Bois Review: Social Science Research on Race* 3, no. 1 (2006): 37–57.

Gans, Herbert. "Sociology in America: The Discipline and the Public; American Sociological Association 1988 Presidential Address." *American Sociological Review* 54 (February 1989): 1–16.

Gerth, Hans, and Saul Landau. "The Relevance of History to the Sociological Ethos."

In *Sociology on Trial,* edited by Maurice Stein and Arthur Vidich, 26–34. Englewood Cliffs, NJ: Prentice-Hall, 1963.

Gibson, Donald B. Introduction to *The Souls of Black Folk,* by W. E. B. Du Bois, vii–xxxv. New York: Penguin, 1989.

Giddens, Anthony. *Capitalism and Modern Social Theory: An Analysis of the Writings of Marx, Durkheim, and Max Weber.* New York: Cambridge University Press, 1971.

Gilbert, David. *No Surrender: Writings from an Anti-imperialist Political Prisoner.* Montreal: Abraham Guillen Press, 2004.

Gilmore, Craig, Donna Hunter, Christian Parenti, Dylan Rodriquez, Cassandra Shaylor, Nancy Stoller, and Julia Sudbury, eds. "Critical Resistance to the Prison-Industrial Complex." Special issue, *Social Justice* 27, no. 3 (2000).

Ginsberg, Allen. *Howl and Other Poems.* San Francisco: City Lights Books, 1959.

Givhan, Robin. "Condoleezza Rice's Commanding Clothes." *Washington Post,* February 25, 2005, C1.

Goffman, Erving. *Asylums: Essays on the Social Situation of Mental Patients and Other Inmates.* New York: Doubleday, 1961.

Goodman, Amy. "Honduran Immigrants in New Orleans: Fleeing Hurricanes Mitch, Katrina, and Now the U.S. Government." *Democracy Now!* September 13, 2005. http://www.democracynow.org/ article.pl?sid=05/09/13/1354211.

Gouldner, Alvin W. "Anti-Minotaur: The Myth of a Value-Free Sociology." In *Sociology on Trial,* edited by Maurice Stein and Arthur Vidich, 35–52. Englewood Cliffs, NJ: Prentice-Hall, 1963.

Greenberg, Judith. "Wounded New York." In Greenberg, *Trauma at Home,* 21–35.

———, ed. *Trauma at Home: After 9/11.* Lincoln: University of Nebraska, 2003.

Griffin, Farah Jasmine. Introduction to *The Souls of Black Folk,* by W. E. B. Du Bois, xv–xxviii. New York: Barnes and Noble Classics, 2003.

Hammad, Suheir. "first writing since." In Greenberg, *Trauma at Home,* 139–143.

Haney, Craig W., Curtis Banks, and Philip Zimbardo. "Interpersonal Dynamics in a Simulated Prison." *International Journal of Criminology and Penology* 1 (1973): 69–97.

Hardisty, Jean. *Mobilizing Resentment: Conservative Resurgence from the John Birch Society to the Promise Keepers.* Boston: Beacon, 1999.

Hersh, Seymour M. *Chain of Command: The Road from 9/11 to Abu Ghraib.* New York: Harper, 2004.

———. "Torture at Abu Ghraib." *New Yorker,* May 10, 2004, 42–47.

Heyen, William, ed. *September 11, 2001: American Writers Respond.* Silver Spring, MD: Etruscan Press, 2002.

Higginbotham, Leon A. "An Open Letter to Justice Clarence Thomas from a Federal Judicial Colleague." In *Race-ing Justice, En-gendering Power: Essays on Anita Hill, Clarence Thomas, and the Social Construction of Reality,* edited by Toni Morrison, 3–39. New York: Pantheon, 1992.

Hine, Darlene Clark. "'In the Kingdom of Culture': Black Women and the Intersection of Race, Gender, and Class." In *Lure and Loathing: Essays on Race, Identity, and the*

*Ambivalence of Assimilation,* edited by Gerald Early, 337–351. New York: Penguin, 1993.

———. "Rape and the Inner Lives of Black Women in the Middle West: Preliminary Thoughts on the Culture of Dissemblance." In *Words of Fire: An Anthology of African-American Feminist Thought,* edited by Beverly Guy-Sheftall, 380–387. New York: New Press, 1995.

Hochschild, Arlie Russell. *The Managed Heart: Commercialization of Human Feeling.* 2nd ed. Berkeley: University of California Press, 2003.

Hondagneu-Sotelo, Pierrette. "Blowups and Other Happy Endings." In Ehrenreich and Hochschild, *Global Woman,* 55–69.

Hoodfar, Homa. "The Veil in Their Minds and on Our Heads: Veiling Practices and Muslim Women." In Lowe and Lloyd, *Politics of Culture,* 248–279.

hooks, bell. *Black Looks: Race and Representation.* Boston: South End Press, 1992.

Horne, Gerald. *Race Woman: The Lives of Shirley Graham Du Bois.* New York: New York University Press, 2000.

Huizer, Gerrit, and Bruce Mannheim, eds. *The Politics of Anthropology: From Colonialism and Sexism toward a View from Below.* Paris: Mouton Publishers, 1979.

Hull, Akasha Gloria. *Soul Talk: The New Spirituality of African American Women.* Rochester, VT: Inner Traditions, 2001.

Hull, Gloria T., Patricia Bell Scott, and Barbara Smith, eds. *All the Women Are White, All the Blacks Are Men, But Some of Us Are Brave: Black Women's Studies.* New York: Feminist Press, 1982.

James, Joy, ed. *Imprisoned Intellectuals: America's Political Prisoners Write on Life, Liberation, and Rebellion.* New York: Rowman and Littlefield, 2003.

Jenkins, Lee. "After the Deluge, A Football Foothold in Houston." *New York Times,* September 10, 2005, B15.

Kelley, Robin D. G. *Freedom Dreams: The Black Radical Imagination.* Boston: Beacon, 2002.

Kellner, Douglas. "Baudrillard, Globalization and Terrorism: Some Comments on Recent Adventures of the Image and Spectacle on the Occasion of Baudrillard's 75th Birthday." *International Journal of Baudrillard Studies* 2, no. 1 (January 2005). http://www.ubishops.ca/BaudrillardStudies/vol2_1/kellner.htm.

———. *From September 11 to Terror War: The Dangers of the Bush Legacy.* Lanham, MD: Rowman and Littlefield, 2003.

———. *Media Spectacle.* New York: Routledge, 2003.

Kihss, Peter. "Benign Neglect." *New York Times,* March 1, 1970, A1, 69.

Kimmel, Michael S. "Masculinity as Homophobia: Fear, Shame, and Silence in the Construction of Gender Identity." In Barbara Balliet and Patricia McDaniel, eds., *Women, Culture, and Society: A Reader* (Dubuque: Kendall/Hunt, 1998), 227–242. Quoted in Consalvo, "Monsters Next Door," 31.

Kimmel, Michael S., and Matthew Mahler. "Adolescent Masculinity, Homophobia, and Violence." *American Behavioral Scientist* 46, no. 10 (June 2003): 1439–1458.

King, Martin Luther, Jr. "Honoring Dr. Du Bois." In *W. E. B. Du Bois Speaks: Speeches and Addresses 1890-1919,* edited by Philip Foner, 12-20. New York: Pathfinder, 1970.

———. "I Have a Dream." In *I Have a Dream: Writings and Speeches That Changed the World,* edited by James M. Washington, 101-106. New York: HarperCollins, 1986.

Kobaytashi, Audrey, and Linda Peake. "Racism Out of Place: Thoughts on Whiteness and an Antiracist Geography in the New Millennium." *Annals of the Association of American Geographers* 90, no. 2 (2000): 392-403.

LaFay, Laura. "Abu Ghraib in Virginia." *Southern Exposure* 32 (Winter 2005): 11-13.

Laub, Dori. "Bearing Witness *or* the Vicissitudes of Listening." In *Testimony: Crises of Witnessing in Literature, Psychoanalysis, and History,* edited by Shoshana Feldman and Dori Laub, 57-74. New York: Routledge, 1992.

Lawrence, Bruce. Introduction to *Messages to the World: The Statements of Osama bin Laden,* by Osama bin Laden, edited by Bruce Lawrence, xi-xxiii. New York: Verso, 2005.

Lemann, Nicholas. "Without a Doubt." *New Yorker,* October 14 and 21, 2002, 164-179.

Lemert, Charles. *Sociology after the Crisis.* Boulder, CO: Paradigm, 2004.

Lengermann, Patricia Madoo, and Gillian Niebrugge. *The Women Founders: Sociology and Social Theory, 1830-1930.* New York: Waveland, 2007.

Leonnig, Carol D. "More Join Guantánamo Hunger Strike: Detainees Demand Hearings, Allege Beatings by Guards." *Washington Post,* September 13, 2005, A3.

Lewis, David Levering. Introduction to *Black Reconstruction in America, 1860-1880,* by W. E. B. Du Bois. New York: Free Press, 1998.

———. *W. E. B. Du Bois: Biography of a Race, 1868-1919.* New York: Henry Holt, 1993.

Lifton, Robert Jay. "Conditions of Atrocity." *Nation,* May 31, 2004, 4-5.

Lindsey, Delario. "To Build a More 'Perfect Discipline': Ideologies of the Normative and the Social Control of the Criminal Innocent in the Policing of New York City." *Critical Sociology* 30, no. 2 (July 2004): 321-353.

Lorde, Audre. *A Burst of Light.* Ithaca, NY: Firebrand, 1988.

———. *The Cancer Journals.* 2nd ed. San Francisco: Spinsters Ink, 1980.

———. *Sister Outsider.* New York: Crossing Press, 1984.

———. *Zami: A New Spelling of My Name.* Boston: Persephone Press, 1982.

Lowe, Lisa. "Work, Immigration, Gender: New Subjects of Cultural Politics." In Lowe and Lloyd, *Politics of Culture,* 354-374.

Lowe, Lisa, and David Lloyd, eds. *The Politics of Culture in the Shadow of Capital.* Durham, NC: Duke University Press, 1997.

Loy, David R. "The Means/Ends Problem in Modern Culture." *International Studies in Philosophy* 26, no. 4 (2002): 47-67.

Lugones, María. "Playfulness, 'World' Travelling, and Loving Perception." In *Making Face, Making Soul/Haciendo Caras: Creative and Critical Perspectives by Women of Color,* edited by Gloria Anzaldúa, 390-402. San Francisco: Aunt Lute Foundation Books, 1990.

Lukes, Steven. *Emile Durkheim: His Life and Work.* New York: Harper and Row, 1972.

Mackay, Neil. "The Pictures That Lost the War." *Sunday Herald,* May 2, 2004, 12.

MacQuarrie, Brian, and Tatsha Robertson. "For Many, Frustrated Attempts to Reunite." *Boston Globe,* September 7, 2005, 3rd edition, A12.

Mai, Rebecca Y., and Judith Albert. "Separation and Socialization: A Feminist Analysis of the School Shootings at Columbine." *Journal for the Psychoanalysis of Culture and Society* 5, no. 2 (Fall 2000): 264–284.

Malinowski, Sharon, and Anna Sheets, eds. *The Gale Encyclopedia of Native American Tribes.* Vol. 1. Detroit: Thomson Gale, 1998.

Mandela, Nelson. *Long Walk to Freedom: The Autobiography of Nelson Mandela.* London: Abacus, 1994.

Marable, Manning. *How Capitalism Underdeveloped Black America.* Boston: South End Press, 1983.

———. *W. E. B. Du Bois: Black Radical Democrat.* Boston: Twayne, 1986.

Marcuse, Herbert. *Eros and Civilization.* New York: Vintage, 1955.

———. *One-Dimensional Man.* Boston: Beacon, 1964.

Martí, José. *José Martí: Selected Writings.* Translated and edited by Esther Allen. New York: Penguin Books, 2002.

Martinez, Theresa A. "The Double-Consciousness of Du Bois and the 'Mestiza Consciousness' of Anzaldúa." *Race, Class, and Gender* 9, no. 4 (2002): 158–176.

Martinot, Steve, and Jared Sexton. "The Avant-garde of White Supremacy." *Social Identities* 9, no. 2 (2003): 169–181.

Marx, Karl. *Capital: Volume 1.* New York: Penguin Classics, 1990.

———. *The Economic and Philosophic Manuscripts of 1844.* Edited by Dirk J. Struik. New York: International Publishers, 1964.

———. "The German Ideology: Part I." In *The Marx-Engels Reader,* edited by Robert C. Tucker, 146–200. New York: Norton, 1978.

———. "Manifesto of the Communist Party." In *The Marx-Engels Reader,* edited by Robert C. Tucker, 469–500. New York: Norton, 1978.

Masters, Jarvis Jay. *Finding Freedom: Writings from Death Row.* Junction City, CA: Padma, 1997.

McFadden, Robert D., with contributions by Cara Buckley, Roja Heydarpour, Daryl Kahn, and Angela Macropoulos. "Police Kill Man after a Bachelor Party in Queens." *New York Times,* November 26, 2006, A1.

McKelvey, Tara. "Unusual Suspects: What Happened to the Women Held at Abu Ghraib." *American Prospect,* February 2005, 18–24.

Milgram, Stanley. *Obedience to Authority.* New York: Harper Perennial, 1983.

Mills, C. W. *The Power Elite.* New York: Oxford University Press, 1956 [1970].

———. *The Sociological Imagination.* New York: Oxford, 1959.

Mitzman, Arthur. *The Iron Cage: An Historical Interpretation of Max Weber.* New York: Grosset and Dunlap, 1969.

Moraga, Cherríe, and Gloria Anzaldúa, eds. *This Bridge Called My Back: Writings by Radical Women of Color.* New York: Kitchen Table Women of Color Press, 1983.

Morrison, Toni. *Beloved.* New York: Plume, 1987.

————. *The Bluest Eye.* New York: Washington Square Press, 1972.

————. "The Dead of September 11." In Greenberg, *Trauma at Home,* 1–2.

Newman, Katherine S., Cybelle Fox, David J. Harding, Jal Mehta, and Wendy Roth. *Rampage: The Social Roots of School Shootings.* New York: Basic Books, 2004.

Nguyen, Tram. *We Are All Suspects Now: Untold Stories from Immigrant Communities after 9/11.* Boston: Beacon, 2005.

Nhat Hanh, Thich. *For a Future to Be Possible: Commentaries on the Five Mindfulness Trainings.* New York: Parallax Press, 1993.

————. *The Miracle of Mindfulness: A Manual on Meditation.* Boston: Beacon Press, 1975.

————. *Peace Is Every Step.* New York: Bantam Books, 1992.

Norrell, Brenda. "Louisiana Tribes Receive No Federal Aid." *Indian Country Today,* October 5, 2005, A4.

————. "Tunica-Biloxi Shelter Storm Refugees." *Indian Country Today,* September 7, 2005, A1.

Ong, Aihwa. "The Gender and Labor Politics of Postmodernity." In Lowe and Lloyd, *Politics of Culture,* 61–97.

Pampel, Fred C. *Sociological Lives and Ideas: An Introduction to the Classical Theorists.* New York: Worth, 2000.

Parkin, Frank. *Max Weber.* London: Routledge, 1982.

Parreñas, Rhacel Salazar. "The Care Crisis in the Philippines: Children and Transnational Families in the New Global Economy." In Ehrenreich and Hochschild, *Global Woman,* 39–54.

Patterson, Orlando. "When 'They' Are 'Us.'" *New York Times,* April 30, 1999, 34.

The Plaid Adder. "The Pictures from Abu Ghraib." *Democratic Underground,* May 5, 2004. http://www.democraticunderground.com/plaidder/04/21.html.

Puri, Jyoti. *Encountering Nationalism.* Malden, MA: Blackwell, 2004.

Ranalli, Ralph. "Evacuees Say They Were Told Little before Arrival." *Boston Globe,* September 10, 2005, B7.

Rath, Richard Cullen. "Echo and Narcissus: The Afrocentric Pragmatism of W. E. B. Du Bois. *Journal of American History* 84, no. 2 (September 1997): 461–495.

Rich, Adrienne. *Blood, Bread, and Poetry: Selected Prose, 1979–1985.* New York: Norton, 1986.

Ritzer, George. *Sociological Theory.* 4th ed. New York: McGraw-Hill, 1996.

Roediger, David R. Introduction to *Black on White: Black Writers on What It Means to Be White,* edited by David Roediger, 3–26. New York: Schocken Books, 1998.

Rollins, Judith. *Between Women: Domestics and Their Employers.* Philadelphia: Temple University Press, 1985.

Romero, Mary. *Maid in the USA.* New York: Routledge, 1992.

Ross, David, and Michael Parenti. "Exposing the Terrorist Trap: David Ross Interviews Michael Parenti." *International Socialist Review,* no. 24 (July 20, 2002): 20–23.

Roy, Arundhati. *An Ordinary Person's Guide to Empire.* Boston: South End Press, 2004.

Ruether, Rosemary Radford. "The War on Women." In *Nothing Sacred: Women Respond to Religious Fundamentalism and Terror*, edited by Betsy Reed, 3–10. New York: Thunder's Mouth Press, 2002.

Rushdie, Salman. *The Ground beneath Her Feet*. New York: Henry Holt, 1999.

Sack, Joetta L. "Teachers' Jobs in Hurricane-Ravaged Areas in Limbo." *Education Week*, November 16, 2005, 3, 17.

Scaff, Lawrence A. "Remnants of Romanticism: Max Weber in Oklahoma and Indian Territory." In *The Protestant Ethic Turns 100: Essays on the Centenary of the Weber Thesis*, edited by William H. Swatos and Lutz Kaelber, 77–110. Boulder, CO: Paradigm Books, 2005.

Schweitzer, Sarah. "Elite Colleges' Welcome Brings Unexpected Boon." *Boston Globe*, September 10, 2005, A1, 13.

Scott-Heron, Gil, and Brian Jackson. "Peace Go with You, Brother." On *Winter in America*, TVT Records, 1998.

Segrest, Mab. *Born to Belonging: Writings on Spirit and Justice*. New York: Rutgers, 2002.

Seidman, Steven. *Contested Knowledge: Social Theory in the Postmodern Era*. Cambridge, MA: Blackwell, 1994.

Sica, Alan, ed. *Social Thought: From the Enlightenment to the Present*. New York: Pearson, 2005.

Singh, Amardeep. "'We Are Not the Enemy': Hate Crimes against Arabs, Muslims, and Those Perceived to Be Arab or Muslim after September 11." *Human Rights Watch*, November 2002, 3–42.

Sontag, Susan. *Regarding the Pain of Others*. New York: Farrar, Straus and Giroux, 2003.

———. "Regarding the Torture of Others." *New York Times*, May 23, 2004, 1–6.

Stannard, David E. *American Holocaust: Columbus and the Conquest of the New World*. New York: Oxford University Press, 1992.

"Storm and Crisis: Government Responses." Photo with caption, "After two weeks, a rescue." *New York Times*, September 14, 2005, national edition, A23.

Tawney, R. H. *Religion and the Rise of Capitalism*. New York: Transaction Publishers, 1998.

Telhami, Shibley, Fiona Hill, Abdullatif A. Al-Othman, and Cyrus H. Tahmassebi. "Does Saudi Arabia Still Matter? Differing Perspectives on the Kingdom and Its Oil." *Foreign Affairs* 81, no. 6 (November/December 2002): 167.

Thompson, Becky. *A Hunger So Wide and So Deep: A Multiracial View of Women's Eating Problems*. Minneapolis: University of Minnesota Press, 1994.

———. *A Promise and a Way of Life: White Antiracist Activism*. Minneapolis: University of Minnesota Press, 2001.

———. "Time Traveling and Border Crossing: Notes on White Identity." In *Names We Call Home: Autobiography on Racial Identity*, edited by Becky Thompson and Sangeeta Tyagi, 92–109. New York: Routledge, 1996.

Thompson, Ken. *Émile Durkheim*. New York: Routledge, 2002.

Tibi, Bassam. *Islam between Culture and Politics.* 2nd ed. New York: Palgrave, 2005.

Tohidi, Nayereh. "Gender and Islamic Fundamentalism: Feminist Politics in Iran." In *Third World Women and the Politics of Feminism,* edited by Chandra Talpade Mohanty, Ann Russo, and Lourdes Torres, 251–270. Bloomington: University of Indiana Press, 1991.

Tutu, Desmond. *No Future without Forgiveness.* New York: Doubleday, 1999.

Walker, Margaret. *Jubilee.* New York: Bantam Books, 1966.

Watts, Michael. "Revolutionary Islam: A Geography of Modern Terror." In *Violent Geographies: Fear, Terror, and Political Violence,* edited by Derek Gregory and Allan Pred, 175–203. New York: Routledge, 2007.

Weber, Marianne. *Max Weber: A Biography.* New Brunswick, NJ: Transaction Books, 1988.

Weber, Max. *From Max Weber: Essays in Sociology.* Edited by H. H. Gerth and C. W. Mills. New York: Oxford University Press, 1946.

———. *The Protestant Ethic and the Spirit of Capitalism.* New York: Charles Scribner's Sons, 1958.

———. "Science as a Vocation." In *From Max Weber,* edited by H. H. Gerth and C. W. Mill, 129–156. New York: Oxford University Press, 1967.

Wells, Jennifer. "Leashes, Lynchings, and Lynndie England." *Toronto Star,* February 20, 2005, A13.

West, Cornel. *The Cornel West Reader.* New York: Basic Civitas Books, 1999.

———. "Exiles from a City and from a Nation." *Observer,* September 11, 2005, 19.

———. *Race Matters.* Boston: Beacon, 1993.

Wideman, John Edgar. Introduction to *The Souls of Black Folk,* by W. E. B. Du Bois, xi–xvi. New York: Vintage, 1990.

———. "In Praise of Silence." In *The Writing Life: Writers on How They Think and Work,* edited by Marie Arana, 111–117. New York: Public Affairs, 2003.

Williams, Patricia J. *The Alchemy of Race and Rights: Diary of a Law Professor.* Cambridge, MA: Harvard University Press, 1991.

———. "From Birmingham to Baghdad." *Nation,* December 13, 2004, 12.

———. "The View from Lott's Porch." *Nation,* September 26, 2005, 10.

Worsley, Peter. *Marx and Marxism.* New York: Routledge, 1982.

Zernike, Kate. "Behind Failed Abu Ghraib Plea, a Tangle of Bonds and Betrayals." *New York Times,* May 14, 2005, national edition, A1, A13.

Zimbardo, Philip G. "The 'Trophy Photos': Abu Ghraib's Horrors and Worse." October 25, 2005. http://www.zimbardo.com/downloads/Trophy%20Photos%20OP%20ED%20.pdf.

Zinn, Howard. "The Scourge of Nationalism." *Progressive,* June 2005, 12.

# INDEX

Abood, Eddie, 219n50

Abood, Sally, 219n50

Abu Ghraib prison abuses: and absence of laws of governance, 100; Abu-Jamal analysis of, 140; and alienation from species being, 122–125; and alienation in postindustrial capitalist economy, 121–125, 143–145, 187; audience for photographs of, 137–143; compared with lynchings, 139; compared with prison abuses in US, 134–135, 222–223nn16–18; Darby's exposure of, 146; and dissociation or doubling, 132, 137; and double consciousness, 143; England's and Graner's participation in, 112–113, 121–125, 131–135, 138–139, 141–142, 147, 187, 219n1; examples of, 136; and Iraqi women prisoners, 223n19; Iraqis in photographs of, 135–137, 184; and Marx on alienation, 3, 4, 10, 14, 121–126, 131–132, 143; and Milgram experiment, 124; military members taking photographs of, 121–122, 132–135, 137, 219n1; and nudity of Muslim prisoners, 112–113; and photographs as fetishes, 131–132; photographs of, 3, 14, 112–113, 121–127, 131–143, 184; pornographic nature of photos of, 138–140; portrayal of Graner and

England as "bad apples," 187, 219n1; racial dynamics of white woman and darker-skinned prisoners, 112–113; and trauma theory, 4, 10, 15, 137–138, 140–141; and Weber's iron cage, 7; and whites' historical memory of slavery, 203; and Zimbardo experiment, 124

Abu-Jamal, Mumia, 140

Abu-Lughod, Janet, 90

Addams, Jane, 180

affirmative action, 30, 32

Afghanistan: justifications of US war against, 101–103, 218n39; Soviet invasion of, 94–95; Taliban in, 19; US war against, 1, 14, 96, 97, 98–99, 101–102, 144, 150, 179, 218n39; women's rights and Islamic fundamentalism in, 218n39

African American studies, 7, 18

African Americans. *See* blacks; Hurricane Katrina; slavery

African National Congress (ANC), 183, 198

AIDS crisis, 12

al-Qaeda, 98–99, 101–105, 107–108, 182–183, 185

Alpert, Judith, 175

alienation: and Abu Ghraib prison abuses, 3, 4, 10, 14, 121–126, 131–132,